LANGUAGE AND DECADENCE IN THE
VICTORIAN FIN DE SIÈCLE

LINDA DOWLING

Language and Decadence in the Victorian Fin de Siècle

🌱

1986

PRINCETON UNIVERSITY PRESS

Copyright © 1986 by Princeton University Press
Published by Princeton University Press,
41 William Street, Princeton, New Jersey 08540
In the United Kingdom: Princeton University Press,
Oxford

ALL RIGHTS RESERVED
Library of Congress Cataloging in Publication Data will be
found on the last printed page of this book

ISBN 0-691-06690-6
ISBN 0-691-01472-8

First Princeton Paperback printing, 1989

Publication of this book has been aided by a grant from
The Andrew W. Mellon Foundation

This book has been composed in Linotron Monticello

Clothbound editions of Princeton University Press books
are printed on acid-free paper, and binding materials
are chosen for strength and durability

Printed in the United States of America
by Princeton University Press
Princeton, New Jersey

FOR MY PARENTS,
FRANK AND DOROTHY CRABILL

TABLE OF CONTENTS

Preface
ix

PREFACE

The tradition in studies of the Victorian fin de siècle has been to identify such figures as Oscar Wilde and Aubrey Beardsley with a tendency then and now known as Decadence, and in Decadence to see a cultural episode with sensational or lurid overtones. This is the controlling impulse, for instance, behind Rupert Croft-Cooke's portrayal of Wilde in *Feasting with Panthers*, a treatment that may well linger as the last reminder of the older view. There is Wilde pursuing his insatiable way from one male prostitute to the next, Wilde reclining on a couch talking of poetry and art and ancient Rome, pressing candied cherries from his own lips to those of his young companion, Wilde leaving tipsily for the night with his chosen catamite (" 'Oscar doesn't care what he pays if he fancies a chap' ").[1] And like so many established views, this one contains its measure of truth; Croft-Cooke's source for all this is the court records of Wilde's trial for homosexual practices in 1895, a proceeding that remains emblematic not least because Decadence, too, was on trial.

Yet the truth of this older view of Decadence is that of rumor or gossip, a truth doomed to exhaust itself in the mere telling, which is doubtless why in recent years there has emerged a more serious view of Decadence as a cult of artifice in art and literature, an impulse or movement defined by what Michael Riffaterre has called its "ostentation

---

[1] Rupert Croft-Cooke, *Feasting with Panthers: A New Consideration of Some Late Victorian Writers* (New York: Holt, Rinehart and Winston, 1967), p. 274.

of artifice."[2] This is the Decadence of Wilde's Sphinx, of Arthur Symons's ballet-girls and Theodore Wratislaw's orchids:

> The silver lips of lilies virginal,
> The full deep bosom of the enchanted rose
> Please less than flowers glass-hid from frosts and
>   snows
> For whom an alien heat makes festival.[3]

This Decadence emerges, in short, as a counterpoetics of disruption and parody and stylistic derangement, a critique not so much of Wordsworthian nature as of the metaphysics involved in any sentimental notion of a simple world of grass and trees and flowers. The world as it then survives in Decadent writing is by contrast a belated world, a place of hesitations and contrarieties and exhaustions.

The idea of Decadence as counterpoetics and critique, though scattered through various articles by various critics and as yet nowhere fully developed, possesses wherever it occurs a genuine power of illumination. The idea gives force, for instance, to Riffaterre's remarks on stylistic artifice, to J. Hillis Miller's contention that certain Victorian writers take as their subject not Nature but "a sublimation of Nature into signs for subjective states,"[4] or to Gayatri

[2] Michael Riffaterre, "Decadent Features in Maeterlinck's Poetry," *Language and Style* 7 (1974): 15.

[3] Theodore Wratislaw, "Hothouse Flowers," *Orchids* (London: Leonard Smithers, 1896), p. 23.

[4] J. Hillis Miller, "Nature and the Linguistic Moment," in *Nature and the Victorian Imagination*, ed. U. C. Knoepflmacher and G. B. Tennyson (Berkeley and London: University of California Press, 1977), p. 445. Miller terms the "linguistic moment" that moment "when language as such, the means of representation in literature, becomes problematic, something to be interrogated, explored, or thematized in itself" (p. 450). In this study I shall use the term "post-philological moment" to stress the public character of this linguistic realization and its origins in a specific body of philological science.

Spivak's argument that Decadent writing refers, not directly and unproblematically to the world of nature, but instead to a world at one remove, a world already made into artifice.[5] Every such argument draws its power to illuminate, surely, from a shift away from the titillations of literary gossip and towards the genuinely problematic sphere of language and style. Yet the idea of Decadence as a cult of artifice is not yet wholly linguistic or stylistic, it seems to me, for beneath the sophistication of such arguments there lingers a notion of cultural content conditioned by the older view, a Decadence of rouge and gaslight and orchids and patchouli reflecting, though at great intellectual remove, the lurid lights of an earlier sensationalism.

The theory of literary Decadence developed in the following pages, at any rate, completes the shift towards language and style, for my argument is that Decadence, even on the cultural level, emerged from a linguistic crisis, a crisis in Victorian attitudes towards language brought about by the new comparative philology earlier imported from

[5] See Gayatri Spivak, "Decadent Style," *Language and Style* 7 (1974): 227-34. More recently, Marilyn Gaddis Rose has attempted to describe "the Decadent love-hate relationship with language" in terms taken over from information theory as consisting in "the redundancy-entropy nexus." See her "Decadence and Modernism: Defining by Default," *Modernist Studies* 4 (1982): 195-206. John R. Reed's *Decadent Style* (Athens: Ohio University Press, 1985) ambitiously undertakes to propose a general definition of Decadence that will be applicable to the several arts of fiction, poetry, music, and graphic art. In Reed's view Decadent style, whatever the medium, is characterized by a superabundance of details that subvert or disintegrate form while simultaneously inviting the aesthetic audience to participate in reconstituting the formal unity of the work on subtler or more unexpected terms. Meanwhile, in a sort of critical counter-movement, Suzanne Nalbantian has revived the older view of Decadence as the literary expression of moral "perversity, paradox and perplexity" in order to discuss works not usually considered Decadent, namely, novels of Dostoyevsky, James, Zola, Hardy, and Conrad. See Suzanne Nalbantian, *Seeds of Decadence in the Late Nineteenth-Century Novel* (New York: St. Martin's, 1983).

the Continent. For it was the new linguistic science, the investigations of Bopp and Grimm and the Neogrammarians, that raised a spectre of autonomous language—language as a system blindly obeying impersonal phonological rules in isolation from any world of human values and experience—that was to eat corrosively away at the hidden foundations of a high Victorian ideal of civilization, an ideal earlier identified by Coleridge with written language in general and with the English of Shakespeare and Milton and the King James Bible in particular. In the immediate background of literary Decadence, that is, there lies the silent emergence of that new linguistic order described by Michel Foucault:

> Perhaps changes in the mode of being of language are like alterations that affect pronunciation, grammar, or semantics: swift as they are, they are never clearly grasped by those who are speaking and whose language is nevertheless already spreading these mutations; they are noticed only indirectly, for brief moments; and then the decision is finally indicated only in the negative mode—by the radical and immediately perceptible obsoleteness of the language one has been using. It is probably impossible for a culture to become aware in a thematic and positive manner that its language is ceasing to be transparent to its representations, because it is thickening and taking on a particular heaviness. As one is in the act of discoursing, how is one to know—unless by means of some obscure indices that one can interpret only with difficulty and badly—that language (the very language one is using) is acquiring a dimension irreducible to pure discursivity?[6]

[6] Michel Foucault, *The Order of Things: An Archaeology of the Human Sciences* (New York: Vintage, 1973), pp. 281-82.

One reason for Foucault's clairvoyant sense of autonomous language in *The Order of Things* undoubtedly is his awareness that Ferdinand de Saussure's epochal distinction between the synchronic and the diachronic, as well as the metaphysical rupture inevitably occasioned by it, had a *history*; that is, even as Saussure altered modern thought by calling the very notions of history-as-cause or history-as-explanation into question, his own work was made possible by an apprenticeship in comparative philology, and in particular by a brilliant early career in the orbit of the Neogrammarians. This insight is the beginning of Foucault's theory of the discourse, which very quickly carries him far away from anything like my concerns in the following pages. Yet Foucault, writing as he does from our own side of the metaphysical rupture brought about by Saussurean linguistics, speaking along with such thinkers as Jacques Derrida and Gilles Deleuze for language as a relentlessly autonomous system of signification obeying no logic but its own, remains a presence on the distant horizons of my argument. For what has emerged in our time as Foucault's theory of discourse or Derridean deconstruction is none other than that dark spectre of autonomous language that haunted literary Decadence.

The story traced in my argument, however, looks not forward to Foucault and Derrida but back to the beginning of the eighteenth century. In particular it looks to the emergence, along with John Locke's *Essay Concerning Human Understanding* (1690) and its empiricist epistemology of association, of a new theory of language that deeply threatened every older notion of language as logos, of words or speech as the revelation of a divine or a divinely-bestowed intelligence. For in Lockean epistemology began those materialist theories of language that, as in the more radical associationism of a Condillac or the speculative etymologizing of a Horne Tooke, made language into little more than another physical reality in a universe now wholly governed by physical laws. It was in a spirit of opposition to this sceptical and powerfully reductive vision of language, in turn, that J. G. Herder was to write *On the Origin of Language (Über den Ursprung der Sprache)*, his great prize essay of 1770; with Herder's essay was born the movement, anticipated in certain respects in England by such writers on language as Bishop Lowth and Lord Monboddo, that I shall be calling Romantic philology.

As it was to contribute in immediate terms to a high Victorian ideal of civilization, Romantic philology was itself a doctrine of the logos, for Herder's was in one sense an attempt to rescue the theological notion of language by relocating it within human society, viewing language or speech as *Volksstimme*, the outward expression of the inner essence of a nation or people. The authority of Herder's theory of language lies in turn behind Coleridge's notion of written English as the *lingua communis* of England and its national clerisy, and of written English as embodied at its noblest in a literary tradition extending back to Shakespeare and the English Bible. And in Coleridge's notion of the *lingua communis*, finally, originated the Victorian vision of English as a world language, the conviction, in an age of empire and imperial ambition, that the tongue of Shakespeare and Milton was destined to carry the values of an advanced English civilization to the remote corners of the globe.

Yet the same tradition of Romantic philology, even as it was to inspire, through Coleridgean idealism, an ennobling Victorian vision of high civilization, was to bring about, through a submerged countercurrent of philological theory, its eventual collapse. For Herder's notion of the *Volksstimme*, identifying language as it did with the living speech of a people, was in the first instance to generate that emphasis on spoken dialects that led to a new comparative philology, and much later to motivate those phonological investigations that, as in the studies of the Neogrammarians, led to the theory of language as a wholly autonomous system. In this guise did the scepticism and materialism of Condillac and Horne Tooke reappear as a source of specifically Victorian cultural anxiety, for English as an autonomous language, developing apart from any sphere of human values in blind obedience to impersonal phonological laws, could no longer be taken as the *lingua communis* of Victorian civilization, the logos-within-history of a noble English cultural destiny.

The new comparative philology was in this context to bring about nothing less than a Victorian cultural crisis, and some consequences of that crisis—along with the valiant but doomed attempts of such figures as Max Müller to hold it at bay—are traced in the following pages. Yet literary Decadence as it was to emerge from the Victorian linguistic crisis was no attempt to oppose in direct terms the spectre of disintegration or collapse, but rather was an attempt to save something from the wreck by turning to literary advantage what had otherwise appeared only as one of the incidentally bleak implications of the new linguistic science: the idea that written language, the literary tongue of the great English writers, was simply another dead language in relation to living speech. My account of Decadence begins, then, in the story behind Walter Pater's attempt, in *Marius the Epicurean* (1885) and other of his later writings, to employ English as a classical dialect, to bestow a belated and paradoxical vitality on a literary language that linguistic science had declared to be dead.

My research for this study was substantially aided by two fellowships: a Rockefeller Humanities Fellowship in

1982-1983, which allowed me to work for a year in the libraries of Great Britain, and an Alexander von Humboldt Fellowship, which during 1984-1985 allowed me to complete my work in nineteenth-century German philology. It is a pleasure to acknowledge my gratitude to the Rockefeller and Alexander von Humboldt foundations, and to the people whose personal generosity did so much to aid my studies abroad: in Edinburgh, Professor Peter Jones of the University of Edinburgh, who arranged for my use of special collections at the University Library; in Cologne, my AvH *Gastgeber* Professor Jon Erickson, whose conversation helped with several important points in my study and whose hospitality made my year in Cologne a delight; and Dr. Gottfried Krieger, Frau Gudrun Anhut and Frau Tanya Klein, all of whom offered timely practical support at crucial points in my work.

Some other debts must be mentioned as well, the earliest being to Professor Barbara K. Lewalski, then of Brown, now of Harvard University, who as my dissertation director gave me an education in primary scholarship that was to bear fruit in a project neither of us could have then foreseen. Friends at the University of New Mexico and elsewhere have been generous with advice and assistance; I want particularly to thank James Barbour, William C. Dowling, Wendell V. Harris, Phillip Herring, Hugh Witemeyer, and, for comments on my argument that were of great help in my final revision of the original manuscript, James G. Nelson of the University of Wisconsin at Madison and Daniel T. O'Hara of Temple University. Finally, I should like to thank the staff of the Scottish National Library and, in New Mexico, Dorothy Wonsmos, head of Interlibrary Loan at Zimmerman Library, for a generosity of effort well above the call of bibliographical duty.

LANGUAGE AND DECADENCE IN THE VICTORIAN FIN DE SIÈCLE

I

Romantic Philology and Victorian Civilization

The spirit does but mean the breath.
—TENNYSON, *In Memoriam*

Even today, when Walter Pater's importance as a Victorian writer seems ever more obviously to reside in his later work, *Studies in the History of the Renaissance* (1873) continues to be his most famous book. The most notorious part of the book remains, of course, the "Conclusion," that unintended manifesto of a new aestheticism that was to earn Pater a reputation as cerebral hedonist and corrupter of youth. As everyone knows, Pater suppressed the "Conclusion" in the second edition of *The Renaissance* (1877), lest it "mislead some of those young men into whose hands it might fall."[1] And as everyone knows, the gesture did no good at all, for the "Conclusion" continued to inflame the imaginations of certain young men through the end of the century, to the point where it has been taken as the inspiration behind the cultural movement or episode known as Decadence. Pater's *The Renaissance*, Oscar Wilde was to say later, "is the very flower of decadence: the last trump should have sounded the moment it was written."[2]

On one level, it is not mistaken to see in the Pater of *The*

[1] Walter Pater, *The Renaissance: Studies in Art and Poetry*, ed. Donald L. Hill (Berkeley and London: University of California Press, 1980), p. 186n.
[2] Quoted in *The Autobiography of William Butler Yeats* (New York: Macmillan, 1965), p. 87.

3

Renaissance the theorist of that cultural aestheticism that was to have so great an influence in England in the later nineteenth century, for so far as the "Conclusion" represented an urgent invitation to a life of passionately charged experience, a mysterious hinting at the allure of "strange dyes, strange colours, curious odours," it was to alter the lives of a thousand undergraduates at Oxford and Cambridge and elsewhere. Yet this is an aestheticism of the cultural surface, the aestheticism of Oscar Wilde's green carnations and Gilbert and Sullivan's *Patience* (1881), which as an impulse was to emerge only from a submerged crisis in Victorian attitudes and assumptions. And the writer who plays a crucial role in this deeper crisis is the Pater of *Marius the Epicurean*, who describes the Romans of a declining empire sitting in their great amphitheater and gazing outward at a

> blazing arena, covered again and again during the many hours' show, with clean sand for the absorption of certain great red patches there, by troops of white-shirted boys, for whom the good-natured audience provided a scramble of nuts and small coin, flung to them over a trellis-work of silver-gilt and amber, precious gift of Nero, while a rain of flowers and perfume fell over themselves, as they paused between the parts of their long feast upon the spectacle of animal suffering.[3]

Even here, in *Marius*, it is the decadence of the surface that is likely to overwhelm our attention, for the Roman scene Pater is describing, one of indolence, luxury, and torture, would seem to embody the very matter of Deca-

---

[3] Walter Pater, *Marius the Epicurean: His Sensations and Ideas*, 2 vols. (London: Macmillan, 1914), 1:235.

dence culturally conceived. Yet the clue to the underlying crisis of assumptions that was to generate literary Decadence in England is not *what* Pater is describing, but the *way* he is describing it: his famous style that, in its studied delays and delicate hesitations, was to lead so many contemporaries to remark that Pater wrote English as a classical language. To grasp the full implications of the remark is to understand Pater's actual role as the progenitor of literary Decadence, the first major writer of Victorian literature in its post-philological moment, seeking a fugitive victory for art by acquiescing in the pronouncement of a new linguistic science that English as a written or literary language was nothing more than an artificial dialect, a petrifaction, a dead tongue. The nature of Pater's enterprise directs us, in turn, to the origins of that Victorian crisis in a deeper intellectual crisis that had emerged, together with Lockean epistemology, nearly two centuries before.

❦

The grave threat to orthodox religious belief and theological assumptions about the world posed by Locke's *Essay Concerning Human Understanding* (1690) was visible almost immediately; by the middle of the eighteenth century, when Locke's own reasonable Christianity had given way to the coruscating scepticism of David Hume, the crisis of belief was an open matter of philosophical controversy, and the crisis would, of course, deepen further in the following century when Pater began to write. Almost unnoticed, however, in this larger movement towards an openly-declared scepticism and materialism, unnoticed probably because Locke's *Essay* had concerned itself only in the most incidental way with linguistic matters, was a similar threat specifically to theological views of language. For it was the very notion of God as Logos, the idea of human language as participating in the divine intelligence or divine speech, that Locke unwittingly threatened when, in a tangential observation in Book III of the Essay, he said,

> It may also lead us a little towards the Original of all our Notions and Knowledge, if we remark, how great a dependance [*sic*] our *Words* have on common sensible *Ideas*; and how those, which are made use of to stand for Actions and Notions quite removed from sense, *have their rise from thence, and from obvious sensible Ideas are transferred to more abstruse significations*, and made to stand for *Ideas* that come not under the cognizance of our senses; *v. g.* to *Imagine, Apprehend, Comprehend, Adhere, Conceive, Instill, Disgust, Disturbance, Tranquillity*, etc. are all Words taken from the Operations of sensible Things, and applied to certain Modes of Thinking. *Spirit*, in its primary signification, is Breath; *Angel*, Messenger: And I doubt not, but if we could trace them to their sources, we should find, in all Languages, the names, which stand for Things that fall not under our Senses, to have had their first rise from sensible *Ideas*.[4]

In Locke's observations, however, we still feel the force of the entirely orthodox assumption that language derives from thought. The assault on orthodoxy begins, then, in those theories of language that, employing a more radical

[4] John Locke, *Essay Concerning Human Understanding*, ed. Peter H. Nidditch (Oxford: Clarendon, 1975), p. 403. Hans Aarsleff stresses the central importance to subsequent linguistic history of this tangential passage in *The Study of Language in England, 1780-1860* (Princeton: Princeton University Press, 1967), p. 33.

Lockean associationism against Locke, were to invert this assumption and declare that thought derived from language. Much of the great nineteenth-century debate between the linguistic idealists and materialists, and later, between the Romantic and "scientific" philologists is in effect prefigured in the conflicts among Locke's various eighteenth-century inheritors. The materialist position, for example, finds early expression in the Abbé de Condillac's declaration in his *Essai sur l'origine des connaissances humaines* (1746) that "The ideas are connected with the signs, and it is *only by this means*, as I shall prove, that they are connected with each other."[5] To be sure, the radical scepticism implicit in Condillac's analysis was not to take immediate shape as a new linguistic theory. It led more directly to unrestrained bouts of speculative etymologizing, especially in England, where legions of amateur philologists pursued the sort of superior parlor game that William Cowper was making fun of when he ridiculed "learn'd philologists, who chase/ A panting syllable through time and space,/ Start it at home, and hunt it in the dark,/ To

[5] Etienne Bonnot, Abbé de Condillac, *An Essay on the Origin of Human Knowledge, Being a Supplement to Mr. Locke's Essay on the Human Understanding*, trans. Thomas Nugent (London: printed for J. Nourse, 1756; reprinted New York: AMS Press, 1974), p. 7. My emphasis. In a series of essays stressing the importance of French linguistic thought, Hans Aarsleff has vigorously disputed the traditional, German-centered account of Romantic language theory and linguistic history invoked by M. H. Abrams, René Wellek, and others. Readers should consult Aarsleff's *From Locke to Saussure: Essays on the Study of Language and Intellectual History* (Minneapolis: University of Minnesota Press, 1982). The present study largely follows the traditional, German-centered view because it concerns itself with Victorian attitudes towards language and literature, and the Victorians assumed— mistakenly, it may be—that there was a decisive break between the theories of Locke and those of the Romantics, and further, that German philology was largely responsible for it. Aarsleff's study, in short, seeks to rectify the history of truth, while we shall be concerned in large part here with the no less interesting history of error.

Gaul, to Greece, and into Noah's ark."[6] Nonetheless, such essentially innocent play with linguistic derivations, by emphasizing the material or even arbitrary nature of the connection between word and idea, prepared the ground for the overtly sceptical and materialist analysis that John Horne Tooke was to propose at the end of the eighteenth century when, in a notorious pronouncement, he declared, "The Latin anima is in truth nothing but the breath of the body: and conversely the soul is of material origin just as is the spirit."[7]

The emergent materialism of such eighteenth-century views in turn became the occasion of J. G. Herder's Berlin Academy prize essay *On the Origin of Language*, published in 1772. Paradoxically, Herder's ostensible target in this essay is not linguistic materialism as such, but that older theory of the Logos initially called into question by Lockean empiricism, and in particular those eighteenth-century theorists who were still pleading for the divine origin of language on linguistically untenable grounds. Yet Herder opposes this older theological view only because he wishes to oppose to materialist views of language his own

[6] William Cowper, "Retirement" (lines 691-94), in *The Poems of William Cowper*, ed. John D. Baird and Charles Ryskamp, 2 vols. (Oxford: Clarendon, 1980), 1:395. The notion, common during the eighteenth century, that in etymology the consonants count for little while the vowels count for less is traditionally ascribed to Voltaire. Cf. also Samuel Johnson, "Preface to the *Dictionary*," in *Selected Poetry and Prose*, ed. Frank Brady and W. K. Wimsatt (Berkeley: University of California Press, 1977), p. 279: "This uncertainty [of pronunciation] is most frequent in the vowels, which are so capriciously pronounced and so differently modified by accident or affectation, not only in every province but in every mouth, that to them, as is well known to etymologists, little regard is to be shown in the deduction of one language from another."

[7] John Horne Tooke, ΕΠΕΑ ΠΤΕΡΟΕΝΤΑ, *or, The Diversions of Purley*, 1st ed. (London, 1786), quoted in L. A. Willoughby, "Coleridge as a Philologist," *Modern Language Review* 31 (1936): 179n.

theory of the logos, one that sees the origin of language in the human intelligence operating within the boundaries of human history. In this essentially triangular conflict among materialist, theologically orthodox, and emergently Romantic linguistic theories, Herder in effect appropriated the field position of orthodoxy and the tactics of materialism in order to establish and defend his own Romantic humanist view.

The degree to which Herder's interpretation of language represents a secularization of the orthodox belief in the Logos, reinforced at crucial points by the empirical discoveries of the linguistic materialists, becomes clearer when we examine the use Herder made of one of his predecessors, the Anglican Bishop Robert Lowth. Lowth's *Lectures on the Sacred Poetry of the Hebrews* (1753) became the stimulus for Herder's thinking on language, because in them Herder could see the obvious signs of an unstable logical synthesis, a failure to hold in any convincing balance two perspectives soon to reveal themselves as mutually incompatible. For Lowth's position, as an Anglican clergyman and Christian believer, is the orthodox view that Hebrew is divinely inspired, "an emanation from heaven . . . the Priestess of divine truth, the Internunciate between earth and heaven."[8] Yet in Lowth's actual treatment of Hebrew poetry, Herder was able to recognize the first dim stirrings of an idea that, through the thought of Herder himself and writers philosophically attuned to similar assumptions, would eventually issue in the radical historicism of Hegel, the idea, that is to say, of the unique individuality of a given people as it is formed by a specific time and specific circumstances. The language and poetry

[8] Robert Lowth, *Lectures on the Sacred Poetry of the Hebrews*, translated from the Latin by G. Gregory, 2 vols. (London: printed for J. Johnson, 1787; reprinted New York: Garland, 1971), 1:46-47.

of the Hebrews in Lowth's account are at once the result of divine inspiration and of local conditions, with the pervasive poetic image of a flood or torrent, for example, arising from the Hebrews' experience in the mountainous topography of Palestine.

The genesis of Romantic philology in Herder's *Origin* is due to the boldness with which he was to expose Lowth's paradox. To Lowth, for instance, the highly metaphorical nature of Hebrew proved in an indirect way its divine inspiration; but to Herder the same metaphors derived from the historical roots of language itself, and amounted to a kind of linguistic tumult that worked *against* any notion of the divine origin of language ("Was God so lacking in ideas and words that he had to have recourse to that kind of confusing word usage?"[9]). Elsewhere, Herder employs a version of the same strategy against those who had proposed an argument from linguistic design. In his *Proof that the Origin of the Language of Man is Divine (Beweis, daß der Ursprung der menschlichen Sprache göttlich sey)* of 1766, for instance, J. P. Süßmilch had insisted that a divine economy was obviously at work in the fact that all the sounds of all the known languages could be reduced to a mere twenty-odd letters. Herder, animated by a phonetic sense that in its keenness looks forward to the investigations of the Neogrammarians in the next century, as well as by a sense of history that leaves no room for weak theodicies, dismisses this out of hand: "There is no language whose living tones can be totally reduced to letters, let alone to twenty. All languages—one and all—bear witness to this fact" (Herder, *Origin*, pp. 92-93).

[9] J. G. Herder, *Essay on the Origin of Language*, in *On the Origin of Language: Jean-Jacques Rousseau, Essay on the Origin of Languages; Johann Gottfried Herder, Essay on the Origin of Language*, trans. John H. Moran and Alexander Gode (New York: Frederick Ungar, 1966), p. 149.

At the same time, Herder's concentration on the sounds of living speech here is no matter of mere polemical convenience, something beginning and ending in a response to Süßmilch's argument concerning the divine economy of the written alphabet. For Herder saw in the reality of living speech nothing less than the basis of a new metaphysics of the logos, and in his argument now we discover the origins of that valorization of speech over writing that was to survive as the controlling impulse not only of Romantic philology but of the scientific or comparative philology of the next century. The argument begins, specifically, as an argument about Hebrew, which earlier writers had declared to be the Adamic tongue, and which most obviously exposes the radical deficiency of Süßmilch's argument that the written alphabet perfectly—and hence providentially—contains all the sounds of spoken language. For in the traditional Hebrew alphabet, of course, it is only the consonants that are written, and Herder argues that this is so because Hebrew vowels, the very embodiment of the living tongue, could not be captured by written marks: "Their pronounciation was so alive and finely articulated, their breath so spiritual and etherlike [*geistig und ätherisch*] that it evaporated and eluded containment in letters" (Herder, *Origin*, pp. 94-95).

Even in an argument as specific as this, one purporting to account only for the orthographic conventions of a single ancient language, it is possible to glimpse the outlines of an emergent metaphysics. For Hebrew is a dead language not least because it is mummified in the transcription of its consonantal structure merely: "what dead language can be called to life? The more alive a language is—the less one has thought of reducing it to letters, the more spontaneously it rises to the full unsorted sounds of nature" (Herder, *Origin*, p. 93). And the self-sounding Hebrew vowels that have eluded transcription are "alive" for Herder because they are coincident with the exhalations of the human breath, arising invisibly, without consonantal friction or gutteral stop, from the inmost recesses of the human being. Thus the living breath becomes in Herder's account of language what animates the dead letters of the written language by bestowing upon them "the spirit of life" (Herder, *Origin*, p. 95).

At just this point, however, Herder's theory encounters the obstacle that always lies in wait for idealist accounts of language, for in identifying language with breath he has granted the derivation of the conceptual from the material, the utter dependence of mind or thought on the brute reality of sound itself. The boldness of Herder's solution may explain why his *Origin of Language* was to have so powerful a subsequent influence; language, he argued, is consequent neither upon reason nor materiality in their pure states, but instead arises from the distinguishing mark [*Merkmal*] that reflection [*Besonnenheit*] *simultaneously perceives and bestows* upon a sensuous image amid that "vast ocean of sensations which permeates [man's soul] through all the channels of the senses." Thus does reflection have the power to "single out one wave, arrest it, concentrate [the soul's] attention on it . . . so that he will know that this object is this and not another" (Herder, *Origin*, pp. 115-16). Thus does language at a stroke become coincident with thought:

> The sound of bleating perceived by a human soul as the distinguishing mark of the sheep became, by virtue of this reflection, the name of the sheep, even if his tongue had never tried to stammer it. He recognized the sheep by its bleating: This was a conceived sign through which the soul clearly remembered an idea—

and what is that other than a word? And what is the entire human language other than a collection of such words? . . . Language has been invented! (Herder, *Origin*, pp. 117-18)

In positing such an origin for language, however, Herder has really invented something else, namely Romantic philology. Snatched from God in a Promethean gesture, language has been relocated within the soul of man, where it still however breathes the spirit of an immaterial intelligence. This is at once a theory of language and of man, of human culture and of human history, of everything that might be summed up in the notion of Romantic philology. Even now, Herder's great and eloquent delight in man as a creature of language seems irresistible: "Unity and coherence! Proportion and order! A whole! A system! A creature of reflection and language, of the power to reflect and to create language!" (Herder, *Origin*, p. 147). This is the view of language, first enunciated in the *Origin of Language*, that would become so powerful an influence in the nineteenth century. Yet as the phrase "a creature of language" may be seen to imply, the relation between man and language in Herder's account contains an ominous possibility. If language makes man, so language remade can unmake man:

> If anyone, after all these observations, were still ready to deny man's being destined to be a creature of language, he first would have to turn from being an observer of nature into being its destroyer! Would have to break into dissonance all the harmonies shown; lay waste the whole splendid structure of human forces, corrupt his sensuousness, and sense instead of nature's masterpiece a creature full of wants and lacunae, full

of weaknesses and convulsions! (Herder, *Origin*, p. 147)

In retrospect, of course, it seems obvious that Herder is contemplating here some as-yet-unthought-of theory of autonomous language that, as in the straightforward materialism of Condillac or Horne Tooke, would threaten a divorce between sound and meaning, speech and intelligence. And in fact the spectre of a plunge into linguistic relativism and arbitrariness does seem to haunt Herder's radically historical vision of linguistic origins, his conviction that languages come into being "in conformity with the manner of thinking and seeing of the people . . . in a particular country, in a particular time, under particular circumstances" (Herder, *Origin*, p. 150). As in the brilliant comparative researches that would in a few years move Sir William Jones to initiate the line of inquiry that would lead through Bopp and Grimm and the Neogrammarians to Saussure, the idea of a historical or scientific linguistics here seems indissociably bound up with some eventual vision of autonomous language.

Yet this is hindsight merely, for in the moment of its emergence Romantic philology had little trouble immunizing itself against the more unsettling implications of its own historicism. Thus, for instance, Sir William Jones's glimpse of a single Ur-language behind Sanskrit and Greek and Latin was for a considerable time to operate as a new guarantee, behind the vicissitudes of historical accident, of an underlying human universality, and thus Jones himself could make, together with his researches in comparative linguistics, certain important contributions to the Romantic expressive theory of poetry.[10] Yet the

[10] Jones, as M. H. Abrams has described in *The Mirror and the Lamp*, was the first writer in England to weave together the various strands of the ex-

most powerful of these saving gestures, and the one fated to have the greatest impact on Victorian thought, as German Romantic philology came mediated to the Victorians through S. T. Coleridge and his idealist successors, was Herder's own vision of individual languages as the voices of historical cultures, and language itself as *Volksstimme*, the outward expression of the inner essence of a nation or people. In this sense the theory of the *Volksstimme* represents the completion of Romantic philology as such, the relocation of the divine Logos within the boundaries of human history.

𝖂 𝖂

Viewed against the background of an emergent Romantic philology, a number of standard episodes in literary history suddenly appear in a new light, chief among them being that debate on poetic diction between Wordsworth and Coleridge so famously rehearsed in the *Biographia Literaria* (1817). In that debate we encounter for the first time the radically opposing views of speech and writing, language and culture that would shape the Victorian context in which questions of literary and cultural decadence were to be debated later in the century with such urgency and apocalyptic dread. Thus it is that Wordsworth's determined rejection in the preface to *Lyrical Ballads* (1800) of the literary conventions of the eighteenth century, what Wordsworth called "the common inheritance of Poets,"[11]

---

pressive theory into a coherent theory. (M. H. Abrams, *The Mirror and the Lamp: Romantic Theory and the Critical Tradition* [New York: Oxford University Press, 1953].) In Jones's important "Essay on the Arts, Commonly Called Imitative" (1772), he directly controverts the Aristotelian poetic of imitation, doing so in the comparativist mode that Bishop Lowth had specifically recommended.

[11] William Wordsworth, "Preface to *Lyrical Ballads* (1800)," in *The Prose*

in favor of purified rural speech establishes the terms of a central conflict in much Victorian fin de siècle literature, specifically, in those literary works that are bounded temporally and stylistically by Pater's *Marius the Epicurean* of 1885 on one side and Yeats's fervently apocalyptic essay of 1898, "The Autumn of the Body," on the other. For, resurfacing at the end of the nineteenth century, the conflict between two opposing models of language, namely, written language and speech, was to force many fin de siècle writers to choose between the self-consciously elaborate mode of literary Decadence on the one hand, and the aggressively unencumbered mode of the 1890s ballad revival on the other. Although both these fin de siècle modes had been shaped significantly by the philological revolution that had gathered force during the middle years of the nineteenth century, both literary Decadence and the 1890s ballad mode also bear unmistakable traces of their origins in the opening years of the century, their origins, respectively, in Coleridge's ideal of the literary *lingua communis* and Wordsworth's impassioned return to the speaking voice.

Wordsworth's revolutionary appeal to a new standard of purified rural speech obviously participates in the same fervent rejection of aristocratic norms of taste and literary decorum we find in Romantics like Herder. Yet a closer glance will reveal at the same time some crucial differences. For one thing, Wordsworth's rustic standard, unlike Herder's, does not depend on any Romantic idealist conception of the *Volk*. Instead, as Gene W. Ruoff has argued, when Wordsworth describes the poet as a man speaking to men, he is appealing to the older universalist

---

Works of William Wordsworth, ed. W.J.B. Owen and Jane Worthington Smyser, 3 vols. (Oxford: Clarendon, 1974), 1:132.

idea of human mind and experience,[12] the belief of Samuel Johnson's *Rambler No. 60* that "there is such an uniformity in the state of man, considered apart from adventitious and separable decorations and disguises, that there is scarce any possibility of good or ill, but is common to human kind."[13] Yet such an Augustan assumption consorts awkwardly with Wordsworth's Romantic emphasis on the immediate, overflowing expressiveness of speech. In the same way, Wordsworth's expressive poetics is complicated by its incorporation of fundamentally alien psychological and philosophical elements, most notably, the associationism of David Hartley. For when Wordsworth defends his own adoption of "the real language of men," he understands the word "real," as Don H. Bialostosky has persuasively argued, in a specifically Hartleyan sense[14]: "real" in this context means "words connected with the sensations received from *things*." But, to the degree that Wordsworth's "real language" means this, it is decisively removed from Herder's notion of language as the "distinguishing mark" of the spirit.

The most important effect of Wordsworth's blending of these divergent and alien ideas, however, is to isolate Wordsworth, an isolation the poet first feels as his own estrangement from the English literary tradition. Wordsworth, of course, does not reject the whole tradition, because he cannot so lightly dispense with Milton and the English Bible. It is instead the "adulterated phraseology" and all the "motley masquerade of tricks, quaintnesses,

[12] See Gene W. Ruoff, "Wordsworth on Language: Toward a Radical Poetics for English Romanticism," *Wordsworth Circle* 3 (1972): 204-11.

[13] Samuel Johnson, *Essays from the Rambler, Adventurer and Idler*, ed. W. J. Bate (New Haven and London: Yale University Press, 1968), p. 110.

[14] See Don H. Bialostosky, "Coleridge's Interpretation of Wordsworth's Preface to *Lyrical Ballads*," *PMLA* 93 (1978): 912-23.

hieroglyphics, and enigmas" (Wordsworth, *Prose Works*, 1:161-62) that must go. Yet in dismissing these, Wordsworth dismisses Gray's sonnets, Pope's *Messiah*, and the metrical paraphrases of Johnson and Prior. A poetics that can dismiss these figures comes uncomfortably close, as Coleridge was later to see, to dispensing with the central idea of English literature: precisely that "common inheritance of Poets"—a vital and enabling inheritance simply *because* it was held in common—that Coleridge knew was essential, not only for new poets, but for any idea of English culture worthy of the name.

Wordsworth's sense of his own isolation from his immediate poetic predecessors is in turn heightened by his uneasy and at times almost frightened sense of isolation from his very linguistic medium. This uncertainty about the poetic adequacy of speech and the fearful ambivalence about the power of language to undo the world it describes become the underlying concerns of Wordsworth's *Essays on Epitaphs* (composed in 1810).[15] In the *Essays*, Wordsworth's ostensible purpose is to revive and improve the epitaphic literary mode. Yet his fascination with the epitaph clearly centers in the way this written form can guarantee those human and literary values Wordsworth had earlier entrusted to rustic speech. For the necessarily slow and laborious process of carving a funerary inscription on a tombstone encourages, as Wordsworth comes to realize, a correspondingly restrained and simple mode of poetic language in the epitaphic poet. Otherwise the "very form and

[15] For recent criticism concerning these previously neglected Wordsworthian essays, see Frances Ferguson, *Wordsworth: Language as Counter-Spirit* (New Haven and London: Yale University Press, 1977), p. 29; and Geoffrey Hartman, "Wordsworth, Inscription, and Romantic Nature Poetry," in *From Sensibility to Romanticism: Essays Presented to Frederick A. Pottle*, ed. Frederick W. Hilles and Harold Bloom (New York: Oxford University Press, 1965), pp. 389-413.

substance of the monument which has received the inscription . . . might seem to reproach the author who had
given way upon this occasion to transports of mind, or to
quick turns of conflicting passion" (Wordsworth, *Prose
Works*, 2:60). Here, then, is a mode of writing that is
wholly free from the defects of ordinary literary writing,
wholly distinct from what Wordsworth calls "proud writing shut up for the studious" (Wordsworth *Prose Works*,
2:59). Unlike the literary mode of the class-bound book,
epitaphic writing is democratically open to everyone en-
tering the churchyard. Unlike the fluttering and superfi-
cially imprinted pages of the book, the epitaph is deeply
cut and permanent. Most of all, in epitaphs, words maintain a direct, in Hartley's sense, a "real" relation to things
by being physically connected to them: the epitaphic poet
can anchor words in things by literally writing *upon*
things.

Yet beneath the hopefulness of the analogy between the
classless permanence of the rural epitaph and the enduring
value of a poetry based on rural speech there lurks a deeper
anxiety about language itself, about treacherous linguistic
autonomy and impermanence:

> Words are too awful an instrument for good and evil
> to be trifled with: they hold above all other external
> powers a dominion over thoughts. If words be not (re-
> curring to a metaphor before used) an incarnation of
> the thought but only a clothing for it, then surely will
> they prove an ill gift; such a one as those poisoned
> vestments, read of in the stories of superstitious times,
> which had power to consume and to alienate from his
> right mind the victim who put them on. Language, if
> it do not uphold, and feed, and leave in quiet, like the
> power of gravitation or the air we breathe, is a

counter-spirit, unremittingly and noiselessly at work
to derange, to subvert, to lay waste, to vitiate, and to
dissolve. (Wordsworth, *Prose Works*, 2:84-85)

In the face of this radical anxiety about language, Words-
worth's more confident pronouncements in the Preface to
Lyrical Ballads seem ingenuously utopian. The *Essays on
Epitaphs* strike just that note of demoralization about the
Romantic logos that, in a more urgently apocalyptic key,
Victorians were to hear in literary Decadence: Words-
worth's linguistic counterspirit would reappear as Walter
Pater's profane "soul in style," and the sensual presence
and insinuating voice of this counterspirit would haunt the
pages of the central Decadent *topos*, the fatal book.

The disturbing autonomy and materiality Wordsworth
senses in language reveals how very far he is from sharing
Herder's belief in the identity of words and thought. Indeed, as Stephen K. Land has recently argued in a brilliant
essay, it is Wordsworth's continuous attempt to control or
circumvent the dangerously independent powers of words
that shapes the overt motives of his poetic: the return to the
simple speech and occasions of the rural peasant, the identification of poetry with pre-verbal feelings rather than
with their verbal expression.[16] In the Romantic philology
shaped by men such as Herder, speech is privileged over
writing so that the spiritual may in the end prevail over the
material. But Wordsworth's appeal to rural speech over
conventional texts only *seems* to invoke spirit over matter
or letter, for language always retains a disturbing materiality. Language can be subdued in epitaphic writing,
made simple as a stone. Or, taking as its model rural
speech, it can be made, as Land suggests, so transparent as

[16] See Stephen K. Land, "The Silent Poet: An Aspect of Wordsworth's
Semantic Theory," *University of Toronto Quarterly* 42 (1972-73): 157-69.

to leave a very minimum of verbal interposition between the reader and the feeling of the poet, so that it becomes almost as transparent as "gravitation or the air we breathe." But such is Wordsworth's mistrust of words and their potentially ungovernable associations (a mistrust that identifies him so obviously as the heir of Locke) that he can portray them as poisonous, deranging, corrupting, dissolving, counter to the spirit.

Wordsworth thus did not seek so much to collapse the Enlightenment polarity of word and thing into a new "incarnational" unity of word and thing as to reverse the axis of that polarity *from* words *to* things or feelings. But the ultimate consequence of Wordsworth's preference for the pre-verbal "language of the heart" is a retreat into silence, "a deliberate attempt to construct by means of poetry situations which necessarily transcend language precisely because they are fitting subjects for poetry. Inarticulateness is not a mere *device* within Wordsworth's poetic fictions but rather a necessary correlative to the semantic theory upon which his theory of poetry rests" (Land, "Silent Poet," p. 168). As long as the primacy Wordsworth confers upon feelings is sustained by a universalist belief in the commonality of such feelings among men, the poet can trust in the real language of men or even in the eloquent situations of the "silent Poet" to make his meaning known. With the decay of the belief in the Augustan universal, however, the redeeming potentialities of both natural speech and silence as genuinely communicative poetic modes will be transformed.

In grounding his poetics in an alien ontology, Wordsworth thus commits himself to a world of experience and value that exists outside of language: pursued faithfully enough by a sensibility "organic" enough, the meditational habit will at last produce descriptions of objects and

21

sentiments "of such a nature and in such connection with each other, that the understanding of the being to whom we address ourselves, if he be in a healthful state of association, must necessarily be in some degree enlightened, his taste and his affections ameliorated" (Wordsworth, *Prose Works*, 1:126). But the moral community that here finds expression *in* language clearly preceded that expression: both poet and reader may now trust language to unite them only because they trusted the "essential passions" and "elementary feelings" *first*. And this is in Wordsworth's own terms a fatal contradiction. To immunize poetry from the treacheries of language by referring poetic vision to a world forever outside language is ultimately to abandon the aim of regenerating society through poetry.

The larger issues of Wordsworth's later disagreement with Coleridge, of what literary history has transmitted to us as a narrow dispute about poetic diction, in fact turn on just this crucial question of whether literary language may be viewed as an agent of moral regeneration—not, as in Wordsworth's uneasy apprehension of his own poetry, a mere secondary expression of moral community, but a means of bringing such community into existence. Beneath Wordsworth's view of language in the *Essays on Epitaphs* lies a barely repressed realm of anxiety about the relation between language and culture, about the very possibility of anything noble and enduring in human life. In Coleridge's opposing view, on the other hand, lies a grand equation of language and civilization itself, an equation that would collapse only with that implosion of Victorian cultural values from which literary Decadence would emerge in the *fin de siècle*.

In Coleridge, too, we encounter the first really profound impact of that German philology that was to play so decisive a role in Victorian views of language and civiliza-

tion. In 1798-1799, when William and Dorothy Wordsworth were living their closely sequestered life in the little
town of Goslar, Coleridge took up residence in Göttingen,
then one of the leading university centers of Germany.
There Coleridge entered the intellectual orbit of C. G.
Heyne, the presiding genius of Göttingen and the father of
Altertumswissenschaft, the sympathetic exploration of the
classical past embraced at its broadest cultural extent: language, literature, history, myth, philosophy, geography,
art. This was the Heyne who was so vivid a hero to Carlyle

> as the founder of a new epoch in classical study; as the
> first who with any decisiveness attempted to translate
> fairly beyond the letter of the Classics; to read in the
> writings of the Ancients, not their language alone, or
> even their detached opinions and records, but their
> spirit and character, their way of life and thought;
> how the World and Nature painted themselves to the
> mind in those old ages; how, in one word, the Greeks
> and the Romans were men, even as we are.[17]

This sonorous conception of the past, so obviously echoing
the thought of Herder and Bishop Lowth, would reach
forward through Coleridge decisively to influence Walter
Pater, Lionel Johnson, and Oscar Wilde.

The *Altertumswissenschaft* of Heyne, whom Coleridge
came to know personally during his year in Göttingen, derived in direct terms from the Herderian belief that a nation or civilization possessed a unique inner life conditioned by its own special circumstances and expressed
most fully and characteristically in its language and liter-

---

[17] Thomas Carlyle, "The Life of Heyne" [1828], in *The Works of Thomas
Carlyle*, 30 vols. (London: Chapman and Hall, 1899; reprinted New York:
AMS Press, 1969), 26:350-51. Carlyle is here reviewing a biography of
Heyne for the *Foreign Review*.

ature. It was Romantic philology, that is to say, the philological thought of Herder and Heyne, which Coleridge first encountered in Göttingen, as well as the work of Friedrich Schlegel and Wilhelm von Humboldt, which Coleridge would later encounter in England, that convinced him that language was "so beautiful, so divine a subject."[18] And Coleridge, in his turn, was to persuade the Victorians who followed him that the English language possessed an intrinsic beauty and vital interest all its own. The specific insights Coleridge gained from Romantic philology—and as L. A. Willoughby has demonstrated, they are many[19]—were to prove less important than the presiding sense Romantic philology awakened in Coleridge of language both as the characteristic voice of a specific culture or nation and as an organic whole at once possessing a history and capable of growth and decline. In specific terms, the idealist conception of a national essence living beyond or beneath the lives of a nation's individual citizens is what allowed Coleridge to view language both as part of "the collective Mind of a Country" and as "a magnificent History of acts of individual minds."[20] The linguistic interaction Coleridge then posited between collective and individual minds would become a central belief among Victorians.

The notion that language is not wholly autonomous, that for all its embodiment of the spirit of a nation or people it could be improved by individual speakers, is curiously exemplified in Coleridge's remark that "in all socie-

[18] S. T. Coleridge, *Table Talk and Omniana of Samuel Taylor Coleridge*, ed. T. Ashe (London: George Bell, 1909), p. 70.
[19] See L. A. Willoughby, "Coleridge as a Philologist," *Modern Language Review* 31 (1936): 176-201.
[20] Quoted in Alice D. Snyder, *Coleridge on Logic and Learning* (New Haven: Yale University Press, 1929), p. 138.

ties there exists an instinct of growth, a certain collective, unconscious good sense working progressively to desynonymize those words originally of the same meaning."[21] For Coleridge's own contribution to language in this instance was the word "desynonymize," his own invention and a telling illustration of the impact he thought gifted individuals could have on their language. In this, Coleridge was diverging from German philological thought, which shifted the initiative away from individuals towards the collective linguistic creativity of the *Volk*. Jacob Grimm, for example, assumed (with Wordsworth) that untutored speakers possess a naturally judicious taste in linguistic matters. Coleridge, however, always valuing literature above speech, reserved a special place for individual masters of language: "A man of Genius using a rich and expressive Language (the Greek, German, or English) is an excellent instance and illustration of the ever individualizing process and dynamic Being of Ideas" (Snyder, *Coleridge*, p. 138). The notion that language might in this case be using the man of genius to express *itself*, though undeniably present, is so far suppressed. Hence, too, Coleridge's much abused attempts to coin new words. As one Victorian was to object, "Minds not so subtile or metaphysical as that of Mr. Coleridge would scarcely recognize the necessity of such terms as these," listing *influencive*, *exhaustive*, *extroitive*, *retroitive* and *productivity*, all taken from *On the Constitution of Church and State*.[22] The objection that such neologisms have an uncertain linguistic fate misses the point, which is nothing other than Coleridge's

[21] S. T. Coleridge, *Biographia Literaria*, ed. J. Shawcross, 2 vols. (London: Oxford University Press, 1907), 1:61.

[22] Matthew Harrison, *The Rise, Progress and Present Structure of the English Language*, 2nd American ed. (Philadelphia: E. C. and J. Biddle, 1856), p. 111.

determination to participate in the life of his own language.

Even when he seems most to move against the current of Romantic philology, however, Coleridge's thinking about language and civilization betrays a profound debt to his German experience. Here, for instance, Coleridge's belief that gifted individuals have the power to transform language, much as it may express the collective spirit of a nation or *Volk*, traces to the same year in Göttingen, for it was in Göttingen that Coleridge learned that Luther's translation of the Bible had done more than simply turn the Vulgate into German, but had in effect transformed literary German into itself:

> In Luther's own German writings, and eminently in his translation of the Bible, the *German* language commenced. I mean the language as it is at present *written*; that which is called the HIGH-GERMAN, as contra-distinguished from the PLATT-TEUTSCH, the dialect of the flat or northern countries, and from the OBER-TEUTSCH, the language of the middle and Southern Germany. The High German is indeed a *lingua communis*, not actually the native language of any province, but the choice and fragrancy of all the dialects. From this cause it is at once the most copious and the most grammatical of all the European tongues. (*Biographia*, 1:140)

Thus where Herder found written German woefully impoverished and imprecise compared to the "living" spoken dialects, Coleridge would come to praise High German because it seemed to represent an important cultural ideal—an organic yet humanly perfected language capable of voicing an idealized national life.

The phrase *lingua communis* returns us to Coleridge's

quarrel with Wordsworth in the *Biographia*, where Coleridge in fact has few real grounds of disagreement with his friend: for both are vitally interested in the relationship of poet to audience and both perceive this relationship to involve more than just poetry. Yet Wordsworth and Coleridge, though in full agreement about the heightened experience of human community that poetry can bring about, disagree irreconcilably about the best model for poetic communication. When he proposes substituting *lingua communis* for the "real language of men" in *Biographia* 17, Coleridge does so not because in his movement towards a hierarchical view of society he now resists Wordsworth's revolutionary devotion to human equality and fraternity, but because he believes that it is only through written language—through literature—that language becomes permanent and accessible enough to be held in common and through time by people otherwise widely different. This is a genuinely radical disagreement: where Wordsworth privileged purified rural speech because of its simplicity and immediacy and its intimate connection with the things of the palpable world, Coleridge sees in rustic speech only the narrowest and most evanescent of communicative modes. Far from providing an all-embracing medium as Wordsworth had imagined, dialectal speech as it really is, Coleridge argues, locks itself entirely within the narrow circle of idiosyncracy, occupation, and region, preserving its few intimations of the larger world only in degraded form.[23]

---

[23] Cf. Coleridge, *Biographia*, 2:40: "If the history of the phrases in hourly currency among our peasants were traced, a person not previously aware of the fact would be surprised at finding so large a number, which three or four centuries ago were the exclusive property of the universities and the schools; and, at the commencement of the Reformation, had been transferred from the school to the pulpit, and thus gradually passed into common life."

The meaning of Coleridge's great contribution to the Victorian ideal of civilization thus derives from this moment of his quarrel with an earlier Wordsworth, from his intensifying conviction that speech, or language as embodied merely in speech, is impermanent. This is the great function of the *lingua communis*, for where Wordsworth can only hope that the "real language of men" will become more common, Coleridge rejoins that only language firmly held in common can be truly real to all men. For, spoken nowhere but intelligible everywhere, only the *lingua communis* of literature can lift men above their contingent, partial lives and bring them into communion with the higher life of ideas. Similarly, within the stable and capacious universe of discourse opened by the *lingua communis*, attachments to more than just one's neighbor become possible. Freed from the trivial but all-determining accidents of rustic life—"the accidental character of the clergyman, the existence or non-existence of schools; or even, perhaps, as the exciseman, publican, or barber, happen to be, or not be zealous politicians, and readers of the weekly newspaper *pro bono publico*" (Coleridge, *Biographia*, 2:42)—and sustained by a permanent form of language that links past with present for the sake of the future, men may conceive of themselves as belonging to a larger cultural and historical whole.

In the relation between the *lingua communis* and an enduring civilization lies, too, the meaning of Coleridge's famous vision of a national clerisy. For it is as members of the clerisy that Coleridge's gifted individual contributors *to* language become guardians *of* language. Though such a book as the English Bible has worked in the past as a "holdfast" against linguistic decay,[24] Coleridge is urgently

[24] Cf. Coleridge, *Table Talk*, p. 49: "Our version of the Bible is to be loved

persuaded that the *lingua communis* of literature and the higher organic life it expresses must have beyond this human partisans working on its behalf. This is the role of the clerisy (Coleridge's Englishing of the German *clerisei*), that "permanent, nationalized, learned order," one part of which was to "remain at the fountain heads of the humanities, in cultivating and enlarging the knowledge already possessed," and the other larger portion of which was to "be distributed throughout the country, so as not to leave even the smallest integral part or division without a resident guide, guardian, and instructor."[25] And behind Coleridge's notion of the clerisy there lies, once again, the authority of that organic conception of language and culture he had absorbed from German thought. We hear the voices of Herder and Heyne in those later words of Friedrich Schlegel that would echo down to the end of the nineteenth century:

> The care of the national language I consider as at all times a sacred trust and a most important privilege of the higher orders of society. Every man of education should make it the object of his unceasing concern, to preserve his language pure and entire, to speak it, so far as is in his power, in all its beauty and perfection. . . . A nation which allows her language to go to ruin, is parting with the last of her intellectual independence, and testifies her willingness to cease to exist.[26]

---

and prized for this, as for a thousand other things,—that it has preserved a purity of meaning to many terms of natural objects. Without this holdfast, our vitiated imaginations would refine away language to mere abstractions. Hence the French have lost their poetical language; and Mr. Blanco White says the same thing has happened to the Spanish."

[25] S. T. Coleridge, *On the Constitution of Church and State*, ed. John Colmer, in *The Collected Works of Samuel Taylor Coleridge*, ed. Kathleen Coburn, 16 vols. (Princeton: Princeton University Press, 1976), 10:69, 43.

[26] Friedrich Schlegel, *Lectures on the History of Literature, Ancient and*

Wordsworth's ultimate failure, then, the failure that brings him back in the *Biographia* as Coleridge's symbolic antagonist on the great question of speech and language, is to have abandoned "that prospectiveness of mind, that *surview*" (Coleridge, *Biographia* 2:44) which the *lingua communis* grants, in favor of the disjunctiveness, the undeliberateness, the mere factuality of peasant speech. In later years Coleridge would protest even more vehemently against the notion that general illumination could proceed, as he put it, *per ascensum ab imis*: "You begin, therefore, with the attempt to *popularize* science: but you will only effect its *plebification*. It is folly to think of making all, or the many, philosophers, or even men of science and systematic knowledge" (Coleridge, *Constitution*, p. 69). But even as early as the *Biographia*, Coleridge's great effort is visibly to resist the downward levelling tendencies he felt were implicit in all "democratic" schemes of education and explicit in Wordsworth's championing of rustic speech over the "proud writing" of the English literary tradition. Coleridge's concerted effort in the *Biographia* is thus "an attempt both to save Wordsworth for Literature and to save Literature from Wordsworth, preserving its traditional and relational properties from the leveling onslaught of [spoken] Language" (Ruoff, "Wordsworth on Language," p. 211).

To save literature from Wordsworth was, in this context, to define and preserve an idealized relationship between literature and civilization. Indeed, this relationship, as well as the task of its defense, was to become Coleridge's enduring bequest to the Victorian generations that succeeded him. For what we mean by high Victorian culture,

---

Modern (New York: J. and H. G. Langley, 1841), pp. 236-37. This is J. G. Lockhart's 1818 translation of Schlegel's very popular lectures, *Geschichte der Alten und Neuen Literatur* [1815].

with its distinctive ethos of earnestness and energy and supreme cultural confidence, is founded, as upon a rock, on Coleridge's identification of literature and civilization, that interanimating synthesis of outward expression and inward essence or spirit by which civilization brought forth literature and literature articulated civilization. The argument between Wordsworth and Coleridge as it is represented in the *Biographia* thus turns less on such local issues as poetic diction than on an underlying issue of linguistic, and ultimately cultural, anxiety. What Coleridge had seen with a kind of uneasy clairvoyance was that any attempt, such as Wordsworth's, to ground poetry in living speech must inevitably expose poetic language to the erosive forces of time and historical circumstance. Even more ominously, in doing this, a speech-based poetics must eventually expose the civilization that had produced it to the anarchic forces of ignorance and mere change. Given the linguistic and cultural danger posed by such a poetics as Wordsworth's, Coleridge attempted to publicize the danger by insisting upon the identity of a nation and its literature, the ideal dialect of the *lingua communis*. This identification of a civilization and its literature the Victorians, as we have said, were to embrace as a rich inheritance. But Coleridge's tactic obviously harbors a deep vulnerability: for if anything should call into question, or undermine, the ideal character of the *lingua communis*, then the civilization with which the *lingua communis* is inseparably identified will also be called into question. And this vulnerability, too, the Victorians were to inherit.

❦ ❦ ❦

Coleridge, as we have seen, drew upon the expanding resources of Romantic philology in order to discredit Wordsworth's speech-based aesthetic and establish the *lingua communis* of literature as a commanding cultural ideal. Coleridge appropriated German philological thought in the name of spirit, for he was, of course, a committed philosophical idealist, intent on the defeat of materialism and the overthrow of all mechanistic systems of thought and social order. And Wordsworth's speech-based poetics, as we have also seen, manifestly did contain disturbing elements of materialism, at times even betraying a mistrust of its own linguistic medium.[27] Coleridge's identification of inward spirit with written language thus makes a certain obvious sense, particularly when we view it in its original polemical context.

Yet it must always be remembered that Coleridge's vesting of spirit in written language violated at a deep level Romantic assumptions about language, assumptions that habitually and instinctively identified spirit, not with written language, but with speech or the speaking voice. In the earlier years of the nineteenth century, Coleridge's incarnation of national spirit in written language made much polemical sense and little practical difference, for Romantic philologists such as Herder's intellectual heirs Friedrich Schlegel and Wilhelm von Humboldt did not distinguish with any great sense of urgency between written and spoken forms of the language. Only later, when the more generous, "mystic" assumptions of Romantic philology would be forced to yield before the rigorous distinctions of a newer and aggressively "scientific" philology, would Coleridge's incarnation of national spirit in written language be exposed to a devastating critique, and ultimately,

[27] For the political aspect of Wordsworth's and Coleridge's linguistic theories, see Olivia Smith, *The Politics of Language 1791-1819* (Oxford: Clarendon, 1984). I became aware of this author's work too late, unfortunately, to take full account of her argument here.

to contemptuous dismissal. In the meantime, however, Coleridge's Victorian successors had adopted his identification of national spirit and written language, and made this essentially problematical basis serve as the foundation for more and more of their cherished hopes and cultural beliefs.

Coleridge's ideal of culture in the broadest sense, or, to give it its most appropriate name, of civilization,[28] had already achieved a triumphant expression by the middle years of the Victorian epoch, when J. H. Newman imperturbably declared in 1854 that although there were doubtless other civilizations and societies scattered over the globe,

> yet this civilization, together with the society which is its creation and its home, is so distinctive and luminous in its character, so imperial in its extent, so imposing in its duration, and so utterly without rival upon the face of the earth, that the association may fitly assume to itself the title of "Human Society," and its civilization the abstract term "Civilization."[29]

Indeed, the same unruffled conviction of Western cultural accomplishment and hegemony had as early as 1832 prompted the young Tennyson in "The Palace of Art" to speak of "the supreme Caucasian mind." The mood that Newman and Tennyson share clearly represents a moment of buoyant cultural confidence in which England is felt to be the final and inevitable heir to all Western achievement,

---

[28] See Michael Timko's discussion of the term and the concept of civilization among the Victorians in "The Victorianism of Victorian Literature," *New Literary History* 6 (1974-75): 607-627.

[29] John Henry Newman, "Christianity and Letters," in *The Idea of a University*, ed. Charles Frederick Harrold (New York and London: Longmans, Green, 1947), p. 219.

in which the culture that had formerly been shared among the Western nations as a patrimony is now to be wholly possessed by England as a birthright. Such sublime confidence, as yet undiminished by economic reverses or by the anthropological perspective that in the closing years of the nineteenth century would shrink all such claims of national superiority to fit the disparaging scale of cultural relativism, was, naturally, further swelled by England's continuing commercial and imperial conquests. But its core was always constituted by an essentially ideological belief in England's providential destiny among its fellow nations, and not simply by a momentarily favorable conjunction of shipping tonnages and square miles of territory possessed.

The vision of high civilization manifest in Newman's or Tennyson's utterance inevitably found its center in written language, for when Victorians began to concern themselves with civilization as a social construct and ideal, it was the public mode of written language—Coleridge's *lingua communis*—that inevitably rose into ascendancy over spoken language as a model for discourse. It was not simply that the new conditions of Victorian civilization, whether actual or ideal, required written language, whether traditionally spelled or (as many in the simplified spelling movement demanded) reformed; rather, written language, as Carlyle realized, was the very condition of civilization, because it represented a surviving memento of vanished precursor civilizations, and because the possibility of writing made historicity possible and, with it, the nineteenth-century historicist idea of civilization. The Victorians had discovered that any notion of civilization presupposes writing. It is this implicit priority of writing to civilization that dictates the Victorian privileging of written language over speech.

The vision of civilization as something embodied in a written *lingua communis* in turn completes itself, through a kind of necessity of cultural logic, in an ultimate equation between civilization and literature. It is here that the German tradition of Romantic philology that Coleridge mediated to Victorians was to have so decisive an impact on their thought, for the same tradition that declared a nation's language to be the expression of its inner spirit made no rigorous distinction, as a later "scientific" philology was to do, between language and literature. This explains, for instance, the enormous influence of Wilhelm von Humboldt on Coleridge's idealist successors. J. W. Donaldson in his early and influential book *The New Cratylus* (1839), for example, devoted several pages to direct translation of Humboldt's great work, *The Heterogeneity of Language and Its Influence on the Intellectual Development of Mankind (Über den Verschiedenheit des menschlichen Sprachbaues und ihren Einfluß auf die geistige Entwickelung des Menschengeschlechts)*, citing Humboldt's view that "language is the outward appearance of the intellect of nations: their language is their intellect and their intellect their language: we cannot sufficiently identify the two."[30] Thus language came to be seen not as an outward "pedigree" of a nation (as Samuel Johnson had described it in the previous century), but as the revelation of its inner reality. As a writer for the *Nineteenth Century* rendered Humboldt, language became "an accurate index to the grade of intellectual comprehension attained by [a race of people], and the intellectual progress of the race may be traced in the gradual development of its speech."[31]

[30] J. W. Donaldson, *The New Cratylus, or Contributions Towards a More Accurate Knowledge of the Greek Language*, 2nd rev. ed. (London: J. W. Parker, 1850), p. 43.

[31] G. Croom Robertson, "How We Come By Our Knowledge," *Nineteenth Century* 1 (March 1877): 116-17.

The influence of Coleridge and, through him, of Romantic philology on Victorian civilization is most obvious at moments like this, when language is taken to express the inner essence of a nation, and the nation, as in Victorian England, sees itself as possessed of a high historical mission. Yet a less obvious consequence of the Romantic view was to have effects just as momentous in the long run. This is the premise of Romantic organicism, which, in positing the living integrity and growth of all organisms, moved easily from the idea that language or literature was the living expression of a civilization to the idea that language or literature in turn actively molded culture. Literature was thus simultaneously an effect of civilization and a partial cause. This peculiar but characteristically idealist form of reciprocal causality allowed an American editor of Friedrich Schlegel's *Lectures on the History of Literature* to declare, "At once the result of opulence, and refined cultivation, literary pursuits become also the means of increasing and perpetuating the civilization from which they originate" (Schlegel, *Lectures*, p. iii). So too Carlyle, following Schiller, pronounced literature both the "daughter" and the "nurse" of all that was spiritual in man, while writers for the *Edinburgh Review* termed literature "an index and a school of national character," as well as "the storehouse and the guardian of knowledge."[32] This insistence upon the double function of literature as both expres-

---

[32] Carlyle, "The Life of Schiller" in *Works*, 25:200: "The daughter, she [i.e. Literature] is likewise the nurse of all that is spiritual and exalted in our character"; [Rowland Prothero], "Modern Poetry," *Edinburgh Review* 163 (April 1886): 467: "As an index and a school of national character the importance of poetry can hardly be exaggerated"; [Henry Reeve], "The Literature and Language of the Age," *Edinburgh Review* 169 (April 1889): 328: "The prime duty and glory of literature is to be the storehouse and the guardian of knowledge."

sive and formative of civilization is one we have come to consider typically Victorian.

It is against the background of Romantic philology, then, against the Coleridgean-idealist notion of literature as the inner speech of an idealized nation, that we are to locate Matthew Arnold's project as embodied in such works as *Essays in Criticism* (1865) and *Culture and Anarchy* (1869). The project that Arnold there proposes, the renovation of imaginative letters as a secular but nonetheless saving scripture, was undertaken, as William Buckler has said, "with the urgency of a desperate hope," and forms "the current which runs steadily, expansively, sometimes turbulently from Carlyle in the 1820s to Hardy in the 1920s. The modern world needed a new testament, and literature was the only mode in which it could be made available."[33] Yet this is to introduce at the same time a pressing dilemma: literature could become an "inevitable" mode of imaginative salvation only if one believed, as the idealists did, that literature communicated with a noumenal realm of value. With what justice could it be said to do so? Because literature was specifically wrought out of language, the idealist argument affirmed, it necessarily participated as language did in the noumenal realm, either because it was a divinely bestowed gift or (as we have seen Herder argue) because rationality itself, the capacity to distinguish among images reflectively, resided in the human power to create an inner distinguishing mark or word. Thus in the short term, whether one accepted the orthodox theological view or the secular interpretation of the Romantics, the logos——the unity of inward idea and outward sign——was guaranteed.

[33] William Buckler, *The Victorian Imagination: Essays in Aesthetic Exploration* (New York and London: New York University Press, 1980), p. 4.

The Romantic notion of literature as the logos relocated within human history may explain, for instance, Schlegel's view of literature as "the comprehensive essence of the Intellectual Life of a Nation" (Schlegel, *Lectures*, p. ix). The influence of this view on the Victorian conception of civilization is caught, in turn, in Carlyle's description of literature as the "essence of philosophy, religion, art; whatever speaks to the immortal part of man."[34] This is why Carlyle's transformation of literature into a secular scripture represents so important a moment in Victorian attitudes toward language. Unlike Coleridge, who preferred that common men and women read only their Bibles, Carlyle was unafraid of opening the Gospel of Imagination to all classes, provided of course that it was the right gospel ("Close thy *Byron*; and open thy *Goethe*") and that it was read in the right way (" 'What!' cries the reader, 'are we to *study* Poetry? To pore over it as we do Fluxions?' ").[35] If poetry, as Wordsworth had taught, was the culture of feelings, it was from the Victorian point of view imperative that those inner feelings be educated in the etymological sense, "led out" into wider public responsibilities, especially when the public that harbored those feelings was itself growing wider and wider.

The triumph of literature in Carlyle's compelling vision, and with it the triumph of Coleridge's hope for a *lingua communis* adequate to the demands of an idealized English civilization, is thus in displaced form the victory of Romantic philology within the confines of an emergent Victorian intellectual culture. For this was the view of literature as scripture, or literature as secularized logos, that in an important sense defines what we mean by Victorian

[34] Carlyle, "Life of Schiller," in *Works*, 25:200.

[35] Carlyle, *Sartor Resartus* [1833], in *Works*, 1:153; Carlyle, review of Goethe's *Collected Works*, *Foreign Review* 2 (1828): 116.

culture, whether in Matthew Arnold's consideration of the
Bible as poetry in 1871, or in John Davidson's poetic foot-
note to Carlyle still later in the century:

> the Bible seems
> A volume with the closing chapters gone,
>
> . . . .
>
> And where are those lost leaves?—in other books,
> Sweet scripture of these latter times, the lay
> Of modern minstrel, the romance of days
> We love in. What's the Bible but the truth?
> Especially the truth of God and man?
> And that is sacred be it here or there,
> In Middlemarch or Palestine.[36]

The same movement of ideas carries us irresistibly towards such late-Victorian developments as Aestheticism,
in which the equation between literature and logos was to
be made almost literal. Even today, when the description
of Aestheticism as a Religion of Beauty has become commonplace, Arthur Machen's version of the idea retains a
certain capacity to shock: "Style . . . is the outward sign of
the burning grace within," "literature [is] the language of
the Shadowy Companion," "literature is the expression,
through the aesthetic medium of words, of the dogmas of
the Catholic Church, and that which in any way is out of
harmony with these dogmas is not literature."[37] Though
Carlyle would never have worshipped in the Aestheticist
chapel, he laid its cornerstone nonetheless.

[36] John Davidson, *Diabolus Amans: A Dramatic Poem* (Glasgow: Wilson
and McCormick, 1885), p. 45. Cf. also *The George Eliot Letters*, ed. Gordon
S. Haight, 9 vols. (New Haven: Yale University Press, 1954-1978), 6:340:
" 'George Eliot's I don't rank as Novels but as second Bibles.' "

[37] Arthur Machen, *Hieroglyphics* [1902] (London: Unicorn, 1960), pp.
40, 76, 176-77.

To see literature as the secularized scripture of Victorian civilization is also to see the underlying relationship between many widely scattered features of Victorian life: the cultivation of family reading-parties as a social institution, or the huge appetite for public readings of the sort given by Charles Dickens; the public perfection of conversational powers by men like Oscar Wilde (of whom Yeats marvelled, "I never before heard a man talking with perfect sentences, as if he had written them all overnight with labour"[38]), or the attempts of Dr. Bowdler to keep books, even Shakespeare or the Bible, from bringing a blush to the cheek of modesty. For even behind the evident excesses of Bowdlerism lies the conviction that the state and fate of civilization itself, or at least of "our English civilisation," were inextricably bound up with the state of English language and literature; words, Coleridge had taught, "are moral acts."[39]

The enormous influence of Romantic philology here lies once again in the immediate background. Because words, in the Romantic idealist view of language, were not inert vessels for meaning, but instead were "living powers," they had to be restrained as living powers of will and passion were restrained—through inward repression and outward check. "There is a fact of immense moral significance," declared G. P. Marsh in his popular *Lectures on the English Language*, a fact only recently made known, thanks largely to the then-new study of language, and it was that

language is not a dead, unelastic, passive implement, but a POWER, which like all natural powers, reacts on

[38] W. B. Yeats, *The Autobiography of William Butler Yeats* (New York: Macmillan, 1965), p. 87.

[39] S. T. Coleridge, *The Friend*, ed. Barbara E. Rooke, 2 vols., in *Collected Works*, 4:I, 77.

that which it calls into exercise. . . . [The] mere giving of verbal utterance to any strong emotion or passion, even if the expression be unaccompanied by any other outward act, stimulates and intensifies the excitement of feeling to that degree that when the tongue is once set free, the reason is dethroned, and brute nature becomes the master of the man.[40]

The emergence of a Victorian standard of public discourse, one suppressing immoral or obscene or just simply idiosyncratic language, thus derives in direct terms from the Romantic idealist notion of language as a moral force. This explains the sometimes violent reactions against the private or purely expressive use of language that so many Victorians were to discover in the poetry of the Spasmodics and Pre-Raphaelites or in literary Decadence. It also explains the tremendous rise during the Victorian period of what might be called linguistic nationalism. Inspired by the patriotic stress within Romantic philology, the stress that had led Schlegel, for example, to urge European nations, including his own, to throw off the tyranny of French, Victorian linguistic nationalism finds its comic apotheosis in the gravely smug observation of Dickens's Mr. Podsnap to the hapless Frenchman, "Ours is a Copious Language, and Trying to Strangers." Yet serious students of language like R. C. Trench could declare without Dickens's satire that the love of one's own language was

[40] G. P. Marsh, *Lectures on the English Language*, First series (New York: Charles Scribner; London: Sampson, Low, Son, 1865), p. 233. First delivered at Columbia University in 1858-1859, Marsh's lectures were widely popular and influential—both Max Müller and Matthew Arnold (who later became acquaintances of Marsh's when he was U.S. Minister to Italy) were indebted to them. Because Marsh was at once the American secretary of the Philological Society of London and a convinced "Saxonist," believing in the manifest destiny of the "Anglican" people of England and the United States, I have drawn upon his work in this study as characteristic of certain aspects of Victorian attitudes towards language and the study of language.

but "the love of our country expressing itself in one particular direction";[41] and J. C. Hare could argue that

> he who does not know how to prize the inheritance his ancestors have bequeathed to him, will hardly better or enlarge it. A man should love and venerate his native language, as the first of his benefactors, as the awakener and stirrer of all his thoughts, the frame and mould and rule of his spiritual being, as the great bond and medium of intercourse with his fellows, as the mirror in which he sees his own nature, and without which he could not even commune with himself, as the image in which the wisdom of God has chosen to reveal itself to him. He who thus thinks of his native language will never touch it without reverence. Yet his reverence will not withhold, but rather encourage him to do what he can to purify and improve it. Of this duty no Englishman in our times has shewn himself so well aware as Coleridge.[42]

The great aim of British philology in the nineteenth century, an aim that finds its supreme monument in the *Oxford English Dictionary*, was thus to become the recovery of the English linguistic past. And, under the inspiration of that Romantic philology that seemed so persuasively to identify the nation with its literature, the same impulse led to the canonization of those "volumes paramount" that represented the nation in its ideal and eternal aspect. In the King James Bible and Shakespeare's plays and Milton's poetry could be found, Victorians believed, "among the most potent agencies in the cultivation of the

---

41 R. C. Trench, *English Past and Present* [1854], in *On the Study of Words and English Past and Present* (New York: E. P. Dutton, [1927]), p. 3.

42 J. C. Hare, *Guesses at Truth*, 3rd ed. (London: Macmillan, 1867), p. 235.

national mind and heart, the strongest bond of union in a homogenous people, the surest holding ground against the shifting currents, the ebb and flow, of opinion and taste" (Marsh, *Lectures*, p. 17). Coleridge had been much struck by the example of Germany, where linguistic and literary nationality preceded, and seemed likely at last to produce, political nationality. Newman expressed much the same idea when in his wonderful peroration on literature he declared, "By great authors the many are drawn up into unity, national character is fixed, a people speaks."[43] And the idea retains its power even when translated into the coarse journalistic prose of one T. C. Horsfall in 1880: "Nothing perhaps except an invasion would do so much to bring people of different classes nearer together than they now are in England, as the possession by many persons in every class of familiar knowledge of even one great book."[44]

The ultimate impact of Romantic philology on the Victorian ideal of civilization is registered, however, only in a last countercurrent that, having moved outward from a purely linguistic view of language to an ideal of literature as the logos of a society or nation, returns on its philological origins in an imperial vision of English as the destined language of an emergent world civilization. This is a vision of culture in which literature retains its privileged centrality, a future in which "the world is circled by the accents of Shakspeare and Milton,"[45] but it is a vision drawing its strength from the new science of historical and com-

[43] John Henry Newman, "Literature: A Lecture in the School of Philosophy and Letters," in *Idea of a University*, p. 255.

[44] [T. C. Horsfall], "Painting and Popular Culture," *Fraser's Magazine* 101 o.s., 21 n.s. (June 1880): 855-56.

[45] Thomas Watts, "On the Probable Future Position of the English Language," *Proceedings of the Philological Society* 4 (1848-50): 212.

parative philology. This is the context, for instance, in which Victorian commentators on language never tired of quoting the opinion of the great German philologist and lexicographer Jacob Grimm that English was destined to prevail as a world language, or in which the linguistic character of English as a "mixed" tongue, a hybrid of the Germanic and Romance lines, would come to appear not as an impurity but as a glorious advantage:

> It would be difficult not to believe, even if many outward signs said not the same, that great things are in store for the one language of Europe which thus serves as connecting link between the North and South, between the languages spoken by the Teutonic nations of the North and by the Romance nations of the South; which holds on to and partakes of both; which is a middle term between them. (Trench, *Past and Present*, p. 28)

In such a sentiment as this, the radical identification between language and civilization is complete.

At the end of the intellectual movement that originates in the Romantic philology of Herder and issues in the noble linguistic imperialism of Coleridge's Victorian heirs, then, we encounter a complex of values and attitudes in which linguistics and literature, the study of language and the embodiment in language of all that is ideal about a nation or people, each hold their honorable place. In the very grandeur of the vision there is a kind of illusive stability, an impression that the greatness being spoken about has somehow already been achieved:

> I can believe that the English language is destined to be that in which shall arise, as in one universal temple, the utterance of the worship of all hearts. Broad and

deep have the foundations been laid; and so vast is the area which they cover, that it is co-extensive with the great globe itself. For centuries past, proud intellectual giants have laboured at this mighty fabric; and still it rises, and will rise for generations to come: and on its massive stones will be inscribed the names of the profoundest thinkers, and on its springing arches the records of the most daring flights of the master minds of genius, whose fame was made enduring by their love of the Beautiful and their adoration of the All Good.[46]

Yet even as this vision, in all its power and generosity, is finding its voice, there is simultaneously devouring away at its foundations an altogether opposing view of language, a view to be advanced resistlessly by a newer philology in the name of scientific objectivity and truth.

[46] George Washington Moon, *The Dean's English: A Criticism of the Dean of Canterbury's Essays on the Queen's English* (New York: George Routledge, 1868), p. 122. Moon was an American Fellow of the Royal Society of Literature.

II

The Decay of Literature

What we are accustomed to call languages, the
literary idioms of Greece, and Rome, and India, of Italy, France, and Spain, must be considered as artificial, rather than as natural
forms of speech. The real and natural life of
language is in its [spoken] dialects.

—MAX MÜLLER,
Lectures on the Science of Language

To look forward to literary Decadence as it will emerge
from the disintegration of a high Victorian ideal of English
civilization is to perceive, as we have seen, the sense in
which that ideal arose from a grand equation between civilization and language, the specific legacy of a Romantic
philology that saw in language the outward expression of
the inner essence of a nation or people. Nor was it yet a
pressing worry that the same Romantic legacy contained
certain unstable or destabilizing elements, such as an organic metaphor giving nations and languages their own
cycles of growth and decay, or a focus on spoken utterance
that made language identical with the living speech of
drovers and peasants; for this was the anxiety Coleridge
had managed so persuasively to circumvent with his saving notion of the *lingua communis*, an ideal of written language that identified the nation with its literature, England with the English of Shakespeare and Milton and the
King James Bible.

At its high point, too, we have seen, this Victorian ideal

took the specific form of imperial ambitions for English as a world language, the silent imperial triumph for which England's colonial and commercial empire was to serve only as an advance guard. And as the Victorian cultural ideal had originated in an older Romantic philology, the emergent imperial vision seemed guaranteed by a newer descriptive and comparative philology. For English as a convergence of the Teutonic and Romance linguistic lines seemed uniquely suited to its imperial destiny. "Great things are in store," we have heard one Victorian writer declare, "for the one language of Europe which thus serves as connecting link between . . . the languages spoken by the Teutonic nations of the North and by the Romance nations of the South; . . . which is a middle term between them."[1]

The speaker here is Richard Chenevix Trench, Dean of Westminster and later Archbishop of Dublin, whose career as a writer on language serves almost as a parable of Victorian linguistic optimism, of a belief that the new philology, courteously welcomed and respectfully treated, could serve as a powerful ally in the war against materialism and unbelief. What Trench and his fellow commentators on language could scarcely recognize at the time, of course, was that it was only their own unconscious moralizing of the new philology that was transforming a potential enemy into a temporary and uneasy ally. Thus, though Trench's two very popular books on language, *On the Study of Words* (1851) and *English Past and Present* (1854), drew upon the investigations of historical and comparative philology, he did not emphasize the revolutionary character of the new study of language, nor did he

---

[1] R. C. Trench, *English Past and Present*, in *On the Study of Language and English Past and Present* (New York: E. P. Dutton, [1927]), p. 28.

pursue the origin-of-language question that had absorbed so fruitlessly the attention of so many eighteenth- and nineteenth-century students of language. Instead Trench steered a middle course between philosophical speculation and philological minutiae, always locating his discussion of language fully within the great traditions of Romantic and humanistic philology:

> Trench shared with the Lockeian school, Tooke and the Utilitarians, the belief that words contained information about thought, feeling, and experience, but unlike them he did not use this information to seek knowledge of the original, philosophical constitution of mind, but only as evidence of what had been present to the conscious awareness of the users of words within recent centuries; his interest was not in etymological metaphysics, not in conjectural history, but in history; not in material philosophy, but in the spiritual and moral life of the speakers of English.[2]

Trench's treatment of language was widely accessible to Victorians precisely because he limited it to narrow grounds, considering individual words rather than linguistic structures, and looking at English words of the modern period rather than the whole linguistic history of the language. Similarly, as a churchman and the author of a book on the Christian parables, Trench treated words and linguistic phenomena homiletically, that is, in a way both familiar and soothing to his Victorian readers, accustomed as they were to hearing weekly homilies in church on the words of the Bible. Words were not merely "fossil poetry" as Ralph Waldo Emerson had said, but fossil eth-

[2] Hans Aarsleff, *The Study of Language in England, 1780-1860* (Princeton: Princeton University Press, 1967), p. 238. I am indebted to Aarsleff's account for details of the early history of comparative philology in Britain.

ics and fossil history as well; words, said Trench, drawing upon a simile which both his teacher J. C. Hare and Coleridge had used before him, were like "the amber in which a thousand precious and subtle thoughts have been safely embedded and preserved. It has arrested ten thousand lightning flashes of genius, which, unless thus fixed and arrested, might have been as bright, but would have also been as quickly passing and perishing as the lightning" (Trench, *Past and Present*, p. 22).

As moralized by Trench and other Victorian writers on language, the new philology could thus be made to lend its aid to an enduring vision of civilization, an optimistic and even exhilarating Victorian ideal. Yet in reality, of course, the new philology was working towards a notion of language that would emerge as a profound threat to all enduring ideals of civilization, as that autonomous and treacherous counterspirit that had haunted Wordsworth's uneasy poetics of living speech, as the very embodiment of all that is arbitrary and valueless in human culture. For as we have seen, the emergent study of language, particularly as it developed in Germany and England, combined a number of disparate and even antagonistic motives. In the earlier years of the nineteenth century, when Romantic humanist assumptions appeared to prevail, the historico-comparative study of language became the fortress of idealists seeking protection from the assaults of such linguistic materialists as Horne Tooke. But as the historico-comparative study of language developed, as it pursued the implications of its own assumptions and of subsequent empirical discoveries, this increasingly "scientific" philology became a less and less hospitable sanctuary for idealists hoping to guarantee the logos on secular terms.

Yet even this dispossession of the idealists from their accustomed refuge in Romantic theories of language would not have proved so momentous for Victorian intellectual and literary history had not Coleridge and his heirs made literature into the foundation for the Victorian ideal of civilization. As it was, however, the ineluctable transformation of historico-comparative philology from a benign Romantic ally to a baleful "scientific" foe threatened far more than the anti-materialist arguments in the pages of Victorian philological journals. As Frederic Farrar recognized in 1860, when the dimensions of the Victorian investment in literature as well as the changed nature of philology had become all too clear, any profound change in views of language would bring with it a profound change in the Victorians' intellectual and spiritual environment, in which "shifting deserts and treacherous waves of conjecture and doubt" reduced all religion and morality—and by extension, civilization itself—to a "shadowy superstructure built upon moving and trembling sands."[3]

Even as he confidently proclaims the destiny of English as a world language, then, Archbishop Trench's high-Victorian linguistic optimism is haunted by the spectre of an eventual disintegration, a collapse out of which would emerge, at the end of the century, such movements as literary Decadence. And the story of that collapse is in one important sense identical with a story that lies in the immediate background of Trench's pronouncements, and of his career as the author of such works as *On the Study of Words* and *English Past and Present.* This is the story of the migration, initially from the eighteenth-century England of Sir William Jones and Horne Tooke to the nineteenth-century Germany of Bopp and Grimm, and then from that Germany back to Victorian England, of a new

[3] Frederic Farrar, *An Essay on the Origin of Language, Based on Modern Researches, and Especially on the Works of M. Renan* (London: John Murray, 1860), p. 156.

historical and comparative philology that would at first seem a potent ally in the Victorian struggle against scepticism and unbelief, and would then at last stand revealed as the adversary of religion and theological faith. It is in the latter baleful guise, as the embodiment of language seen to be autonomous and purely arbitrary, that the new Continental philology would play so powerful a role in subverting the hopeful equation of civilization and literature that lay at the heart of the Victorian ideal.

♈

Britain at the beginning of the Victorian era was a country rich in philological resources, and yet relatively poor in philological achievements. It was, to be sure, Sir William Jones whose revolutionary suggestion about the common origin of Sanskrit and the major Western languages laid the foundation of the new historico-comparative study of language, but after Jones, Englishmen had contributed relatively little to the development of the new science. Even Britain's great wealth of Anglo-Saxon manuscripts had for the most part enriched the linguistic investigations of foreign rather than native scholars. It was the Germans Friedrich Schlegel and Franz Bopp who journeyed to the East India House in London to study its Vedic manuscripts, and it was the Danish philologist Rasmus Rask who in 1817 published an Anglo-Saxon grammar five years before the first such work (far inferior to Rask's) was produced in England by Joseph Bosworth. So too, it was "the Danish Carlyle," N.F.S. Grundtvig, who amused British librarians with the sight of a Dane assiduously transcribing their unregarded Anglo-Saxon manuscripts.

Yet the philological traffic was not all one-way. In 1826, Benjamin Thorpe went to Copenhagen to study for four years under Rask, an apprenticeship that produced his influential English translation of Rask's Anglo-Saxon grammar and confirmed Thorpe as the first professional English philologist. And in the same spirit of ambitious apprenticeship J. M. Kemble began corresponding with Jacob Grimm in the early 1830s. Kemble, a Trinity College, Cambridge graduate and a member of the Cambridge Apostles (with Trench, Tennyson, A. H. Hallam, and F. D. Maurice), was a formidably aggressive and self-confident man. Thus we may estimate something of the isolation and frigid disregard in which serious philological study was held in England in 1833 by his complaint to Grimm that his spirits were "nearly sinking under the painful consciousness that I was working day & night upon a subject that scarcely anyone regarded. There is nothing so miserable as the thought that one is alone in one's studies, and now that poor Price [Richard Price (1790-1833), Anglo-Saxon philologist and antiquary] is gone, Thorpe and I are so; still my courage is strong, and Please God! we will make a change in the matter."[4]

In fact, the change came in the next year. Kemble used his review of Thorpe's compendium of Anglo-Saxon readings in the *Gentleman's Magazine* as an occasion to lash his "idle" British colleagues with unfavorable comparisons to their industrious Continental counterparts. Had it not been for the Germans and the Danes, Kemble declared, "we might still be where we were, with idle texts, idle grammars, idle dictionaries, and the consequences of all these—idle and ignorant scholars" (Aarsleff, *Study*, p. 196), a view of the matter that is particularly ironic when we recall that some fifty years before, J. G. Herder had

---

[4] *John Mitchell Kemble and Jacob Grimm: A Correspondence 1832-1852*, ed. Raymond A. Wiley (Leiden: E. J. Brill, 1971), p. 39.

held up the industry of Thomas Warton and Thomas Percy as a model for "idle" German scholars. The ensuing controversy between the "old Saxonists" and the new ensured not only that the hostility of the British amateurs was turned against the new Continental philology, but also that the attention of the educated reading public was for the first time turned towards it.

The new philology was welcomed in England initially because it seemed so obviously to provide an arsenal against the speculative etymologizing of Horne Tooke, a tradition that, beginning in the empiricism and associationism of Lockean psychology, had been taken over in the nineteenth century by such proponents of rationalism and materialism as Jeremy Bentham and James Mill. Since truth, according to Horne Tooke's most notorious etymology, was not vested in a noumenal world of value but was simply what a man *troweth*, the Utilitarians pursued their Lockean task of ensuring that men's opinions were framed in words cleansed of ambiguities. Hence Bentham's many efforts in neology (so like those of his mighty opposite, Coleridge), which included *utilitarian*, *codification*, and *international*, as well as those ungainly and unpronounceable words of Greek derivation that made Hazlitt complain, "His works have been translated into French—they ought to be translated into English."[5] In coining new words, Bentham was doing more than minting a more efficient linguistic currency; he was demonstrating his contempt for the uncritical reverence of the past that, in his estimate, had allowed English law to become an engine for the oppression of the English people. Yet in treating language as merely the product of the as-

---

[5] William Hazlitt, "Jeremy Bentham," in *The Spirit of the Age, or Contemporary Portraits* [1825] (London: Oxford University Press, 1960), p. 16.

sociative operations of the mind—operations assumed to be the same for all men in all times—Horne Tooke and Bentham cut themselves off from the new fields of language study that would prove the most fruitful during the next several decades: the historical and the comparative.

The historical and comparative philology that initially was to provide so potent a weapon against thinkers like Horne Tooke and Bentham had originated, as we have seen, in that same Romantic philology that contributed its idealizing impulse to the Victorian vision of civilization, the Romantic idealism of Herder. Its most influential heir in England was to be Julius Charles Hare, who appropriately enough was not only partly educated in Germany but was also partly reared by the widow of Sir William Jones. Hare became an assiduous visitor to the aging Coleridge at Highgate, carrying back Coleridgean gleanings to Trinity College and his tutee F. D. Maurice (who, though eager for Coleridge's ideas, was too shy to attend the great man in person). Hare was unusual among his contemporaries in deriving his interest in Germany and German thought directly rather than at second hand, as Carlyle, for instance, had done through Coleridge and Madame de Staël. Due in part to his position at Trinity, which he held until 1832, and to *Guesses at Truth*, the enormously successful collection of Coleridgean meditations upon various subjects that Hare first published with his brother Augustus in 1827, Hare's influence upon professional philologists and historians as well as lay students was vast, and was to continue even after he left Cambridge: "[Hare's influence] was still active," Graham Hough has said, "in expounding the ideas of Coleridge and 'the German school' to the next, the Tennysonian, generation of undergraduates."[6]

[6] Graham Hough, "Coleridge and the Victorians," in *The English Mind:*

It was Hare's influence as the chief of the "Germano-Coleridgeans" that was in turn to open the way, at first at Trinity and later more widely, to the new Continental philology. When Grundtvig visited Hare's Trinity in 1831, he found more "Germanism" there than anywhere else in England. Not only were the discussions of the Cambridge Etymological Society conducted along the lines of a German university seminar, but also its associated publication (edited by Hare), the *Philological Museum*, was dedicated to raising British philology from the sad desuetude into which it had fallen during the 1820s. To harbor such an ambition was inevitably to look towards Germany, where the brilliant achievements of Heyne and Wolf in *Altertumswissenschaft* had been augmented by the efforts of Bopp and Grimm in *Sprachwissenschaft*, and where Wilhelm von Humboldt had established philology as the master discipline among German university studies. Yet as Hans Aarsleff has emphasized, neither the Etymological Society nor what in a sense was its successor, the Philological Society of London (founded 1842), devoted itself particularly to Germanic philology or German philological methods. The *Philological Museum*, it is true, published Kemble's article "On English Preterites," the first exposition in English of Grimm's analysis of the forms of the Germanic verb, and Hare affirmed that one of his chief purposes in the journal was "to acquaint the English student of classical literature with the new views that have been taken, and the discoveries that have been made, of late years by the scholars upon the Continent, that is to say by a very pardonable synecdoche, the scholars of Germany" (Aarsleff, *Study*, p. 220). Nonetheless, Hare's jour-

---

Studies in the English Moralists Presented to Basil Willey, ed. H. S. Davis and George Watson (Cambridge: Cambridge University Press, 1964), p. 184.

nal, like the *Proceedings* (later to be called the *Transactions*) *of the Philological Society*, largely concerned itself with classical and English dialectal philology, concerned itself, that is to say, with the two interests traditionally pursued by British students of language.

This curious situation is due not least to the irritation of a sensitive national pride by German philological pre-eminence. This is an irritation we hear, for instance, when the anthropologist E. B. Tylor reviews Max Müller's *Lectures on the Science of Language*: "It is by no means pleasant to find ourselves here much worse placed than in many other fields of art and science. Towards the end of the last century we had actually grasped the clue which was to lead to the great philological discoveries of the present; but it was for the most part by Continental explorers, especially by Germans, that this clue was followed up."[7] And we certainly hear it in the peevish complaint of Henry Sweet in 1880:

> When I first began it, I had some hopes of myself being able to found an independent school of English philology in this country. But as time went on it became too evident that the historical study of English was being rapidly annexed by the Germans, and that English editors would have to abandon all hopes of working up their materials themselves, and resign themselves to the more humble rôle of purveyors to the swarms of young program-mongers turned out every year by the German universities, so thoroughly trained in all the mechanical details of what may be called "parasite philology" that no English dilettante

[7] [E. B. Tylor], "The Science of Language," *Quarterly Review* 119 (April 1866): 394.

can hope to compete with them—except by German-
izing himself and losing all his nationality.[8]

The new German philology was able finally to triumph
over such resistance not least because of a larger ethno-
centrism that identified the imperial ambitions of the Victorians with a more vague and general notion of Germanic
or Teutonic supremacy in the modern world. It is in this
context, for instance, that we hear Charles Kingsley declaring with a breathtaking blandness to an audience of
Cambridge students in 1864 that "the welfare of the Teutonic race is the welfare of the world,"[9] or another Victorian writer tracing in linguistic history the clear—and
clearly providential—progress of a chosen race:

> [The] most singular fact connected with this social
> metempsychosis [of imperial power from the Aryans
> through the Greeks, Romans and Teutons to the Eng-
> lish] is, that the Saxon should now rule with uncon-
> trolled sway over that antique land, whence the heri-
> tage he so gloriously holds was originally transmitted
> to him, and should there impart to his Hindostanic
> brethren a civilization whose germs had been planted
> by their common ancestors, at a period when the vast
> mountain barrier that bounds that luxuriant realm
> still gleamed with mythic radiancy athwart the gloom
> of hoar antiquity.[10]

[8] Quoted in Arthur G. Kennedy, "Odium Philologicum, or, A Century of
Progress in English Philology," in *Stanford Studies in Language and Literature*, ed. Hardin Craig (Stanford: Stanford University Press, 1941), p. 26.

[9] Charles Kingsley, *The Roman and the Teuton* (London: Macmillan,
1864), p. 305.

[10] I. A. Blackwell, "Remarks on Bishop Percy's Preface," in *Northern An-
tiquities*, trans. Bishop Percy, ed. I. A. Blackwell (London: Bell and Daldy,
1873), p. 45.

For all the persistent misgivings about German *Sprach-wissenschaft*, then, it is nonetheless clear that the German example in philology was a source of constant stimulation to the Victorians, spurring the recovery of the English linguistic and literary past that had been for so long shamefully ignored or misrepresented, and at the same time, the German example vastly improving—as Kemble had said it would improve—British standards in editing and scholarship, an improvement to which the long line of sterling editions sponsored by the Early English Text Society (founded 1864) would testify. And finally, though obviously the Victorians could look back upon a distinguished lexicographical achievement in Samuel Johnson's *Dictionary*, it was German works of scientific etymology like Franz Passow's *Handwörterbuch der griechischen Sprache* [1819-1823] and the Grimms' *Deutsches Wörterbuch* (begun in 1838, first volume published in 1851, completed in 1960) that supplied the model for the almost unimaginable labors undertaken, first by the Philological Society, and later by James A. H. Murray and his sub-editors, in compiling Britain's own linguistic monument to its national development, the *Oxford English Dictionary*.

A number of important developments in Victorian attitudes toward language thus trace in immediate terms to J. C. Hare's sympathetic reception of German scientific philology at Trinity College, Cambridge. Even more powerfully influential, especially upon the lay reading public, was the hope Hare inspired in his friend William Whewell that linguistic science might reconcile the competing claims to truth of science and Biblical scripture. Hare's brilliant student F. D. Maurice had been able in 1838 to oppose Horne Tooke's disturbing derivation of *truth* from *troweth*, and the whole spectre of linguistic materialism and moral relativism raised by such etymologies, by rhe-

torical and homiletical means: "These are the slights of
hand," Maurice said, "by which this distinguished ety-
mologist robs those who gave heed to him of that [i.e. absolute truth] for which all the silver and gold in the universe would be no compensation."[11] It was a "notorious
fact" that Horne Tooke's materialist analysis of language
had led many people to believe that words, like false coins,
had been passed off on them as stamped with precious and
genuine names like Truth and Right, but in fact carrying
only a purely conventional value. In the face of Horne
Tooke's materialist and atheist view of language, it was vital, Maurice declared with a rising urgency, that people
understand that

> words do indeed bear witness to man's connection
> with that which is earthy and material, because he *is*
> so connected, and because everything which he does
> and utters must proclaim this truth: but that if you
> look them fairly in the face, they are also to testify, and
> that not weakly or obscurely, of man as a spiritual
> being; nay, that it is impossible steadily to meditate
> upon the history of any single word without carrying
> away conviction that he is so, which all the material-
> ism in the world cannot set aside. (Maurice, "On
> Words," pp. 51-52)

Yet Frederic Farrar, who as we have heard, saw in the linguistic materialism of Horne Tooke only "treacherous
waves of conjecture and doubt" that threaten the foundations of religion and morality, is able to turn with an innocent optimism to the new philology, declaring the baleful *truth/troweth* etymology to be a piece of linguistic

[11] F. D. Maurice, "On Words" [1838], in *The Friendship of Books and
Other Lectures* (London: Macmillan, 1874), p. 50.

analysis "as erroneous as the inference drawn from it is dangerous and false."[12]

It is against this background, then, that Archbishop Trench stands forth as an emblematic figure, drawing at once upon the idealist tradition of Herder and Romantic philology and upon the newer scientific philology of Bopp and Grimm, and managing to hold the contrary and mutually destructive impulses within this evolving study of language in a kind of temporary equipoise. As we have seen, it is Trench who equates love of one's native language with love of country; and it is Trench, writing during the fearful uncertainties of the Crimean War, who quotes Schlegel on the vital connection between language and civilization, words that deeply colored the Victorian imagination and persuaded many Victorians to see the later emergence of literary Decadence in a peculiarly apocalyptic light. Yet it is also Trench who in his famous call for a new English dictionary, the work that would become the *OED*, declares that the business of its compiler must be ever "to collect and arrange all the words, whether good or bad, whether they do or do not commend themselves to his judgment," and it is Trench who urges that English literature be considered for the purposes of scientific lexicography simply a vast source of data, a "surface" to be culled for words.[13]

Yet Trench's optimism and confidence are, as we have said, haunted by the spectre of a disintegration in which the new scientific philology would erode the foundations of the Victorian ideal of civilization and threaten its eventual collapse. If the instability of that equipoise in which

[12] Farrar, *Origin*, p. 156. Farrar credited Richard Garnett, Sr. with disproving Horne Tooke's *truth/troweth* etymology.

[13] R. C. Trench, "On Some Deficiencies in Our English Dictionaries," *Transactions of the Philological Society* (1857-59): 5.

Trench's writings held the older idealism and the newer scientific spirit of philology did not trouble his first readers, it was because the promises of the new philology seemed too sanguine, its descent from Romantic humanist assumptions too plain. Similarly, the generation of young men taught by J. C. Hare at Trinity, the generation of Trench and Kemble and Tennyson, could with little difficulty sustain both their belief in the importance of serious, professional, and scientific study of language and their faith that language represented and upheld the spiritual and immaterial part of man. If the next generation of Victorians could not maintain this poise, the generation of Swinburne and Pater and, beyond them, the generation of Wilde and the young men of the 1890s, it is largely because the results of such serious, professional, and scientific language study were to become much more apparent and abundant. That the essential nature and newer findings of scientific philology became clear, disturbingly clear to many Victorians, is largely the great and at times unwitting work of Friedrich Max Müller.

❦ ❦

Although Max Müller was able to communicate to his Victorian audiences a sense both of intellectual excitement and steady reassurance about the new order of language, he was not able entirely to suppress the revolutionary elements in the new philology that most threatened the Victorians' settled beliefs about language and literature. Specifically, Müller could not avoid taking into account two premises central to the scientific analysis of language: the premise that language was organized on purely linguistic principles independent of both men and representation, and the premise that language was essentially constituted by sound. Not only were these two assumptions heavily emphasized in Müller's famous lectures, but because they received such emphasis there, they became in turn twin foci for Victorian anxieties about the new order of language and the subversion of culture that order seemed to portend—anxieties, that is to say, that even Müller himself could not in the end assuage.

As the linguistic science of Bopp and Grimm made language visible, it simultaneously made language opaque, that is, it taught students to see in language elements— roots, affixes, and so on—that referred to nothing outside the linguistic inquiry. Combining and varying according to regular but purely linguistic principles, these elements constituted a hitherto unperceived patterning in language, an order of meaning completely detached from the representational order, from the ostensible meaning of word or sentence. Hence the Victorians' sense that suddenly words "mean more than they ever meant before"[14] testifies not only to their enhanced awareness of the etymological history of individual words (a history that had been inculcated so engagingly by Archbishop Trench), but it reveals as well a new consciousness that words mean more than their representational meaning. Yet this linguistic order of meaning seemed at the same time to threaten meaning of the traditional sort. Victorians could recall that when Trench analyzed words, he exposed to their view the beautiful thoughts and images, the imagination and feeling of past ages those words recorded. When the linguistic scientist anatomized words, on the other hand, he reduced them to such unimaginably bare linguistic particles as the Indo-European roots *ī* and *as*. The linguistic concept of

[14] [Marie von Bothmer], "German Home Life—V: Language," *Fraser's Magazine* 91 o.s., 11 n.s. (June 1875): 774.

roots seemed to annihilate words understood as Trench's "beautiful thoughts and images" or as Emerson's "fossil poetry," setting in their place, one writer protested, "visible forms of nothing in particular."[15]

Linguistic science thus seemed not simply to make words independent of their meanings, but as it repelled the a priori speculations of human reason, seemed to make language disturbingly independent of man as well. It was the purpose of Müller's lectures to demonstrate that the new order of language *was* humanly comprehensible if only it were viewed in the proper linguistic terms. At the same time, however, Müller emphasized that language remained detached from man. That is, whereas earlier Romantic philologists had portrayed language as the true *Volksstimme*, such successors as Bopp and Müller and August Schleicher seemingly shifted the emphasis away from man when they stressed that the morphological and phonological being of language took its course beyond man's control. In Müller's celebrated formulation, "It is in the power of one individual to change empires, to abolish laws, to introduce new customs, new forms of government and new ideas, [but] no King or Dictator has ever been able to change the smallest law of language."[16] Though

[15] [M. T.], "A Few Words on Philology," *Fraser's Magazine* 87 o.s., 7 n.s. (March 1873): 310.

[16] [Max Müller], "Comparative Philology," *Edinburgh Review* 94 (October 1851): 330. A somewhat less forceful version of this statement appears in Müller's *Lectures on the Science of Language, Delivered at the Royal Institution of Great Britain in April, May and June 1861,* First series, 2nd rev. ed. (New York: Scribners, 1862), p. 49. The conventional Victorian assumption opposing this view may be represented by [Archibald Alison], "Ancient and Modern Eloquence," *Blackwood's Edinburgh Magazine* 68 (December 1850): 658-59: "[W]ho made the ancient languages at once so copious and condensed? It was the ancients themselves who did this. It was they who moulded their tongues into so brief and expressive a form, and, in the course of their progressive formation through successive centuries, rendered them

Müller here speaks of individual men rather than general-ized mankind, the effect of his statement was, in the words of one Victorian, to persuade his audiences "that languages existed apart from man."[17]

It is precisely here, as the new philology divorced language from literature and valorized sound laws instead of poetic license, that it began to threaten the Victorian ideal of civilization. Even more subversive of that ideal, how-ever, was the second major premise of linguistic science, namely, that language must be treated as a totality of sounds distinct from the written symbols used to tran-scribe them. Though the phonetic character of language was not acknowledged as primary by the first great Ger-man philologists—witness Grimm's customary reference to "letters" when he meant sounds and Bopp's principal interest in Indo-European morphology—the essential ba-sis of language in sound soon became dogma. Thus did the new philology further undermine established assumptions about language as it demonstrated that the apparent sta-bility of the written word was illusory: orthographical conventions varied wildly, a single letter could mask a number of entirely different sounds, and so on. On the other hand, sound, "mere vibrations in the atmosphere" (Farrar, *Origin*, p. 38), persisted in the new linguistic or-der. Its changes could be traced with great certainty and codified into linguistic laws, laws indeed so regular, as the Continental Neogrammarians of the 1870s and 1880s were to argue, that they admitted of no exceptions.

---

daily more brief and more comprehensive. It was the men who made the lan-guage—not the language the men. It was their burning thoughts which cre-ated such energetic expressions, as if to let loose at once the pent-up fires of the soul."

[17] Charles Whibley, "Language and Style," *Fortnightly Review* 71 o.s., 65 n.s. (January 1899): 100.

To a Victorian ideal of civilization founded on the equation of literature and nation, however, a far more menacing implicaton of the phonetic premise was that language was identical with living speech. From the viewpoint of comparative philology, noted G. W. Cox in the *Edinburgh Review*, "the vulgar idiom of the peasant" was "no less than the refined dialect of the philosopher; the uncouth articulation or scream of the savage not less than the majestic rhythm of the most exquisite poetry."[18] With the phonetic premise, as many Victorians were to realize, began an assault on written language that would end in the subversion of the idea of literature itself. For within the new linguistic order, literature did not simply become one dialect among many. The phonetic premise, setting war between sound and letter, assumed beyond this that writing in effect froze and falsified speech. In its extreme form, as the Neogrammarian Hermann Paul was to formulate it, the phonetic premise required a divorce of writing from language: "Not merely is writing not language, but it is in no way an equivalent for it. . . . Language and writing bear the same relation to each other as line and number."[19] But even as Max Müller expressed it years earlier, the phonetic premise meant the demotion of literature within the linguistic order of language: "What we are accustomed to call languages, the literary idioms of Greece, and Rome, and India, of Italy, France, and Spain, must be considered as artificial, rather than as natural forms of speech. The real and natural life of language is in its [spoken] dialects" (Müller, *Lectures*, 1:58).

Though philologists appealed to a fully conventional vo-

18 [G. W. Cox], "Max Müller on the Science of Language," *Edinburgh Review* 115 (January 1862): 69.

19 Hermann Paul, *Principles of the History of Language*, trans. H. A. Strong, 2nd ed. (London: Longmans, Green, 1891), p. 434.

cabulary of words like "artificial" and "petrified" and to the dead letter/living sound opposition that had been traditional in discussions of language since Plato's *Cratylus*, the philological eminence of such men as Henry Sweet, Alexander Ellis, and J.A.H. Murray assured that the traditional metaphors took on among Victorians a wholly new authority and weight. We hear Ellis telling the Philological Society, "If we really wish to penetrate into the meaning and growth of languages, we must look behind the conventional written form into the penetralia of living speech."[20] And we find Sweet, displaying the single-minded eccentricity that moved G. B. Shaw to make him the model for Professor Henry Higgins, addressing the same body, "Fonetics alone can breathe life into the ded mass of letters which constitute a writn language."[21] But it was Müller himself who invoked the metaphor most vividly when he portrayed the demotion of literature brought about by the phonetic reconstitution of language. In a memorable and widely quoted passage from his first series of lectures he said:

> After having been established as the language of legislation, religion, literature, and general civilisation, the classical Latin dialect became stationary and stagnant. It could not grow because it was not allowed to change or to deviate from its classical correctness. It was haunted by its own ghost. Literary dialects, or what are commonly called classical languages, pay for their temporary greatness by inevitable decay. They are like stagnant lakes at the side of great rivers. . . . It is during times when the higher classes are either

[20] Alexander Ellis, "Tenth Annual Address of the President: 20 May 1881," *Transactions of the Philological Society* (1880-82): 257.

[21] Henry Sweet, "On the Practical Study of Language" [1884], in *Linguistics in Great Britain*, vol. 1 of *History of Linguistics*, ed. Wolfgang Kühlwein (Tübingen: Max Niemeyer, 1971), p. 125.

crushed in religious and social struggles, or mix again with the lower classes to repel foreign invasion; when literary occupations are discouraged, palaces burnt, monasteries pillaged, and seats of learning destroyed; it is then that the popular or, as they are called, the vulgar dialects which had formed a kind of under current, rise beneath the crystal surface of the literary language, and sweep away, like the waters in spring, the cumbrous formation of a bygone age. (Cox, "Max Müller," pp. 78-79)

Within the new linguistic order, then, literary language, be it the Latin of Horace or the English of Shakespeare, was viewed as dead or decaying just as it succeeded in preserving itself from the ceaseless change and variation of approximate, impermanent human speech. Such language has "passed into an artificial condition of arrested growth and inevitable decay," G. W. Cox declared, paraphrasing Müller. "It has lost the power of regeneration which the [spoken] dialects retain; it is exposed not less than they are to phonetic corruption: it cannot issue out into new forms by any powers of its own" (Cox, "Max Müller," p. 78).

To any Victorian at all aware of the conventional and ennobling equation between the English nation and the language of Shakespeare and Milton, then, the new scientific philology should have seemed an influence so subversive as to portend little less than cultural degeneration and collapse, the sort of apocalypse that would a few years later lead many in the Victorian fin de siècle to see in Decadent writing, with its linguistically sanctioned use of non-literary language and slang, a harbinger of "public calamity, perplexity, war, and revolution."[22] The absence of any such widespread anxiety is largely due to Max Müller's re-

---

[22] [Charles Mackay], "English Slang and French Argot: Fashionable and Unfashionable," *Blackwood's Edinburgh Magazine* 143 (May 1888): 692.

assuring portrayal of scientific philology as the "science of language." For the audiences that assembled in 1861 and 1863 for Müller's Royal Institution lectures heard in his clear albeit German-accented speech the announcement of another kind of revolution altogether, the vast and peaceful turn of science: "The Ptolemaean theory of the universe was not more completely set aside by the system of Copernicus, than all previous conceptions of grammar and speech by the new-born science of language" (Cox, "Max Müller," p. 67). For in Müller's idiosyncratic and soothing version of the new philology, "science" did not diminish literature or subvert the noumenal realm of values that underlay civilization. Instead, "science" came to Müller's Victorian audiences richly clothed in literature, as in this typical passage:

And now, that generations after generations have passed away, with their languages,—adoring and worshipping, the name of God,—preaching and dying in the name of God,—thinking and meditating over the name of God,—there the old word stands still, as the most ancient monument of the human race—*aere perennius*—breathing to us the pure air of the dawn of humanity, carrying with it all the thoughts and sighs, the doubts and tears of our bygone brethren, and still rising up to heaven with the same sound from the basilicas of Rome and the temples of Benares, as if embracing by its simple spell millions and millions of hearts, in their longing desire to give utterance to the unutterable, to express the inexpressible.[23]

[23] Müller, "Comparative Philology," p. 339. Müller incorporated a version of this peroration into a lecture on comparative mythology that he delivered in Edinburgh in 1863. In 1847, Benjamin Jowett saw a sample of the

Nor to many Victorians did Müller's "science" seem unduly to threaten religious faith. Pressed by Victorians eager not only for linguistic information but for a coherent structure of belief in which to set that information, and impelled after his bitter defeat in a contest for the Boden Professorship of Sanskrit at Oxford to demonstrate his own religious orthodoxy, Müller set about reorienting the new linguistic science along familiar axes of belief. Indeed, the resulting science of language frequently sounds like little else than the traditional Biblical account of man and language transposed into the new linguistic terms. When, for example, Müller insists upon an original but now diminished plenitude of linguistic roots—"the spring of speech—to be followed by many an autumn" (Müller, *Lectures*, 1:385)—or when he suggests that the loss (through "phonetic decay") of linguistic forms is balanced by gain (through "dialectal regeneration"), we recognize a structure of argument that owes little to the theories of Bopp and Grimm, but that instead, on a deeper level, was meant to reassure Victorians simply by virtue of its familiar patterns and symmetries borrowed from Christian theology.

Yet what his eager audiences heard as a seamless text of science and literature, science and faith, was in fact a gorgeously tinted patchwork of sound philological information and wildly incautious conjecture, careful etymologiz-

---

young German emigré's writing and decided it needed "a much more artistic working up." In studying to improve his English style Müller must have studied Carlyle. Cf. *Past and Present* [1843], Book 2, Chapter 17: "What thousand thousand articulate, semiarticulate, earnest-stammering *Prayers* ascending up to Heaven, from hut and cell, in many lands, from the fervent kindled souls of innumerable men, each struggling to pour itself forth incompletely, as it might, before the incompletest *Liturgy* could be compiled! The first man who, looking with opened soul on this august Heaven and Earth, this Beautiful and Awful, which we name Nature, Universe, the essence of which remains for ever UNNAMEABLE. . . ."

ing and fervent exhortation. Despite his appropriation of scientific trappings—his lectern at the Royal Institution for the Advancement of Science, his constant appeals to "fact" and the "inductive method"—true scientific procedures never touched Müller's own conclusions in the least, for whatever induction he attempted always followed upon his a priori assumption that language was thought and thought language. Müller was a strict constructionist in the matter of the logos, insisting, *"Without speech no reason, without reason no speech"* (Müller, *Lectures*, 2:69), and in him the Romantic idealist theory of language first shaped by Lowth and enunciated by Herder and Humboldt finds its extreme statement.

Given the privileged status of his assumption that language and reason were identical, everything else in Müller's science followed readily. Even those troubling aspects of linguistic science that we have already noticed—the independence of language from man, the basis of language in sound—were limited, finally, in their power to dismay because the human identity and value they seemed to subvert were in fact continuously guaranteed by Müller's assertion of the logos. That is to say, in Müller's science of language—and it is crucial to distinguish his idiosyncratic "science" from true linguistic science—the new linguistic order can never remain permanently estranged from man; for even as its obscure "growth" proceeds according to its even obscurer "laws," or as its phonetic basis undermines the special claims of literature, the essential and intrinsic meaningfulness of language persists triumphantly.

Müller, however, managed to guarantee the ideal and humanly expressive nature of language to Victorians only by papering over difficulties with rhetoric and conjecture; and in the very violence or foolishness of his attempt to yoke together Romantic and scientific philology, we may measure the distance that now lay between them. At the center of Müller's effort to guarantee the immaterial and spiritual character of language was his theory of linguistic roots. Borrowing (at first without attribution) K.W.L. Heyse's suggestion that roots were "phonetic types," Müller declared, "There is a law which runs through nearly the whole of nature, that everything which is struck rings. Each substance has its peculiar ring. . . . It was the same with man, the most highly organized of nature's works" (Müller, *Lectures*, 1:384). When the majesty of creation first broke in upon the consciousness of man "in his primitive and perfect state," a creative faculty or instinct (later extinguished from disuse) supplied each new conception "as it thrilled for the first time through the brain" with its own distinctive sound (Müller, *Lectures*, 1:384-85). In this way was the foundation of language in the names of sensations—the inescapable linguistic fact that had supported materialist thinkers from Locke to Ernst Haeckel—to be overcome. And thus was the word *spirit* to be shown as more than mere embellished breath: for according to Müller, *spirit* did not imitate the sound of exhaled air; instead *spirit* in its root form expressed the sound of the concept of breathing. In short, far from being "visible forms of nothing in particular," roots became in Müller's science of language forms of everything in general, the mystic nexus between mind and matter.

From this characteristically incautious guess, Müller retreated almost at once, offering modifications and reformulations over the years without, however, entirely disavowing it. Tempted by a Victorian public yearning for answers about the origin of language, Müller boldly and obligingly struck out beyond the high ground of legitimate scientific inference, only to plunge into conjectural regions where, as E. B. Tylor wonderfully remarks, he cut a very odd figure: "It is as if some prosperous London financier, whose occupation with gold and silver has begun with its appearance in ingots and bags of dollars in Threadneedle Street, were to be sent off to Australia to dig up the material in which he has so successfully traded" (Tylor, "Science," p. 425). Having tellingly dismissed the imitative and interjectional explanations of language origin as the "bow-wow" and "pooh-pooh" theories, Müller found, as was perhaps only fair, that his own law of phonetic types was quickly characterized in turn as the "ding-dong" theory.

The discrediting of Max Müller as a linguistic scientist was not sudden, but by the end of the century it was complete. Where George Eliot had once described Müller's published lectures to her friends as his "great and delightful book," and where J. H. Newman had made it his favorite prize-book for students, a generation later Oscar Wilde who, like G. M. Hopkins, discovered Müller's work at Oxford, would dismiss Müller's famous theory that mythology was a "disease of language" with a good deal of witty asperity.[24] Despite the enormous success of his first Royal Institution lectures—enthralling performances that drew Tennyson, Faraday, and J. S. Mill, and persuaded Queen

[24] *The George Eliot Letters*, ed. Gordon S. Haight, 9 vols. (New Haven: Yale University Press, 1954-78), 4: 8 [January 14, 1862]: "I hope you are able to enjoy Max Müller's great and delightful book during your imprisonment. It tempts me away from other things"; Oscar Wilde, "The Truth of Masks" [1885], in *The Artist as Critic: Critical Writings of Oscar Wilde*, ed. Richard Ellmann (New York: Random House, 1968), pp. 418-19: "I have no desire to underrate the services of laborious scholars, but I feel that the use Keats made of Lemprière's Dictionary is of far more value to us than Professor Max Müller's treatment of the same mythology as a disease of language. Better *Endymion* than any theory, however sound, or as in the present instance, unsound, of an epidemic among adjectives!" Müller's mythological theories had been thoroughly ridiculed by Andrew Lang in 1882.

Victoria to invite him to Osborne House to lecture—
Müller, thanks in part to his carelessness and combative-
ness, steadily lost ground to his critics, and at last may be
said to have been driven from the field of linguistics altogether. Yet though Müller earned numbers of critics in
England, notably George Darwin among the evolution-
ists, Andrew Lang among the anthropologists, and Henry
Sweet among the linguists, it was chiefly his great oppo-
nent in America, William Dwight Whitney of Yale, who
succeeded in deflating Müller's extraordinary fame as a
philologist.

Even though Müller had frequently warned his audiences that the answer to their questions about the origin of
language must almost certainly remain hidden in the abyss
of time, he did not hesitate, as we have seen, to vouchsafe
his listeners an informed guess or two about the answer to
this seemingly most crucial question. And even though
Blackwood's in 1864 plainly doubted the theory of "phonetic types," wondering at Müller's "recourse to the bold
expedient that there was some occult connection between
certain roots, or primitive words, and the things signified," Müller felt compelled to invoke his questionable
theory of linguistic roots once again in 1873, when in another set of Royal Institution lectures he rose to meet the
threat explicit in Charles Darwin's view of language: "But
if we deduct that inorganic stratum [of onomatopoeic
words], all the rest of language, whether among ourselves
or among the lowest barbarians, can be traced back to
roots, and every one of these roots is the sign of a general
concept. This is the most important discovery of the Science of Language."[25]

[25] [William Henry Smith], "Müller's Second Series," *Blackwood's Edinburgh Magazine* 96 (October 1864): 402; Müller, "Mr. Darwin's Philosophy of Language: Lecture II," *Fraser's Magazine* 87 o.s., 7 n.s. (June 1873): 677.

The catalyst of the controversy between Müller and Whitney, which was to focus on Müller's theory of linguistic roots and the answer it purported to offer Darwin's conjectures about language in the *The Descent of Man* (1871), was Darwin's son George. It was he who quoted Whitney's authority ("the distinguished philologist, Professor W. D. Whitney") in the pages of the *Contemporary Review*, and he who forced Müller to confront his pitiless American foe directly. Like other readers, Whitney granted Müller genuine abilities, that is to say, his literary gift and his powers of genial assertion, but he adamantly denied that these engaging talents had bestowed upon scientific philology anything in the least valuable:

> It has, perhaps, been my misfortune not to appreciate sufficiently the services rendered by Professor Müller to the science of language; certainly, while fully acknowledging what he has done toward spreading a degree of knowledge of its facts, and, by his *prestige* and eloquence, attracting to them the attention of many who might have been reached in no other way, I have never been able to see that he helped either to broaden its foundations or to strengthen its superstructure.[26]

Instead, Whitney was prepared to argue that Müller's gift for vivid language and memorable phrasing had again and again created obstacles in the path of serious students of language. Such, for example, was the term "Turanian." Müller did not coin the term, but he gave wide currency to it as the designation for all languages that were neither

---

[26] W. D. Whitney, "Are Languages Institutions?" *Contemporary Review* 25 (April 1875): 730. This is Whitney's reply to Müller's harsh remarks about him in "My Reply to Mr. [George] Darwin," *Contemporary Review* 25 (January 1875): 305-26.

Indo-European nor Semitic, a group that he maintained was characterized by its lack of distinguishing characteristics. Whitney characterized Turanian as an "aggregation" that "has for a generation been a stumbling-block in the way of science."[27]

It was, however, Müller's curiously elevated regard for words and his low estimate of the importance of the logical relations among words that provoked Whitney's most intense censure. I have said that Müller's theory of linguistic roots was a function of his belief in the logos, the absolute identity of thought and language. As long as roots could be viewed as "phonetic types," Müller could successfully evade Whitney's charges of self-contradiction and illogic. But with the collapse of this theory, Müller became vulnerable to them. Of Müller's insistence upon the identity of thought and word, Whitney said, "This is merest confusion and absurdity, like maintaining the identity of processes of mathematic reasoning with mathematical signs, or of the hands with tools" (Whitney, *Max Muller*, p. 30); of Müller's assertion of the logos and his contention that the science of language was a physical science, Whitney remarked, "It takes a mind very peculiarly constituted to contain them both without being disturbed by their repugnance. Nor is it every one who could manage to be so far wrong in both the mutually-destructive parts of one theory" (Whitney, *Max Müller*, p. 30). As we have seen, the contradiction Whitney noted between a physical science and its study of immaterial mind found its resolution in Müller's theory of roots as "phonetic types," but this resolution was fleeting, failing almost as soon as Müller proposed it.

[27] W. D. Whitney, *Max Müller and the Science of Language: A Criticism* (New York: Appleton, 1892), p. 49.

To see Müller's theory of roots as a function of his belief in the logos is to see as well that his rhetorical conduct of his lectures is the very enactment of that belief. Quite simply, Müller entrusted so much of his argument to wordplay and metaphor and rhapsodic repetition not merely because he was possessed of a clever foreigner's fondness for puns, but because he believed so strongly that words *are* thought. Thus when, to Whitney's fury, Müller treated the "conventional" theory of language origin as if it proposed an actual convention of hitherto speechless persons, he was, according to what we may call the logic of the logos, exposing a decisive flaw in the theory. In the same way, when Müller explained Grimm's Law by comparing it to the heraldic arms of the Isle of Wight, or when he said that only man is capable of thought because only man "can gather the single under the general; he is capable of it because he has the faculty of speech; he is capable of it—we need not fear the tautology—because he is man" (Müller, *Lectures*, 2:68-69), he did so because he believed the logic is literally *in* the words, not in the logical relations among them.[28]

Whitney was accorded the last word in the *Contemporary Review* exchange. Müller returned to the fray with an elaborate apologia, *In Self-Defense*, published first as a pamphlet and later included in his four-volume collection

[28] Cf. Müller's peculiar faith in the supra-logical efficacy of words when he says of Democritus, "I called his theory on the origin of language the '*Bow-wow*' theory, because I felt certain that, if this theory were only called by its right name, it would require no further refutation." Müller, "Darwin's Philosophy: Lecture II," p. 671. Müller probably derives his fondness for rhetorical tautology from Friedrich Schiller, who uses it extensively in his *Aesthetic Letters* (1795). Müller published some of Schiller's original letter versions of this work in 1875. See Friedrich Schiller, *On the Aesthetic Education of Man, in a Series of Letters*, ed. Elizabeth M. Wilkinson and L. A. Willoughby (Oxford: Clarendon, 1967), pp. cxxi-cxxvi.

of essays.[29] Thereafter Müller declined to contest Whitney, even when his great adversary crowned his long campaign with the monograph *Max Müller and the Science of Language: A Criticism* (1892). By that time, aging, bereaved, and cheerlessly aware that he had lived beyond his time into an inhospitable day, Müller had no appetite for combat. People, he complained, continued to take him to task for his *Essay on the Turanian Languages* (1854) as if it had been published just one year and not forty years before. In his last years Müller turned away from the science of language, that "science of brand-new description"[30] that he had so largely created, and instead devoted his still-formidable energies to the study of comparative mythology, to the "science of thought," and to an English translation of his *primum mobile*, Immanuel Kant.

❦ ❦ ❦

As Whitney's attack upon Müller suggests, it was the idealist or metaphysical or, as Henry Sweet said, "mystical" elements in Romantic philology that would fail to win the assent of the new generation of linguists emerging in the 1870s and 1880s. Thus Karl Brugmann, one of the principal Neogrammarian philologists, would impatiently declare Müller's opinions "confused and in part completely untenable."[31] Yet after a certain point Müller, with his

[29] See Max Müller, *Chips from a German Workshop*, 4 vols. (London: Longmans, Green, 1867-75), 4:473-549.

[30] Fitzedward Hall, *Recent Exemplifications of False Philology* (New York: Scribner, Armstrong, 1872), p. 30: "Philology becomes an easy affair enough, when, from premises to conclusion, it takes the shape of an exercise of the imagination; and 'the science of language,' as thus illustrated by its chief hierophant, reveals itself as indeed a science of brand-new description."

[31] From Brugmann's review of the German version of Müller's *The Science of Language* (*Die Wissenschaft der Sprache* [Leipzig, 1892-93]), quoted by Kurt

metaphysical commitments and rhetorical excesses, became perhaps too easy a target. A more serious measure
of the continuing threat posed to Romantic assumptions
by scientific philology, a better gauge of the unrelenting
nature of its attack, is found in the career of Müller's
great contemporary August Schleicher (1821-1868).
Schleicher is chiefly remembered today for his "Darwinism," his use of so-called starred forms in philological re-
construction, his family-tree model of linguistic development and differentiation (*Stammbaumtheorie*), and his
famous fable composed in Proto-Indo-European. Yet
Schleicher's theory of language at its most scientific was
deeply imbued with Romantic assumptions, a legacy deriving both from Herder and from certain powerful
controlling metaphors in the metalanguage that were
Schleicher's inheritance as a nineteenth-century philologist. For although "stem" and "root" had been established
and seemingly neutral terms in linguistic discourse for
over two hundred years, the metaphorical potency of such
terms, as Whitney and even Müller repeatedly pointed
out, exerted an irresistible and illegitimate influence
within contemporary discussions of language.[32]

R. Jankowsky, *The Neogrammarians: A Re-evaluation of Their Place in the Development of Linguistic Science* (The Hague: Mouton, 1972), p. 178.

[32] Cf. E. B. Tylor, "On the Origin of Language," *Fortnightly Review* 4 (April
1866): 558-59: "Wilhelm von Humboldt's view that language is an 'organism,'
has been considered a great step in philological speculation; but, so far as I can
see, it has caused an increase of vague thinking and talking, and thereby no
small darkening of counsel. If it were meant to say that human thought, language, and action generally, are organic in their nature, and work under fixed
laws, this might be a very different matter; but this is distinctly not what is
meant, and the very object of calling language an organism is to keep it apart
from other human arts and contrivances. It was a hateful thing to Humboldt's
mind to 'bring down speech to a mere operation of the understanding.' 'Man,'
he says, 'does not so much form language, as discern with a kind of joyous wonder its developments, coming forth as of themselves.' " For the influence of

Schleicher's work depended upon the idea that language was "organic," not simply in generalized Romantic organicist terms, but in a specifically linguistic sense, an idea that may be traced to Friedrich Schlegel, whose work in turn drew substantially upon Sir William Jones's Sanskrit studies. Drawing as well on Schlegel's notion of Sanskrit as the *Ursprache*, and adapting to his own purposes the "agglutination theory" of his great teacher Franz Bopp, Schleicher arrived at an "evolutionary theory" of language development that, as he saw, ran closely parallel to the biological theory of Darwin:

> Darwin describes here with striking accuracy the process of the struggle for existence in the field of human speech. In the present period of the life of man the descendants of the Indo-Germanic family are the conquerors in the struggle for existence; they are engaged in continual extension, and have already supplanted or dethroned numerous other idioms.[33]

The last victorious assault on such assumptions was carried out, in turn, by the new generation of Neogrammarians, some of whom Schleicher had in fact taught, who saw in the Bopp-Humboldt-Schleicher theory of language nothing more than an unexamined and scientifically indefensible metaphysics. Languages developed, said the Neo-

---

Schleicher on Müller, see Arno Beyer, *Deutsche Einflüsse auf die englische Sprachwissenschaft im 19ten Jahrhundert* (Göppingen: Kümmerle, 1981), pp. 210-12.

[33] August Schleicher, *Darwinism Tested by the Science of Language*, trans. Alexander V. W. Bikkers (London: John Camden Hotten, 1869), p. 64. Cf. also Frederic W. Farrar, "Philology and Darwinism," *Nature* 1 (1870): 529: "In two capital points, viz., (1), the immense changes which can be effected by infinitesimally gradual changes; and (2), the preservation of the best and strongest form in the struggle for life, Mr. Darwin's hypothesis may be confirmed and verified by the entirely independent researches of the comparative philologist."

grammarians, in accordance with phonetic laws as exceptionless as the laws of the physical sciences. Instead of any scheme of prehistorical development and historical decay, the Neogrammarians proposed a single diachronic continuum of slow and uniform linguistic change. There was no golden age of primal language, no primordial "catastrophe" precipitating linguistic decay, merely a continuous series of infinitesimal changes. Since as scientists they were committed to observation rather than speculation, the Neogrammarians urged the study of the most reliable examples of language, that is, contemporary languages and spoken dialects:

> [Brugmann and Osthoff] refused to accept a reconstruction as scientific, if it was based solely on the oldest linguistic forms extant, since these in their turn first needed elucidation from much younger, i.e. from safer, preferably contemporary forms. Proceeding from the unknown to the known results in distortion of the latter and in needless and fruitless speculation, incompatible with the positivistic approach advocated and employed by all Neogrammarians. (Jankowsky, *Neogrammarians*, p. 132)

With the Neogrammarians, the emphasis of the new philology, now recognizably transforming itself into modern linguistics, thus shifts finally to a conception of language as spoken utterance entirely, and the notion of a language wholly autonomous in its operations may be glimpsed for the first time.

Though we now associate the idea of autonomous language with Ferdinand de Saussure, and with that revolutionary distinction between synchrony and diachrony that was to herald another sort of metaphysical rupture, the theory of linguistic autonomy in fact derived from the investigations of those Neogrammarians among whom Saussure himself had served his apprenticeship as a linguist. For the exceptionlessness (*Ausnahmslosigkeit*) of the sound laws posited by the Neogrammarians indicated that languages underwent change only as a result of innumerable choices among variants made by individual speakers. Such a linguistic choice, if it became established, after a sufficient lapse of time was "detectable in historical perspective and its regular occurrence statable as a sound law" (Jankowsky, *Neogrammarians*, p. 138). The autonomy of language as a system was in fact something that had already been clairvoyantly glimpsed by W. D. Whitney, who was hailed as a great pioneer by the Neogrammarians for his insistence, against Max Müller's mystical view of language as logos, that language was simply an institution established by and only existing through its speakers:

> In the present stage of what we call the growth of language, nothing takes place which is not the effect of human agency; the only obscurity about it grows out of the fact that there is involved the consenting action of a community, since language is a social institution, and exists primarily and consciously for the purpose of communication. But if this is so nowadays, then it was so in the period next preceding, and the one before that; and so on, until the very beginning is reached. For we have no right to assume unnecessarily that the processes of growth have essentially changed; that is to say, if the methods of word-making and form-making as exhibited in the historical period are sufficient to account for the whole existing material of speech, we are not authorized to postulate others. (Whitney, "Institutions," p. 719)

The specific manner in which the Neogrammarian program urged a theory of autonomous language follows directly from such a view of Whitney's. For in insisting upon the exceptionless operation of the sound laws and consequently upon the role therein of the innovating idiolect, the Neogrammarians inevitably insisted that language treated independently of its individual speakers was a dangerously misleading abstraction. Thus language could not be a *Volksstimme* expressing the *Volksgeist*; and thus both the "English language" and the "English national character," which Coleridgeans assumed it expressed, were no more than vague and nostalgic abstractions—like Coleridge's *lingua communis*, spoken of everywhere but existing nowhere. In much the same way, the Neogrammarian analysis irretrievably undermined the Romantic assumption that any organic model of language could serve either linguistic history or linguistic morphology. Instead of a linguistic teleology of inflected perfection (as in the Indo-European parent language) giving way to analytical mutilation and corruption (as in "degenerate" Amerindian or, indeed, such modern European languages as English), the Neogrammarians posited an open-ended chain of uniformitarian processes by which linguistic change could be construed as neither growth nor decay but merely as change. The discrediting of the organic analogy meant, too, that formal elements must increasingly be treated in linguistic analyses independently of meaning. With the dismissal of Müller's programmatically Romantic assertion of the logos (*"Without speech no reason, without reason no speech"*), linguistic scientists were much more inclined to follow Whitney and treat language as the a posteriori tool or sign of thought. For their part, the Neogrammarians did not deny the value of semantic analysis; they merely argued that semantic value could only be known after the primary analysis of form.

If the exceptionless operation of the sound laws formidably armed the Neogrammarians against the Romantic notion of linguistic organicism, there can be no question that this very *Ausnahmslosigkeit* at the same time reaffirmed the primacy of speech over writing. For both the Neogrammarians and the areal linguists of the later nineteenth century argued that all purely spoken dialects brought scientists closer to linguistic reality; Hermann Paul, for example, noted that dialects were closer to the originating idiolect than any standard language was. And not only was dialect more "real," as Kurt Jankowsky has pointed out, it was also more stable: "Changes in dialects occur far less frequently. The changes found can be pinned down more definitely to their causes, since dialectal speech is much less an ideal norm than an actually spoken part of a given community" (Jankowsky, *Neogrammarians*, pp. 157-58). Spoken dialects, that is to say, not only more perfectly reflected language reality than did written languages; they also persisted in their linguistic purity, whereas written languages, already falsified by orthography, compounded their falsity by incorporating the vogue words and constructions of civilized fashion. Thus did nineteenth-century linguistic science end by fully ratifying Wordsworth's belief in rural speech as the real language of men, and by deeply undermining Coleridge's ideal of literature and the literary dialect as a *lingua communis*.

With the triumph of the Neogrammarian program, then, there triumphed not only a powerful new vision of language as an autonomous system working blindly towards ends answerable only to impersonal phonetic laws, but the notion of sound itself as the raw stuff of linguistic change, the reality of language scientifically considered. And in the moment of this triumph was dispelled not only the linguistic metaphysics of that Romantic philology that had earlier led Herder to identify language as the outward speech of nation or people, but the saving gesture with which Coleridge had identified the English of Milton and Shakespeare with English civilization itself. In the linguistic order ushered in by the new comparative philology, the only instance of decay in language was writing, and the only monuments of dead language were works of literature embalmed as books on the shelves of libraries. The threat to Victorian values was manifest and convulsive, and out of that convulsion would emerge the movement known as literary Decadence.

☙ ☙ ☙ ☙

As the very term Decadence reminds us, the imminent cultural collapse so many Victorians were to see in the literary movement that would arise following Pater's *Marius* and fade with the turn of the century was derived from an analogy with Roman civilization, an analogy of rise and decline so deeply rooted in Victorian assumptions that it operated less as an analogy than as the assumed illustration of a general historical law. That the Victorians looked upon Rome this way, and upon their own Decadence as a reenactment of an earlier Roman decadence, is known. What has gone generally unrecognized is the extent to which this was as well a linguistic episode.

The underlying agent of this episode, too, was to be the new comparative and historical philology, that scientific study that seemed at first to guarantee English a noble destiny as an imperial tongue, as a world language that would carry the accents of Shakespeare and Milton, and the values of the civilization that had produced them, to the farthest corners of the globe. As it had deeply undermined that complex of Victorian values of which Shakespeare and Milton were the ornaments, however, so too was the

new philology to subvert the imperial ambitions that identified the spread of English civilization with the spread of
the English language. Moreover, it was to do so by gain-
ing intellectual dominance in England itself, raising the
frightening spectre not only of an empire on the edge of
disintegration or collapse, but of an empire first extended
beyond its own perimeters of cultural cohesion, and then
betrayed by those within its walls.

The displacement of the Roman analogy onto language
and linguistic issues followed almost inevitably from certain premises arising from the Victorian interest in philology. For in the first instance the fall of Rome was identified chronologically and causally (if mistakenly) with the
"decay" of Latin; and the linguistic dimension of the
change was commemorated in the general habit of referring to the "declension" of Rome, as if the territorial disintegration of the Roman Empire and the loss of Latin
grammatical inflections or declensions were the result of
the same inward collapse. In other versions of the linguistic fall of Rome, Latin was portrayed as having "died"
while "giving birth" to the vernacular tongues that succeeded it: "Every extant language," F. W. Farrar declared,
"has grown out of the death of a preceding one" (Farrar,
Origin, p. 204). Even after Max Müller corrected this mis-
apprehension by showing that the European vernaculars
had in fact grown up by the side of Latin, the belief that
"the single language of civilized Rome was succeeded by
linguistic anarchy and barbarism"[34] remained widespread.
In short, to Victorians, the supplanting of English by
French after the Norman Conquest was but an obscure linguistic episode compared to the "death" of Latin.

[34] A. H. Sayce, *Introduction to the Science of Language*, 2 vols. (London:
Kegan Paul, Trench, 1883), 2:350.

So too, the Roman Empire served the Victorians as an implicit structural model for understanding the linguistic processes posited by the new linguistic science. That is, Victorians saw in the Roman expansion and assimilation of foreign peoples an analogue for the ceaseless expansion and assimilation of a "living" language, particularly of course a language as mixed and radically assimilative as English. Yet such a model was inevitably overshadowed by the historical fate of Rome, which, according to the traditional explanation voiced by Montesquieu and others, was due precisely to over-expansion, as Coleridge put it, Rome's "*imperial* character overlaying, and finally destroying, the *national* character."[35]

Thus, though many Victorians cherished for England and the English language hopes of territorial, commercial, and linguistic hegemony as far-reaching as Rome's, they could never forget that Rome had ultimately failed: growing beyond her own institutional foundations, she had at last shattered them; her center no longer determined her circumference, and expanding, Rome collapsed. Victorians insistently asked themselves whether the same pattern of outward expansion and inward collapse would not also apply to Britain's imperial tongue:

> The immense area over which the language now extends in America, Asia, and Africa removes it further from the center in Europe, and whilst English tends to become the language most widely used and spoken in all parts of the globe, it is used and spoken by men less familiar than ourselves with the literary authority which determines its accuracy and fitness.[36]

[35] S. T. Coleridge, *Table Talk and Omniana of Samuel Taylor Coleridge*, ed. T. Ashe (London: George Bell, 1909), p. 245.

[36] [Henry Reeve], "The Literature and Language of the Age," *Edinburgh Review* 169 (April 1889): 349. Cf. also [J. H. Marsden], "Dr. Trench on

Given this resistless linguistic expansion and assimilation, the only safeguard for the English language seemed to lie in linguistic and literary vigilance of the most assiduous and unsleeping sort. According to Schlegel and Coleridge, it was the unofficial clerisy whose familiarity with the sanctioning literary tradition enabled, indeed obliged them to uphold and defend language. If the clerisy slept, or worse, if they abandoned their posts, they betrayed their trust and culture, and in that moment joined the enemies of civilization. Hence Victorians like Henry Reeve declared, in words that recall Schlegel's famous warning at the beginning of the century, "There is no surer or more fatal sign of the decay of a language than in the interpolation of barbarous terms and foreign words. . . . [A] corrupt and decaying language is an infallible sign of a corrupt and decaying civilization. It is one of the gates by which barbarism may invade and overpower the traditions of a great race" (Reeve, "Literature," pp. 348-49).

The clerisy had earlier mounted its defense of linguistic integrity through an appeal to an immemorial grammatic tradition reaching back through Latin to universal reason or law. Thus, for instance, the grammatical pronouncements of any given nineteenth-century schoolmaster were predictably backed by the famous and ubiquitous grammar (2 million copies sold in over 300 editions) of Lindley Murray (1795).[37] Murray in turn based his implacably prescriptionist strictures on Bishop Lowth's influential

---

English Dictionaries," *Edinburgh Review* 109 (April 1859): 376: "[I]t is impossible to overlook the fact, that in the extremities of this wide empire the purity and precision of the language itself are likely to be corrupted and lost. Already, in the United States, in Australia, and in the Western colonies, the vernacular tongue of the people differs widely from the standard of the mother country; and the current literature of the day, being chiefly in the form of newspapers, tends rather to debase than to raise the style of diction."

[37] Edward Finegan, *Attitudes Towards English Usage: The History of a War of Words* (New York: Teachers College Press, 1980), p. 46.

grammar of 1762, and Lowth appealed in turn to the dicta of Varro and Quintilian concerning Latin. Finally, the grammatical authority of Latin assumed its conclusively privileged status because Latin, the "universal language," was believed to represent most fully the logical forms and operations underlying and structuring all thought—and indeed reality itself, a notion of grammar as embodying universal principles that had found its most famous statement in the "Port-Royal grammar" of 1660. This chain of linguistic and grammatical authority, however, the new philology had decisively sundered. Not only was Latin thrust from its privileged position as the grammatic paradigm for all languages, but the linguistic authority of logic and reason were set aside in favor of the authority of empirically determined and specifically linguistic law. Once again, tremendous hopes had been raised in Victorians only to be crushed by the new linguistic science.

Yet the victory of the new philology over older convictions was not immediate, and there is something almost moving in the initial hopes of those Victorians who followed its development that the science of language would bring to light a new realm of universal law. To Max Müller, for instance, comparative grammar revealed that "in language, as elsewhere, the conflict between the freedom claimed by each individual and the resistance offered by the community at large, establish[es] in the end a reign of law most wonderful, yet perfectly rational and intelligible."[38] Thus while we see the emphasis shifting from the traditional natural law towards the idea of a specifically linguistic law or set of laws governing language, the older belief that such a law represents a universal and humanly

[38] Max Müller, "Inaugural Lecture: On the Value of Comparative Philology as a Branch of Academic Study" [1868], in *Chips from a German Workshop*, 4 vols. (London: Longmans, Green, 1867-75), 4:41.

applicable principle persists reassuringly. The perigee of hopeful expectations concerning linguistic law is surely reached by A. H. Sayce when he declares:

> It is not the least practical benefit conferred by comparative philology that it has dissipated the old idea of a fixed and stationary standard in language, and shown that the forms of grammar in which thought expresses itself are but variable accidents dependent on the conditions which surround a people or an age. . . . It is becoming recognized that the minds of the young should be accustomed from the first to the conception of the universal prevalence of law, and efforts are being made to replace the study of language by that of physical science upon this very ground. But it is only the study of language as carried on according to exploded and antiquated methods, that is open to the charge of misleading and perverting the growing intelligence; carried on according to the principles of scientific philology it becomes the surest means of impressing on the mind the great fact of the universality of law amid all the change and development of nature. (Sayce, *Introduction*, 2:334-36)

Yet the Neogrammarians, with their relentless principle of *Ausnahmslosigkeit*, were of course to reveal no new realm of universal law, but only the spectre of a language impersonal and autonomous in its operations, and in this context Victorian commentators were to turn away from linguistics and toward literature, not to the language of Shakespeare and Milton but to Shakespeare and Milton themselves, as the repository of English linguistic purity. In the absence of any national academy such as the French possessed to superintend language, English speakers were obliged to contrive an unofficial jury. "The only authority which can, as it were, legalise and determine the use and meaning of a word," declared J. H. Marsden, "is the consent of good authors" (Marsden, "Dr. Trench," p. 379). And this was the position G. W. Moon took against Henry Alford, the Dean of Canterbury, in a famous Victorian controversy. Moon believed in the puissance of usage in linguistic matters, but he insisted that great writers exert an effect upon language far superior to that of ordinary users: "Great writers may make or may mar a language. It is with them, and not with grammarians, that the responsibility rests; for language is what custom makes it; and custom is, has been, and always will be, more influenced by example than by precept."[39]

This line of defense, however, was doomed to failure as well, for the same comparative and historical philology that insisted on the status of English as a "mixed" language insisted that even its greatest authors were compromised at every turn by its anarchic and inescapable linguistic heterogeneity. Thanks to the peculiar history of English, especially its eclipse as a written language during the 200-year domination of the Norman French, the language had emerged irretrievably as a far more linguistically "analytical" and vexedly exception-riddled tongue than any of its sister European vernaculars. Thus it was far more resistant than they to all attempts at regularization. Indeed, Samuel Johnson became convinced that most of its irregularities were not corrigible defects at all but rather "spots of barbarity impressed so deep in the English language that criticism can never wash them away: these, therefore, must be permitted to remain untouched."[40]

[39] G. W. Moon, *The Dean's English: A Criticism on the Dean of Canterbury's Essays on the Queen's English*, 5th ed. (New York: George Routledge, 1868), p. 3.
[40] Samuel Johnson, "Preface to the *Dictionary*," in *Selected Poetry and*

The earlier history of the language thus explained but could not resolve the "anomaly not found, perhaps, in any literature but ours" described by a writer in *Blackwood's*, namely,

> that the most eminent English writers do not write their mother tongue without continual violations of propriety. With the single exception of Mr. Wordsworth, who has paid an honorable attention to the purity and accuracy of English, we believe that there is not one celebrated author of this day who has written two pages consecutively without some flagrant impropriety in the grammar.[41]

Thus English literature, in Matthew Harrison's view, "furnishes us with no positive and recognized standard of grammatical accuracy" (Harrison, *Rise*, p. 393). And according to R. G. White, creative literary genius apparently neither could nor did "ensure to its possessor a greater certainty of correctness in the use of language than may go with the possession of inferior powers."[42] Instead, White insisted, people must apply a higher law than mere usage, namely, "the law of reason, toward a conformity to which usage itself is always struggling" (White, *Words*, p. iii). But this, of course, was simply to return to the discredited certainties and prescriptions of universal grammar.

Even more damaging to Victorian hopes for the "Copernican Revolution" of linguistic science, however, was the Neogrammarian view that linguistic laws, exception-

---

Prose, ed. Frank Brady and W. K. Wimsatt (Berkeley: Univ. of California Press, 1977), p. 279.

[41] Quoted in Matthew Harrison, *The Rise, Progress and Present Structure of the English Language*, 2nd American ed. (Philadelphia: E. C. and J. Biddle, 1856), pp. 125-26.

[42] R. G. White, *Words and Their Uses Past and Present: A Study of the English Language* (Boston: Houghton Mifflin, 1870), p.v.

less though they might be, represented little else than the systematization of innumerable usage decisions by individual speakers. As Whitney had taught, not only was the connection between sign and signified perfectly conventional, but the changes in the system of signs were due to equally conventional (if not fully conscious) agreements among men. Hence, just as there was "no sign in any human language [that] depends for its value upon an internal and immediately or instinctively apprehensible connection between sign and sense" (Whitney, *Max Müller*, p. 33), so there was no internal or inherent principle within language changing language; there were merely the external changes wrought by innumerable speakers, changes that were only *ex post facto* codified into "law."

Moreover, such agreements among speakers represented not necessarily the best or the most logical or the most eloquent choice, merely the majority's choice. "The speakers of language," Whitney asserted, "thus constitute a republic, or rather, a democracy, in which authority is conferred only by general suffrage."[43] Whitney admitted that books played a part in this linguistic republic: "Each book is, as it were, an undying individual, with whom, often, much larger numbers hold intercourse than any living person can reach, and who teaches them to speak as he speaks" (Whitney, *Language and Its Study*, 1:23). But Whitney insisted that "each work is, after all, only a single person, with his limitations and deficiencies, and with his restricted influence. Even Shakespeare, with his unrivalled wealth and variety of expression, uses but about fifteen thousand words" (Whitney, *Language and Its Study*, 1:23). Besides, as we have seen, the claims to linguistic au-

[43] W. D. Whitney, *Language and Its Study: Seven Lectures*, ed. R. Morris, 2 vols. (London: Trübner, 1876), 2:38.

thority of even a single "undying individual" like Shake-speare were severely limited by linguistic scientists: in their view written language retained some historical interest, but in its "petrified" state it could provide no adequate guide to the living tongue.

This was the context, in particular, in which the analogy of Rome came to exert a potent force; for in removing linguistic authority from great authors and investing it in the populace of an expanding British empire, linguistic science plainly appeared to enfranchise the barbarian usages of the underclass and the "outlandish" voices of the circumference at the expense of the high literary dialect of the capital, the *lingua communis* of Coleridge's clerisy. Not to allow Shakespeare and Milton and the English Bible their special authority was to do nothing other than acquiesce in the democracy of mere usage—spoken usage—proposed by the Neogrammarians. "True it is," conceded G. P. Marsh, "the source of growth in language is in the people," but the guardians of language must never forget that this source was not a well of English undefiled: "though the popular mint yet strikes some coin of sterling gold, the majority of its issues are of a baser metal."[44] For the very idea of a "barbarian" is, of course, a linguistic notion. If the term originally expressed the Greeks' disdain for those un-Hellenic outlanders who stammered (i.e. said *barbar*) when they spoke, the term lost none of its linguistic force when it subsequently came to be used of the vastly expanded and diverse linguistic groups that stammered their obscure dialects inside and outside the borders of the Roman, and now the British, Empire.

With the forces of linguistic purity and cultural custo-

---

[44] G. P. Marsh, *Lectures on the English Language*, First series (New York: Charles Scribner; London: Sampson, Low, 1865), p. 577.

dianship in disarray so deep, and with the extension of an invisible franchise to every speaker of slang and pidgin, it was perhaps inevitable that a new literary naturalism would emerge to claim the space vacated by the great writers of the past. One senses the influence of the new philology, at any rate, behind Thomas Hardy's demand for "a sincere school of Fiction . . . a Fiction that expresses truly the view of life prevalent in its time, by means of a selected chain of action best suited for their exhibition,"[45] that was to open fiction to representations of substandard speech. To be sure, the substandard speech represented by rural dialects had already formed an accepted part of the creative materials of such writers as Sir Walter Scott, Emily Brontë, William Barnes, and Hardy himself. Dickens's brilliant recreation and representation in written language of the dialects of the London poor opened a new vein of substandard speech to writers. In Dickens's work, however, such lower-class characters were never protagonists. When, under the influence of French naturalism, writers like George Moore and Arthur Morrison made heroes of such characters, they accorded substandard speech a legitimacy that many Victorians found disturbing—as when, for example, the speaker of Tennyson's "Locksley Hall Sixty Years After" (1886) insists on rhyming "Zolaism" with "abysm."

Even works like those of the "New Woman" novelists of the fin de siècle, which invoked no naturalistic sanction for their use of colloquial speech, were accused by their Victorian critics of contributing to the degradation of literature by a determined embrace of, in the words of *Punch*,

---

[45] Thomas Hardy, "Candour in English Fiction" [1890], in *Thomas Hardy's Personal Writings*, ed. Harold Orel (Lawrence, Kansas: University of Kansas Press, 1966), p. 126.

"slang and sin."[46] The affinity of "advanced" fictional heroines for the new license in language (which is to say substandard language) was particularly remarked and regretted, and it is clear that the peculiar effect or *frisson* achieved when unmistakable ladies pronounced (or heard) unmistakably forbidden words retained its power well into the twentieth century. It is still in force, plainly, when G. B. Shaw has Clara Eynsford Hill in *Pygmalion* giddily take up and pronounce (for the first time on the English stage) the word "bloody" as the *dernier cri* of fashionable speech; and it is no less apparent when D. H. Lawrence's gamekeeper says "f__" in the presence of Lady Chatterley.

Nor was the popularity of substandard speech entirely a matter of literary fashion. Later Victorian commentators like Charles Mackay noted that the vogue of "the still current speech of the very lowest classes of the people" was widespread among their social superiors, who further amused themselves by taking up American colloquialisms (Mackay, "English Slang," p. 691). Like so many of his colleagues, Mackay blamed "Democracy" as "the real parent of vulgar slang." Yet as we have seen, the spread of lower-class slang and outlandish colloquialisms had less to do with a specifically political development of sympathies between classes than with what Whitney had recognized as the democracy of linguistic usage, where authority was always and irresistibly conferred by general suffrage. Whitney may well have doubted whether any resistance whatever by the educated classes against the spread of substandard, speech-based usage could in reality have a restraining effect. Nonetheless the call for the clerisy to resist linguistic degradation continued to reverberate through every decade of the nineteenth century.

[46] *Punch, or, the London Charivari* (April 27, 1895): 203.

Next to this sanctioned linguistic relativism and permissiveness, nothing in the linguistic order ushered in by the new philology seemed so clearly to signal to Victorian commentators—those anxious members of an invisible clerisy—the imminence of cultural decay and eventual collapse. This is the context in which we hear Mackay, a few months after the publication of the first volume of the *Oxford English Dictionary* in 1888, repeating with renewed urgency the call of Trench and Coleridge and Schlegel: " 'Slang' that was formerly confined to tramps, beggars, gipsies, and thieves . . . has in our day—and more especially within the last half-century—invaded the educated and semi-educated classes in England, America, and France" (Mackay, "English Slang," p. 692). As it did so, insisted Mackay, this linguistic degradation unmistakably signalled inevitable national decay, "a time, perhaps rapidly approaching . . . [of] public calamity, perplexity, war, and revolution" (Mackay, "English Slang," p. 692), a time, in short, much like that described by Max Müller in his lectures years before,

> when literary occupations are discouraged, palaces burnt, monasteries pillaged, and seats of learning destroyed . . . [when] the vulgar dialects which had formed a kind of under current, rise beneath the crystal surface of the literary language and sweep away, like the waters in spring, the cumbrous formation of a bygone age. (Cox, "Max Müller," pp. 78-79)

As the urgency of Mackay's tone makes clear, the *Oxford English Dictionary* was for many Victorians to stand as the very emblem of the linguistic relativism and permissiveness brought about by the new philology, the unlikely harbinger of an era of cultural decay. Proposed to the Philological Society by R. C. Trench in 1857, the new dictionary was intended to establish English etymologies for the first time on a scientific basis. To accomplish this useful end, however, meant that the scientific lexicographer must be free, as we have heard Trench say, "to collect and arrange all the words, whether good or bad, whether they do or do not commend themselves to his judgment." And this in turn meant converting all of English literature into a vast source of historical data; the task ahead would be to "draw the sweepnet over the whole surface of English literature" (Trench, "On Some Deficiencies," p. 5). Only this tremendous and concerted effort would allow the new dictionary to take its place beside the Grimms' *Deutsches Wörterbuch* and Littré's *Dictionnaire* as the great linguistic symbol of national development. And indeed, during the early years of its compilation under Frederick Furnivall's supervision, the dictionary became something of a national pastime as hundreds of volunteer cullers set about drawing the sweepnet (rather inefficiently as it turned out) over the surface of English literature.

Yet as Victorians such as J. H. Marsden were to object, Trench's intention of admitting every word represented in English literature into the new dictionary meant (given the well-known faults of English writers) opening the gates to irresponsible usage: "What is this but to throw down all barriers and rules, and to declare that every form of expression which may have been devised by the humour, the ignorance, or the affectation of any writer, is at once to take rank in the national vocabulary?" (Marsden, "Dr. Trench," p. 369). When a new editor, J.A.H. Murray, succeeded Furnivall, he found himself, as he attempted to honor Trench's counsel, at loggerheads with the new financial sponsor of the dictionary, the Oxford University Press. For Murray's ruling principles in lexicography were yet more radical: where Dr. Johnson's purpose had been "to admit no testimony of living authors," and Trench's was to collect and arrange all the words in English literature, Murray's was to go beyond authors and beyond literature, accepting quotations from newspapers as well as slang and scientific terms. The Delegates of the Press were stunned. In common with many people at that time, the Delegates, as Murray's granddaughter and biographer has said, "still had the illusion that a Dictionary should set a standard of good literary usage."[47] Yet even before the first volume of the *OED* appeared, many Victorians had already come to see how illusory the notion of a canonical dictionary now was. T. L. Kington-Oliphant, for example, in replying to a writer's defense that she had used no word that could not be found in a dictionary, was moved to exclaim, "Imagine the state of mind of any being who thinks that the mass of sewage found in our Dictionaries may safely be raked into for the benefit of our generation!"[48]

When Volume I, comprising A–B, was finally published in 1888, Victorians were thus at once proud and dismayed. On one hand, the volume was visible proof of the advance of Victorian civilization, yet on the other, even as it overwhelmed the mind with concrete linguistic detail, the dictionary suggested the darker possibility of cultural

[47] K. M. Elisabeth Murray, *Caught in the Web of Words: James A. H. Murray and the Oxford English Dictionary* (Oxford: Oxford University Press, 1979), p. 223. Cf. Derwent Coleridge, "Observations on the Plan of the Society's Proposed New Dictionary," *Transactions of the Philological Society* (1860-61): 156: "[T]he office of a Dictionary, a unilingual Dictionary more especially, is eminently regulative—regulative in effect, though declarative in form. It separates the spurious from the genuine, either silently, in the way of exclusion, like the Dictionary of the French Academy, or by careful obelism. In the case of an old and highly cultivated language, like the French or English, it is, or ought to be, zealously conservative."

[48] T. L. Kington-Oliphant, *The New English*, 2 vols. (London: Macmillan, 1886), 2:220.

decline. "One knows everything is to be found there," Henry Reeve conceded, "but one feels that human faculties are inadequate to embrace and penetrate the details of so vast a collection" (Reeve, "Literature," p. 350). Trench's advice and Murray's practice had seemingly produced a chaos of linguistic inclusiveness. Like the Crystal Palace exhibition of 1851, to which Reeve compared it, the new dictionary seemed oppressively inclusive and yet incomplete. And this is the context of Reeve's invocation of the imperial metaphor that we have already noticed, the metaphor of Rome's over-expansion, self-betrayal, and collapse. For as the *Oxford Dictionary* dismissed considerations of literary value in its account of the English language, it subverted the central authority of culture and opened the defensive walls of Victorian literary decorum to attack from every side: "a corrupt and decaying language is an infallible sign of a corrupt and decaying civilization. It is one of the gates by which barbarism may invade and overpower the traditions of a great race" (Reeve, "Literature," pp. 348-49).

Murray, its editor in chief, defended the scientific lexicography of the *OED* by advancing an alternative view: the English language was better to be understood as a center without a circumference, proving itself "a great, cultivated, civilized language" precisely by its illimitable, "vanishing border of special terms, scientific, technical, slang, dialectal, some of which are English to some Englishmen, and undreamt of by others."[49] But as Reeve and Marsden and others recognized, without literature acknowledged as the true central authority for language, voices from the circumference, whether from Africa or In-

[49] J.A.H. Murray, "Ninth Annual Address of the President: 21 May 1880," *Transactions of the Philological Society* (1880-82): 131, 132.

dia or America or from London's own East End, would soon redefine and displace the center:

> The more important is it, that here, in the seat and cradle of our race, under the tutelary sanction of our public schools and universities, with a highly educated class of men engaged in the liberal professions and in public life, and in the very centre of the literary activity of the nation, we should endeavour, as far as possible, to fix and determine the correct meaning and value of those words which are destined to pass current throughout the world, and to express the manifold inflections and varieties of thought, feeling, and perception in so many myriads of men. The greater the extension of the language, the more important does it become to throw around it all the lustre of literary authority, and to preserve it as far as possible from the innovations which tend to vulgarise and degrade it. (Marsden, "Dr. Trench," pp. 376-77)

To Victorians like these, Murray's image of a center with vanishing borders thus suggested nothing so much as an imperial city without defensible walls. In this view, when the *OED*, backed by the new linguistic science, insisted on displacing literary authority and effacing all distinctions between Greek and barbarian, the dictionary proposed a world in which language, abandoned by its guardians, ceaselessly expanded and assimilated until at last the barbarian in effect lived within the city walls, in which language, that is to say, itself became the vehicle of cultural decay.

As a kind of counterpart to the bold and dismaying labors of the *OED* editors, finally, there were the efforts of those missionaries whose aim was to carry English and its civilizing values to every corner of the Empire. As the

OED had ended by betraying the hope that it would fix English forever as the *lingua communis* of a high civilization, the missionary attempt to Christianize and Anglicize the remote regions of the world had ended in evident corruptions of the *lingua communis* it had hoped to export. Colonization, observed Matthew Harrison, "has a tendency not only to add to the words of a language, but also to corrupt it," adducing as proof the practice of Moravian missionaries to the Negroes of British and Dutch Guiana: the Moravians had found it expedient to translate the English of the Authorized Version of the Bible into "talkee-talkee," the local pidgin.[50] In "talkee-talkee," however, the glorious periods of the English Bible were considerably changed, with "a generation of vipers," for example, becoming "snekki-family" ("snaky-family"), and the account of the wedding at Cana concluding:

> But when grandfootboy taste that water, this been turn wine, could he no know from where that wine come-out-of (but them footboy this been take that

[50] Harrison, *Rise of English*, p. 119. The Moravian translation, in use long before it was published by the British and Foreign Bible Society in 1829, was widely cited in Victorian articles on language. Harrison's detestation of pidgin may be constrasted with G. B. Shaw's wholehearted approval of it: "When certain Negro slaves in America were oppressed by a lady planter who was very pious and very severe, their remonstrance, if expressed in grammatic English, would have been 'If we are to be preached at let us not be flogged also: if we are to be flogged let us not be preached at also.' This is correct and elegant but wretchedly feeble. It says in twenty-six words what can be better said in eleven. The Negroes proved this by saying 'If preachee preachee: if floggee floggee; but no preachee floggee too.' They saved fifteen words of useless grammar, and said what they had to say far more expressively." "Excerpts from the Preface by George Bernard Shaw to *The Miraculous Birth of Language*," in *Shaw on Language*, ed. Abraham Tauber (New York: Philosophical Library, 1963), pp. 117-18. Henry Sweet taught Shaw to see that English resembled uninflected monosyllabic languages like Chinese (and pidgin) more than it did the cognate tongues of Latin and Greek.

water well know): he call the bridegroom. He talk to him, every one man use of give first the more sweet wine; and when them drink enough end, after back the less sweety wine: but you been cover that more good wine.[51]

Thus did the movement that was to encircle the globe with the accents of Shakespeare and Milton end in talkee-talkee.

In the corruption of English as a living language and the dissolution of its great literary tradition as an embodiment and standard of high civilization, then, the Victorians of an invisible clerisy could scarcely avoid seeing a decline, of which the collapse of Rome was an ominous prefiguration. And, to adopt the terms of the Liberal Anglican interpretation of history that so powerfully shaped Victorian thought, Rome had fallen from within, from an inward moral collapse: Rome, in a word, had betrayed itself. By establishing the history of Rome as the paradigm for all national history, the Liberal Anglicans raised the example of Rome among Victorians to new and apocalyptic significance.[52] By shifting the source of historical decline from external attacks by barbarians to the internal failure and

---

[51] Quoted in [Robert Southey], "The New Testament in the Negro Tongue," *Quarterly Review* 43 (October 1830): 558. Southey declared that this "mingle-mangle speech" was the result of the Protestant planters' desire to separate religion from knowledge and so more completely subjugate their slaves. Should talkee-talkee rather than English or Dutch become the permanent language of common life, he warned, "it will, eventually, have occasioned more evil than good: for nothing can correct the radical depravity of this mixed speech. . . . [I]t has been adapted in its construction by ignorant persons, of the vulgarest and coarsest minds, to the lowest state of human intellect" (p. 564).

[52] For a fuller treatment of this theme, see Linda Dowling, "Roman Decadence and Victorian Historiography," *Victorian Studies* 28 (1985): 579-607.

betrayal by Rome's guardians, they indelibly impressed Victorians with a sense of their specifically individual responsibility for preserving—or betraying—their own civilization. By seizing upon literature as the essential revelation, not just of past civilizations but of present ones as well, they assured that any contemporary echo of "the sickly literature of the last ages of Greece and Rome"[53] would reverberate among Victorians like the trump of doom.

[53] A. H. Stanley, *Whether States, Like Individuals, After a Certain Period of Maturity, Inevitably Tend to Decay* (Oxford: J. Vincent, 1840), p. 46.

III

The Fatal Book

No single volume paramount, no code,
No master spirit, no determined road.
—Quoted in J. C. Hare,
Guesses at Truth

In the immediate background of literary Decadence, we began by saying, of the moment of Oscar Wilde and Aubrey Beardsley and the *Savoy*, there lies a story, not of cultural decline, but of linguistic demoralization, of the silent subversion of a high Victorian ideal of civilization by the new comparative philology imported from the Germany of Bopp and Grimm. The same displacement of cultural ideals and cultural anxiety onto language explains why we also glimpse in the background of Victorian Decadence no lurid tales of sin and sensation and forbidden experience but a range of stylistic effects, of quiet disruptions and insistent subversions in the prose of Walter Pater. For Pater's writing, both in itself and as it was to set in motion the forces that would converge in literary Decadence, is best understood as an attempt to rescue from the assaults of scientific philology and linguistic relativism an ideal, however diminished and fugitive, of literature and literary culture.

In the immediate background of Pater's enterprise, in turn, lies the final triumph of the new philology in the English universities, the institutional victory that so many Victorians were to regard as a final subversion of civilized and civilizing ideals. Nor was it an error, as we have seen, to perceive in the triumph of scientific philology some ultimate devaluation of literature as an embodiment of cultural values. It is the bluff and unsentimental positivism of the new philology that we hear, for instance, in the accents of J.A.H. Murray as he addresses the Ashmolean Natural History Society: "I am not a literary man, I do not write novels, nor essays, nor poems, nor history, I am not specially interested in Arthur & his knights . . . I am a man of science, and I am interested in that branch of Anthropology which deals with the history of human speech."[1]

The great fear, then, and one by no means unjustified, was that as scientific philology divorced itself from literature, it would cut itself off from the moral and spiritual values Victorians looked to literature to instill. For a time, indeed, some Victorians could hope that literature itself might provide an antidote to relativism in this new guise, serving at the very least as a source of common culture. This was a venerable function: ever since the seventeenth century, as D. J. Palmer has noted, English literature has served as a sort of poor man's classics.[2] And in the nineteenth century, English literature was widely prescribed to the newly literate as an antidote to the febrile infections likely to be spawned by the spread of industrial democracy. Hence the teaching of such literature in schools and in the new colleges. The difficulty, however, was that the examination systems within those institutions quickly converted the study of English literature into the servile

---

[1] K. M. Elisabeth Murray, *Caught in the Web of Words: James A. H. Murray and the Oxford English Dictionary* (Oxford: Oxford University Press, 1979), pp. 292-93.

[2] D. J. Palmer, *The Rise of English Studies: An Account of the Study of English Language and Literature from Its Origins to the Making of the Oxford English School* (London: Oxford University Press, 1965), p. 78.

drudgery of mere fact-cramming. Clearly, if Victorians, particularly those of the less articulate classes, were to be uplifted at all, they would first have to be released from their Gradgrindian servitude to facts, and this, argued reformers like John Churton Collins during the 1880s, could come about only if English literature were taught as one of the liberal arts:

> [People] need aesthetic culture, that life may not only be brightened, but refined and elevated by sympathetic communion with what is truly beautiful and excellent in Art and Literature; they need moral culture, and that on broader lines than when it ran wholly in theological and conventional grooves; they need political culture, instruction, that to say, in what pertains to their relation to the State, to their duties as citizens; and they need also to be impressed sentimentally by having the presentation in legend and history of heroic and patriotic example brought vividly and attractively before them. To the Greek instruction of this kind was conveyed easily and delightfully through the study properly directed of the best literature, and particularly of the best poetry; and of instruction of this kind the best literature and the best poetry may still become the means.[3]

In such an utterance may be glimpsed, obviously enough, the major theme of that moral tradition in English criticism that runs from Matthew Arnold at least to F. R. Leavis, for that tradition has survived. What was more peculiarly Victorian was the anxiety that the enterprise of moral criticism, even as it was establishing itself, had al-

[3] John Churton Collins, *The Study of English Literature* (London and New York: Macmillan, 1891), p. 148.

ready been colonized and subordinated by the new philology. For if philological methods were required to guarantee the intellectual rigor and seriousness of literary study, would philologists not inevitably extend their methods and assumptions over new terrain, desiccating everything they touched and setting themselves up as arrogant and tyrannical arbiters? The note of just this anxiety is caught, for instance, in Henry Craik's warning that the philological partisans of English studies "evolve out of remnants of archaism, that appear to ordinary readers sterile and dull, what they are pleased to believe marvels of genius and of force. . . . Is obscurity thus to be reckoned as a positive merit, that it should suffice to collect a crowd of industrious and painful elucidators?"[4]

Even as a new tradition in English criticism seemed to be emerging—in short, a new program of English studies that might work to counteract any decline or decay of Victorian civilization—it was not clear how even this countermovement could escape the subversive influence of the new philology, be prevented from dwindling into a mode of mere Alexandrianism. And Alexandrianism, of course, itself spelled cultural decline. For as Victorians had been reminded by Max Müller's lectures, the study of literature and language arose only with the decline of Greece; that is, it was only when the grammarians of Ptolemaic Alexandria had to confront the various competing written and spoken forms of Greek arising with the disintegration of the Greek political and cultural hegemony that they took up their close study of the language. The almost superstitious dread of somehow initiating Alexandrian cultural decline through Alexandrian philological studies was such

---

[4] [Henry Craik], "The Study of English Literature," *Quarterly Review* 156 (July 1883): 191.

that G. P. Marsh opened his lectures on the English language by specifically acknowledging the fear:

> It is a trite remark, that the national history and the national language begin to be studied only in their decay, and scholars have sometimes shown an almost superstitious reluctance to approach either, lest they should contribute to the aggravation of a symptom, whose manifestation might tend to hasten the catastrophe of which it is the forerunner. Indeed, if we listen to some of the voices around us, we are in danger of being persuaded that the decline of our own tongue has not only commenced, but has already advanced too far to be averted or even arrested.[5]

Such fears are so vivid that Marsh is compelled to go to extraordinary lengths to dispel them:

> We are, accordingly, not warranted in concluding that, because the creative spirits of ancient and flourishing Hellenic literature did not concern themselves with grammatical subtleties, but left the syntactical and orthoepical theories of the Greek language to be developed in late and degenerate Alexandria, therefore the study of native philology in commercial London and industrial Manchester proves the decadence of the heroic speech, which in former centuries embodied the epic and dramatic glories of English genius. (Marsh, *Lectures*, p. 4)

So ominous is the spectre of cultural decline and decay raised by Marsh's own repeated protestations, in fact, that at last he is forced to confront the intimations of apocalypse

[5] G. P. Marsh, *Lectures on the English Language*, First series (New York: Charles Scribner; London: Sampson, Low, 1865), p. 3.

haunting his own observations: "But although the interest now manifested in the history and true linguistic character of the English speech originated in external movements, yet it must be admitted that it is, at this moment, strengthened in England by a feeling of apprehension concerning the position of that country in coming years—an apprehension which, in spite of occasional manifestations of hereditary confidence and pride, is a very widely prevalent sentiment among the British people" (Marsh, *Lectures*, pp. 6–7). Marsh's intimations coincide with Matthew Arnold's conviction expressed in an 1865 letter to his sister Fan that "there is a real, an almost imminent danger of England losing immeasurably in all ways, declining into a sort of greater Holland, for want of what I must still call ideas, for want of perceiving how the world is going and must go, and preparing herself accordingly. This conviction haunts me, and at times even overwhelms me with depression; I would rather not live to see the change come to pass, for we shall all deteriorate under it."[6]

In the gloominess of Arnold's mood we glimpse the final implications, perhaps, of that demoralization of literary culture in which the relentless advance of the new scientific philology had played so great a part. For with literary language lost to the nation as its authentic outward speech, with the subversion of a great literary tradition as an embodiment of English values, with even an emergent school of English studies apparently contaminated by desiccating philological methods, it was not clear in what direction the guardians of civilization might turn in any hopeful attempt to arrest cultural decline. And, quite beyond this, with the new philology firmly entrenched in

[6] *Letters of Matthew Arnold*, ed. George W. E. Russell, 2 vols. (New York and London: Macmillan, 1895), 1:360.

Oxford and Cambridge, those venerable institutions that Coleridge had seen as the enduring fountainheads of cultural renewal for his guiding national clerisy, it was not clear that even a fugitive minority of contemporary writers might mount any meaningful resistance. This was the darkening background against which Walter Pater, of Brasenose College, Oxford, was to take up his pen as a Victorian writer.

♈

As one of the first major writers of the post-philological moment in Victorian civilization, Pater was to embark on a strategy of what amounts to victory through acquiescence, an attempt to establish a new kind of writing that granted scientific philology its essential claims, and thus neutralized the most destructive of its threats to any sort of coherence in literary culture. Pater's initial version of the strategy took a social or cultural form, as that ethic of personal ecstasy embodied in the famous "Conclusion" to *Studies in the History of the Renaissance*, an injunction to "catch at any exquisite passion . . . that seems by a lifted horizon to set the spirit free for a moment"[7]—the literary embodiment of which is, in turn, the *purpureus pannus* in Pater's essay on Leonardo (1869), with its imperfect verbs drawing the past into the present ("like the vampire, she has been dead many times, and learned the secrets of the grave; and has been a diver in deep seas, and keeps their fallen day about her").[8]

---

[7] Walter Pater, "Conclusion" to *The Renaissance: Studies in Art and Poetry*, ed. Donald L. Hill (Berkeley and London: University of California Press, 1980), p. 189 and p. 274. I quote here the 1873 version of the "Conclusion."

[8] Walter Pater, "Leonardo da Vinci," in *The Renaissance*, p. 99.

Perhaps because the "Conclusion" to *The Renaissance* occasioned so violent a reaction among Victorian readers outraged by what seemed to them a soulless hedonism, perhaps because he saw that a mere ethic of personal ecstasy allowed no mature expression of an increasingly complex intellectual perspective, Pater was subsequently to abandon the overt argument for his position and embody it instead in a mode of writing. By the time of *Marius the Epicurean*, the Pater of *The Renaissance* has been transformed into a character in the story, the young aesthete Flavian whose ruling passion is a "hard-set determination . . . to arrest this or that little drop at least from the river of sensuous imagery rushing so quickly past him."[9] Thus did Pater interpose a narrative and historical distance between his present and younger selves.

In the space established by this interposition, in turn, Pater pursued the stylistic project of his later years, embracing the relentless insistence of the new philology that literary English is quite literally a dead or moribund language, and attempting to establish a new mode of writing on its very morbidity, dissolving the antagonistic opposition between philology and literature in a new vision of the writer as a sort of philologist or scholar of words, and lastly, seeing in the writers and readers of this new mode a fugitive but yet vital remnant of that all-embracing national clerisy envisioned by Coleridge. This is the movement that begins when, as in Pater's description of the aesthete Flavian, the immediacy of personal ecstasy is apprehended through the distance of a history unfolding in linear time. Detached moments of imaginative richness still occur, for instance, to Marius, but now they "occur"

[9] Walter Pater, *Marius the Epicurean: His Sensations and Ideas*, 2 vols. (London: Macmillan, 1914), 1:117.

in the past. For Marius's reminiscent temper, a temper made reminiscent by his friend Flavian's death, makes him look back at his own experience—even *as* he experiences it—as if from the distance of years: "Detached from him, yet very real, there lay certain spaces of his life, in delicate perspective, under a favourable light" (Pater, *Marius*, 1:154), but such moments of distanced and thereby chastened intensity are, for Marius, always already in the past.

In a sense, the linear represents a fallen mode of cognition for Pater, a sort of Kantian category imposed on post-paradisal sensibility. It is how one *must* see once the epiphanic visions of innocence or Wordsworthian childhood—visions such as the sight of the intensely red hawthorn tree ("a plumage of tender, crimson fire out of the heart of the dry wood") described in the autobiographical meditation "The Child in the House" (1878)—have dropped away.[10] In the same way, the historian can no longer see "face to face." Interposing between him and the past moment that he seeks is always a succession of intervening, obscuring moments or years or ages. As Pater realized as early as 1868, "The composite experience of all the ages is part of each one of us: to deduct from that experience, to obliterate any part of it, to come face to face with the people of a past age, as if the middle age, the Renaissance, the eighteenth century had not been, is as impossible as to become a little child, or to enter again into the womb and be born."[11] Such moments insist upon the linear, cumulative nature of personal and historical narrative, for as William Buckler has argued, Pater's subject in *Marius* is always "the human understanding in a state of di-

[10] Walter Pater, "A Child in the House," in *Miscellaneous Studies* (New York: Macmillan, 1907), p. 158.
[11] [Walter Pater], "Poems by William Morris," *Westminister Review* 90 (October 1868):307.

rected motion, consciousness negotiating history."[12] If Pater's historical schema lacks either origin or teleological end, it does possess sequence and direction; and it is this linear pattern which rescues consciousness from mere flux.[13]

Yet in order to win exemption from the flux one must write well. And to write well one must know, first of all, "the true nature of one's own impression . . . a true understanding of one's self being ever the first condition of genuine style" (Pater, *Marius*, 1:155). *Marius the Epicurean* is, of course, the story of this quest for self-knowledge. The second requirement of writing well is to know one's medium, a search for knowledge that is described in both *Marius* and in Pater's great essay of 1889, "Style." It is at this point that our attention begins to be insistently drawn to the persistent analogies between literature and the visual arts in Pater's works, as when, for example, he parallels the sculptor and the prose writer ("as the sculptor with solid form, or the prose-writer with the ordinary language of men"), or when he says, "For in truth all art does but consist in the removal of surplusage, from the last finish of the gem-engraver blowing away the last particle of invisible dust, back to the earliest divination of the finished work to be lying somewhere, according to Michelangelo's fancy, in the rough-hewn block of stone."[14]

[12] William Buckler, "*Déjà vu* Inverted: The Imminent Future in Walter Pater's *Marius the Epicurean*," *Victorian Newsletter*, No. 55 (Spring 1979): 1.

[13] See Peter Allan Dale, *The Victorian Critic and the Idea of History: Carlyle, Arnold, Pater* (Cambridge, Mass.: Harvard University Press, 1977), pp. 171-205: "That Pater both as critic and imaginative writer is, in the end, a good deal more concerned with tracing the historical development of speculative culture or the general consciousness of mankind than he is with burning with a hard gemlike flame is a point that needs more recognition than it has generally received from modern writers" (p. 188).

[14] Walter Pater, "Style," in *Appreciations, with an Essay on Style* (London: Macmillan, 1920), pp. 5-6, 19-20.

Such analogies have suggested to many commentators that Pater's is essentially a "spatial" or "synchronic" notion of literature, that Pater's literary art, in Gerald Monsman's words, "perversely aspires, syntactically, to the atmosphere of a painting or a tapestry: static, pictorial, nonlinear."[15] Indeed, Jerome Bump has pointed out that it "would be difficult to overestimate just how pervasive are the spatial paradigms of literature we have inherited from Pater."[16] Yet Bump goes on to make the more important point that, having inherited this visual paradigm of literature from Pater, modern critics now tend to read it— in fact, over-read it,—back into Pater's own texts, thus ignoring the other, auditory models for language and reading to be found in such works as *Marius*.

There can be no question that such visual arts analogies for literature were powerfully influential during the period in which Pater wrote. But the provenance of these analogies makes clear their actual significance to Pater. For such visual arts analogies in fact belong to the larger Aestheticist inheritance from German aesthetic idealism. They represent in a literal fashion the distinctive stress in idealist aesthetics—and particularly in the aesthetic thought of Kant and Friedrich Schiller—on the importance of form in beauty. Kant's emphasis on the form of the beautiful object has, through a long and complex process of transmission, come to be identified with the physical form or medium of the art object. What was indeterminately intellectual or cognitive activity in Kant, however, has become a physical entity or material in the Aestheticist writers of mid-century.

[15] Gerald Monsman, *Walter Pater's Art of Autobiography* (New Haven and London: Yale University Press, 1980), p. 37.

[16] Jerome Bump, "Seeing and Hearing in *Marius the Epicurean*," *Nineteenth Century Fiction* 37 (1982): 275.

Inevitably this collapse or displacement into the literal occasioned difficulties for those who inherited the visual arts analogies without understanding them. Such difficulties come vividly to light, for example, in the defense the second-generation Pre-Raphaelite poet Arthur O'Shaughnessy made for a group of poems he titled "Thoughts in Marble": "I have kept strictly within the lines assigned to the sculptor's art, an art in which I have as yet failed to perceive either morality or immorality. They are therefore essentially thoughts in marble, or poems in form, and it would therefore be unjustifiable to look in them for a sense which is not inherent in the purest Parian."[17] In asserting the marble/language analogy so baldly, O'Shaughnessy unwittingly raises objections to it that otherwise might have slept: his literal-minded assertion makes obvious how little similarity there can be between truly senseless marble, and language that comes to the artist's hand always pre-inscribed with meaning, "senseless" in fact only when it ceases to be language.

Pater, who appears to have studied both Kant and Schiller, remains aware of the fictive or illustrative nature of such analogies, which is precisely why his appeal to the visual arts never seeks literal-mindedly, like O'Shaughnessy's, to appropriate their illusory simultaneity or spatiality. Instead, Pater understands the Aestheticist cult of form as a call for self-discipline and genuine proficiency. Pater had learned from Gautier and Rossetti, not that language ought to aspire to the condition of paint and marble, but that language ought to be treated with the same respect and technical knowledge as sculptors treated marble or painters paint, a Ruskinian and Pre-Raphaelite ideal of

---

[17] Arthur O'Shaughnessy, "Thoughts of a Worker," *Songs of a Worker* (London: Chatto and Windus, 1881), p. viii.

craftsmanship that J. H. Newman also recommended: "Why may not that be true of literary composition which is true of painting, sculpture, architecture, and music? Why may not language be wrought as well as the clay of the modeller? why may not words be worked up as well as colours?"[18] Implicit in this ideal of craftsmanship is the assumption that the artistic medium can be carefully wrought only when the peculiar nature and limits of its expressiveness have been studied and mastered. In turn, these limits of the medium will determine the subject matter. As Newman said in his essay "Literature," the work that David DeLaura has shown to have powerfully influenced Pater's "Style": "Each of the Fine Arts has its own subject-matter; from the nature of the case you can do in one what you cannot do in another; you can do in painting what you cannot do in carving; you can do in oils what you cannot do in fresco; you can do in marble what you cannot do in ivory; you can do in wax what you cannot do in bronze" (Newman, "Literature," p. 251).

It is precisely this sense of the peculiar, limited, resistant nature of the linguistic medium that Pater emphasizes in "Style," as when, for example, he says that the attentive prose writer will find the "conditions of the literary art arising out of the medium or material in or upon which it works, the essential qualities of language and its aptitudes for contingent ornamentation, matters which define scholarship as science and good taste respectively" (Pater, "Style," p. 21). Ruskin and the Pre-Raphaelites had

---

[18] J. H. Newman, "Literature: A Lecture in the School of Philosophy and Letters," in *The Idea of a University*, ed. Charles Frederick Harrold (New York and London: Longmans, Green, 1947), p. 247. For the Aestheticist disposition to treat language as a "concrete, resisting material," see Aatos Ojala, *Aestheticism and Oscar Wilde*, 2 vols. (Helsinki: Suomalaisen Tiedeakatemian Toimituksia, 1955), 2:14-15.

taught that the nature of the marble will determine the ambitions of the sculptor, if he is wise. Pater, like Newman before him, saw that the literary artist's situation was precisely the same: "all the cautions regarding style arising out of so many natural scruples as to the medium through which alone he can expose that inward sense of things, the purity of this medium, its laws or tricks of refraction" (Pater, "Style," pp. 35-36).

To grasp the full implications of Pater's view of language as an artistic medium is, at the same time, to become aware of his familiarity with the contemporary revolution in philological science, and with the complex linguistic reality that that science had taken as its object of inquiry. Here we become aware in particular of the influence of his Oxford colleague Max Müller, whose *Lectures on the Science of Language*, First and Second series, Pater read in 1867 and 1874 respectively.[19] When Pater says in "Style" that the essential qualities of language require a measure of "science" for their elucidation, it is Müller's science of language that stands in the background. That the linguistic medium *is* complex Pater repeatedly emphasizes, as when

[19] Cited in Stephen Connor, "Myth as Multiplicity in Walter Pater's *Greek Studies* and 'Denys l'Auxerrois,' " *Review of English Studies* n.s. 34 (1983): 39. Connor is drawing upon the research of Billie Andrew Inman. See her *Walter Pater's Reading: A Bibliography of His Library Borrowings and Literary References, 1858-1873* (New York: Garland, 1981), pp. 159-60. Müller's influence also may have come to Pater more indirectly. Pater was impressed by his tutor Benjamin Jowett's lectures on Plato, some of which remained unpublished: "Ever since I heard it, I have been longing to read a very dainty dialogue on language, which formed one of [Jowett's] lectures, a sort of 'New Cratylus.' " A. C. Benson, *Walter Pater* (London: Macmillan, 1906), p. 56. Pater implies that he transcribed or took notes from Jowett's lectures: "They passed very soon into other notebooks all over the University." Jowett may have enlisted Müller's help for the Cratlyus dialogue. See Evelyn Abbott and Lewis Campbell, *The Life and Letters of Benjamin Jowett, M. A.*, 2 vols. (London: John Murray, 1897), 1:250.

he employs a submerged language-as-marble metaphor to speak of "the purity of this medium, its laws or tricks of re-fraction," or when he says, "Product of a myriad various minds and contending tongues, compact of obscure and minute association, a language has its own abundant and often recondite laws, in the habitual summary recognition of which scholarship consists" (Pater, "Style," p. 12). We hear Müller's accents in all this, in the emphasis on lin-guistic laws (Müller gave wide currency to the phrase "Grimm's Law" as a way of describing Grimm's *Lautver-schiebung*), and in the stress upon the enormously long and interculturally rich history of language and of individual words ("And now, that generations after generations have passed away, with their languages . . . there the old word stands still, as the most ancient monument of the human race").

So too does Müller's vivid characterization of the decay of Latin and the rise of the vernacular languages lie behind Pater's portrayal of language in *Marius the Epicurean*. Müller, as we have seen, made use of revolutionary meta-phors to describe how the vulgar spoken dialects rose from beneath the "crystal surface" of the high literary language, at last to "sweep away, like the waters in spring, the cum-brous formation of a bygone age." Müller's portrayal of an explicitly political conflict between written and spoken di-alects is one that Pater draws upon in portraying Flavian's literary program as "partly popular and revolutionary, as-serting, so to term them, the rights of the *proletariate* of speech" (Pater, *Marius*, 1:95). In the same way, Pater's depiction of the increasing "artificiality" of literary Latin and the growing vividness and expressiveness of colloquial speech—and even Pater's habit of using "dialect" to refer to the written form—reflect the themes of Müller's *Lec-tures*: "The popular speech was gradually departing from the form and rule of literary language, a language always and increasingly artificial. While the learned dialect was yearly becoming more and more barbarously pedantic, the colloquial idiom, on the other hand, offered a thousand chance-tost gems of racy or picturesque expression, rejected or at least ungathered by what claimed to be classical Latin" (Pater, *Marius*, 1:94-95).

Pater abides as well by Müller's warning that the origin of language is lost in the abyssal past. Müller, as we have seen, could not himself resist speculating on this origin, but his humiliating failure to say anything sensible about it may account for the change we find in Pater's view of the question. For in his early essay on Wordsworth (1874), Pater appealed to the traditional Romantic notion of language as originating in powerful emotions; indeed, he is doing little other than applying Wordsworth's words to Wordsworth himself: Wordsworth is inspired by "the not wholly unconscious poetry of the language used by the simplest people under strong excitement—language, therefore, at its origin."[20] So too, in *Marius*, Pater shows Flavian caught up in the fervor of his poetic reforms, attempting to "reestablish the natural and direct relationship between thought and expression, between the sensation and the term, and restore to words their primitive power" (Pater, *Marius*, 1:96). Flavian, enchanted by the utter simplicity of Homer's poetic style, hopes to go "back to the original and native sense" of each word, imagining that those earlier Homeric days were "naturally, intrinsically, poetic, a time in which one could hardly have spoken at all without ideal effect" (Pater, *Marius*, 1:96, 101).

In *Marius*, however, Pater makes clear that such a pursuit of linguistic origins is as illusory as contemporary lin-

[20] Pater, "Wordsworth," in *Appreciations*, p. 59.

guistic opinion said it was. Flavian has merely come under
the influence of the "enchanted-distance fallacy" by which
every preceding age and its mode of expression come to
seem simple and unencumbered to the eyes of those living
in the "belated" days that follow. Here Pater understands
a truth that eluded his rival, J. A. Symonds. Symonds, ex-
patiating upon the differences between Elizabethan and
contemporary poetry that absorbed so much Victorian attention, concluded (with a certain regretful satisfaction)
that "it is impossible for people of the present to be as fresh
and native as the Elizabethans were. Such a mighty
stream, *novies Styx interfusa*, in the shape of accumulated
erudition, grave national experiences, spirit-quelling
doubts, insurgent philosophies, and all too aching pressing facts and fears, divides the men of this time from the
men of that."[21]

What Pater grasps so decisively in contrast is that even
Homer's age felt itself "trite and commonplace enough"
before it was made young in and through Homer's art. Flavian, that is to say, can never encounter language "face to
face" in its original freshness, for the originary moment of
primitive power ever recedes as it is pursued. Instead, as
Flavian himself comes to see, all that can be achieved in
these latter days is the self-conscious *imitation* of simplicity: "Perhaps the utmost one could get by conscious effort,
in the way of a reaction or return to the conditions of an
earlier and fresher age, would be but *novitas*, artificial art-
lessness, *naïveté*; and this quality too might have its measure of euphuistic charm . . . but only of a bunch of field-
flowers in a heated room."[22]

[21] J. A. Symonds, "A Comparison of Elizabethan with Victorian Poetry,"
Fortnightly Review 51 o.s., 45 n.s. (January 1889): 58.
[22] Pater, *Marius* 1:102. This theme in Pater shaped Arthur Symons's
opinion that "All Art, surely, is a form of artifice." Cf. Symons's "Lillian:

What sort of literary style, then, is best suited to this complex linguistic medium? In *Marius* the answer is Euphuism. Apuleius's euphuistic *Golden Ass* becomes Flavian's "golden book," inspiring him to follow the example of Apuleius, who in an age "when people, from the emperor Aurelius downwards, prided themselves unwisely on writing in Greek . . . had written for Latin people in their own tongue; though still, in truth, with all the care of a learned language" (Pater, *Marius*, 1:56). Thus Flavian, like his contemporary Apuleius, seeks *novitas* in the contemporary Latin vernacular: he appropriates as a refrain for the poem he plans to write (Pater makes the fictional Flavian the author of the actual *Pervigilium Veneris*) "a snatch from a popular chorus, something he had heard sounding all over the town of Pisa one April night" (Pater, *Marius*, 1:99). But Flavian's literary program does not face simply in one direction towards the new and the spoken: his "neologies" are matched by his "archaisms." And hence Flavian also pursues *novitas* by assiduously studying the writing of earlier Latin authors—"what research for the significant tones of ancient idiom—*sonantia verba et antiqua!*" (Pater, *Marius*, 1:96-97); for in that older idiom Flavian detects a buried freshness of "latent figurative expression"—not genuine newness, but an artificial ingenuousness, a rebirth of linguistic elements that have already lived and died many times before.

Pater makes clear that Flavian's Euphuism arises in part from the young poet's personal situation: quite simply, Flavian seeks fame, as the patrician Marius, seeing in Eu-

---

Proem," *London Nights* (London: Leonard Smithers, 1895), p. 9:

> Yet here, in this spice-laden atmosphere,
> Where only nature is a thing unreal
> I found in just a violet, planted here,
> The artificial flower of my ideal.

phuism "a kind of sacred service to the mother-tongue" (Pater, *Marius*, 1:97), will discover a private refuge. Yet Pater takes great care to show that Euphuism is neither an idiosyncratic personal enthusiasm of the two young men nor a single aberrant literary episode of the second century A.D. Simply calling the rhetorical revival of Apuleius and Cornelius Fronto "Euphuism," of course, sets that movement in a "prescient" relationship to the Elizabethan Euphuism of John Lyly. Moreover, Pater insists upon the historical recurrence of Euphuism by pointing to the similarities amongst its various historical instances: "as with the Euphuism of the Elizabethan age, and of the modern French romanticists [by whom Pater means Baudelaire and his successors], its neologies were the ground of one of the favourite charges against it; though indeed, as regards these tricks of taste also, there is nothing new, but a quaint family likeness rather, between the Euphuists of successive ages" (Pater, *Marius*, 1:98).

Yet Pater is intent upon making even a larger claim than this for Euphuism. Euphuism manifests itself, he declares, "in every age in which the literary conscience has been awakened to forgotten duties towards language, towards the instrument of expression" (Pater *Marius*, 1:97). At first glance, Apuleius's Euphuism may seem to overthrow all "conscientious" notions of style, for it is "full of archaisms and curious felicities in which that generation delighted, quaint terms and images picked fresh from the early dramatists, the lifelike phrases of some lost poet preserved by an old grammarian, racy morsels of the vernacular and studied prettinesses" (Pater, *Marius*, 1:56). But Pater insists that even Apuleius's Euphuism, like the other Euphuisms that arise throughout history to regenerate literary language, "does but modify a little the principles of all effective expression at all times" (Pater, *Marius*, 1:97).

Euphuism, that is to say, is nothing other than a self-conscious care for language, "extreme" only in its assiduous attention to the complex linguistic textures of old and new, archaism and neology.

Beyond this, Pater describes Euphuism in *Marius* as characterized by occasional lapses into "fopperies or mannerisms, not wholly unpleasing perhaps, or at least excusable, when looked at as but the toys (so Cicero calls them), the strictly congenial and appropriate toys, of an assiduously cultivated age, which could not help being polite, critical, self-conscious" (Pater, *Marius*, 1:98). Such sentences as this demonstrate Pater's habit of diluting or dispersing what might be considered objectionable opinions by appending successive, and in their effect cumulative, qualifications. Thus "fopperies" are muted to "mannerisms," "mannerisms" are seen to be but "toys," "toys" are relieved of their childish connotations when Pater notes they are "appropriate" to the age, and the age—cultivated, polite, critical and self-conscious—is fully assimilated to the Victorians' own. The notion of Euphuism as mere foppery has thus somehow been dismissed without ever having been overtly defended, and the literary mode of Apuleius and Flavian stands forth as a regenerating and universally answerable style.

The seriousness with which Pater takes Euphuism as a mode of stylistic regeneration is emphasized in his great essay on "Style." Although Pater there prefers the word "eclecticism" to Euphuism, such Victorian readers as Lionel Johnson realized that Pater, in that essay and elsewhere, was in fact "vindicat[ing] a certain sort of Euphuism," with Euphuism understood as "no dreamy toying with rich and strange expressions."[23] The "quaint family

[23] Lionel Johnson, "The Work of Mr. Pater," *Fortnightly Review* 62 o.s., 56 n.s. (September 1894): 363-64.

likeness" between Euphuism in *Marius the Epicurean* and eclecticism in "Style" becomes yet clearer when we find Pater in that essay recommending to the contemporary writer just those habits of mind and methods of composition that Apuleius and Flavian employed: "Racy Saxon monosyllables, close to us as touch and sight, he will intermix readily with those long, savoursome, Latin words, rich in 'second intention' " (Pater, "Style," p. 16); so too, the modern writer must "make time to write English more as a learned language,"[24] just as Apuleius had done for his disregarded Latin vernacular. There is surely a suppressed humor at work in "Style" when Pater describes Tennyson, Victorian Poet Laureate and by 1889 a revered institution in his own right, in terms that would apply to a Latin Euphuist like Apuleius or a French Euphuist like Baudelaire: "How illustrative of monosyllabic effect, of sonorous Latin, of the phraseology of science, of metaphysic, of colloquialism even, are the writings of Tennyson; yet with what a fine, fastidious scholarship throughout!" (Pater, "Style," p. 17). On another level, however, Pater is perfectly serious, recognizing and praising Tennyson's heterogeneous and linguistically informed writings (for Tennyson, as we have seen, was the intellectual heir of J. C. Hare and the personal friend of R. C. Trench at Trinity College, Cambridge)—a style answerable to the post-philological moment.

Tennyson is being invoked here, clearly, as a magisterial presence in Victorian letters, and Pater wants mainly to borrow his authority to sanction his own unorthodox program of stylistic Euphuism. Yet the only reason Tennyson can be so invoked is that his eclectic style is the

[24] Walter Pater, "English Literature: Four Books for Students of English Literature" [17 February 1886], in *Essays from the "Guardian"* (London: Macmillan, 1910), p. 15.

mode genuinely required both by "this late day" and by
the linguistic "belatedness" of the English language. Pater
is keenly aware that biological science has newly revealed
the world as being almost unimaginably heterogeneous, a
world in which "types of life [evanesce] into each other by
inexpressible refinements of change."[25] And now linguistic science has revealed English to be the most heterogeneous and assimilative of the modern European languages.
Thus writers of English in "this late day" are uniquely
equipped to realize the world most fully and genuinely if
they will but fashion eclectic, Euphuistic prose out of their
own richly heterogeneous linguistic medium, "an instrument of many stops, meditative, observant, descriptive, eloquent, analytic, plaintive, fervid" (Pater, "Style," p. 11).

As Pater's terms at any such moment begin inescapably
to suggest, his program of stylistic Euphuism has all along
had a deeper rationale, nothing other than the urging of
written language—that is, language frozen in writing and
divorced from living speech in the philological sense—as a
literary medium. For to urge composing English "more as
a learned language" is to conceive of the language as a
written dialect, whose spoken form is insignificant or non-
existent. To recommend archaisms is to do the same, for
the etymological weight, the "second intention" that Pater
so prizes in such words, inheres in them only because of
the lexicographical, which is to say, the written tradition.
Pater's own attempt to recover the etymological sense, "to
restore . . . the finer edge of words" (Pater, "Style," p. 16),
emphasizes his conception of language as written dialect,
and diverges significantly from what we find in Swinburne. For though Swinburne, too, self-consciously writes

[25] Pater, "Coleridge," *Appreciations*, p. 66. This essay is a revision of
"Coleridge's Writings" [1866].

in the post-philological moment, he in contrast embraces song as the only adequate remaining model for literary language in the aftermath of the subversion by scientific philology of the written tradition. Thus when Swinburne makes etymological puns, as he frequently does, they are rarely very obvious ones; instead, as Jerome McGann has pointed out, they usually pass by undetected.[26] But we are always aware of Pater's puns: either they are openly attended by quotation marks or by words such as "literally" and "indeed," or their etymological densities are deployed in such a way as to change the texture of the sentence, drawing attention to them.

We see precisely the same divergent practice in the case of literary allusions, for where Swinburne's allusions and quotations are most often completely submerged and unrecognizable in what Swinburne himself calls his "multiform unity of inclusion," Pater makes the presence of his allusions known at every turn—with quotation marks, slightly deformed syntax, or even with a sort of expectant archness of tone. Pater displays his own prose as a deliberately written form, a form that self-consciously takes up its position at the end of the written tradition. Even the "racy morsels" of the spoken vernacular that Pater recommends including, and that he himself includes, are conceived essentially as contrasting elements—their piquant vulgarity set off by quotation marks—in a fundamentally written conception of language. In short, as Pater surely remembered from Newman's "Literature," where the etymology is spelled out, style itself (and hence "Style") derives from the Latin *stilus*, the Roman instrument for writing on wax.

We trace Pater's conception of language even in his ac-

---

[26] See Jerome J. McGann, *Swinburne: An Experiment in Criticism* (Chicago and London: University of Chicago Press, 1972).

tual habits of composition, as A. C. Benson reminds us: "When he had arranged his notes he began to write on ruled paper, leaving alternate lines blank; and in these spaces he would insert new clauses and descriptive epithets. Then the whole was recopied, again on alternate lines, which would again be filled; moreover, he often had an essay at this stage set up at his own expense in print, that he might better be able to judge of the effect; the same device that Tennyson so often used" (Benson, *Walter Pater*, p. 202). Pater composed, in short, not to the measure of the speaking voice, but specifically and literally for the printed page. Moreover, as Edmund Chandler makes clear in his analysis of Pater's revisions of *Marius the Epicurean*, Pater took the compositional unit of written language to be not the paragraph but the sentence: "Pater felt he could dismantle *Marius* into its component sentences, and then revise each as an entity in itself. . . . For though the essay on 'Style' gives little support for such a view, it is clear from the revision that for Pater the art of writing was synonymous with the composition of sentences."[27] And as Anthony Ward's study of Pater's writing in manuscript suggests, it is what we may call the topographical contour of individual sentences that interested Pater as much as their actual meaning: "Often a sentence is plotted out before the meaning of it, what it refers to, is made specific. Gaps are left in the larger structure and several alternative words, often quite different in meaning, are written down above the gap, to be selected on grounds of their denotative meaning."[28] We may say that Pater conceived of prose

[27] Edmund Chandler, *Pater on Style: An Examination of the Essay on "Style" and the Textual History of "Marius the Epicurean"* (Copenhagen: Rosenkilde and Bagger, 1958), p. 82.

[28] Anthony Ward, *Walter Pater: The Idea in Nature* (Worcester and London: MacGibbon and Kee, 1966), p. 189.

as a linear form, not least (to paraphrase Carlyle) because sentences are linear and paragraphs are solid.

Yet even if we had no such biographical evidence available to us, we would doubtless conclude after studying Pater's metaphors of style and the characteristic conduct of his prose that Pater conceived of language as a linear, written form, for Pater's metaphors of style stress the linear nature of written language. Even Pater's appeal to the "architectural sense" in style is a metaphor of *progress through* a shaped structure, "that architectural conception of work, which foresees the end in the beginning and never loses sight of it" (Pater, "Style," p. 21). So too, we find Pater's metaphors from the fine and applied arts—an invocation once again of the craftsmanly ideal—giving way to a metaphor of linear movement: "The literary artist, I suppose, goes on considerately, setting joint to joint, sustained by yet restraining the productive ardour, retracing the negligences of his first sketch, *repeating his steps* only that he may give the reader a sense of secure and restful *progress*, readjusting mere assonances even, that they may soothe the reader, or at least not interrupt him *on his way*."[29] And in Pater's warning against the dangers of digression we find (as perhaps is hardly surprising given Pater's etymological interests) a metaphor of walking vs. wandering:

> Parallel, allusion, the allusive way generally, the flowers in the garden:—he knows the narcotic force of these upon the negligent intelligence to which any *diversion*, literally, is welcome, any *vagrant* intruder, because one can go *wandering* away with it from the immediate subject. Jealous, if he have a really quickening motive within, of all that does not hold directly to that, of the facile, the otiose, he will never depart

[29] Pater, "Style" in *Appreciations*, p. 24. My emphasis.

from the strictly *pedestrian process*, unless he gains a ponderable something thereby. . . . Surplusage! he will dread that, as the *runner* on his muscles.[30]

Yet there is an obvious paradox here, for Pater's own prose seldom fulfills his strictures or follows such recommendations as, "Say what you have to say, what you have a will to say, in the simplest, the most direct and exact manner possible, with no surplusage" (Pater, "Style," p. 34). Even if we notice that Pater takes care to include justifications for elaborate stylists like himself (e.g., "unless he gains a ponderable something thereby" or "if it be right in its elaboration"), we are likely to wonder at the conduct of Pater's own prose. What is the meaning of Pater's frequent diversions from the strictly pedestrian process? The clue is contained in a sentence from "Style": "For to the grave reader words too are grave; and the ornamental word, the figure, the accessory form or colour or reference, is rarely content to die to thought precisely at the right moment, but will inevitably linger awhile, stirring a long 'brain-wave' behind it of perhaps quite alien associations" (Pater, "Style," p. 18).

Pater's answer, in short, is style as enactment. Just as the virtuoso line in Pope's *Essay on Criticism* ("And like a wounded snake drags its slow length along") enacts the crippled progress of an inept alexandrine, so Pater's multiplied examples ("the ornamental word, the figure, the accessory form or colour or reference") themselves delay the "death to thought," that is, the moment of cognitive closure of the sentence in which they appear. In precisely the same way, Pater's striking neology "brain-wave" itself sets up a chain of alien or digressive associations (e.g., is

[30] Pater, "Style" in *Appreciations*, p. 19. Pater emphasizes "diversion"; the other emphases are mine.

"brain-wave" a legitimate scientific term? if so, when was it first introduced? how did Pater come to know of it? and so on), further putting off the moment when the "opaque" phrases become "clear" to the construing mind.

The virtue of such a sentence, then, is that it illustrates Pater's characteristic stylistic conduct, what we may call his aesthetic of delay. Pater, that is to say, puts off the moment of cognitive closure, not least because it *is* a little emblematic death. And he does this not simply by writing long sentences, but by so structuring his sentences as to thwart—at times even to the point of disruption—our usual expectations of English syntax. Hence, for example, Pater's curious use of proleptic reference, his habit of introducing and then widely separating a pronoun from its referent. In "Apollo in Picardy," for instance, the "He" introduced at the beginning of one sentence is maintained as a subject for some twelve lines before finally being identified as the "Prior Saint-Jean."

Hence, too, Pater's habit of inverting his sentences by beginning with the emphatic phrase. Where another writer, as A. C. Benson points out, would say, "That tale of hours, the long chanted English service, develops patience," Pater writes, "It develops patience—that tale of hours, the long chanted English service" (Benson, *Walter Pater*, p. 205). The conclusiveness, the cognitive clinching achieved by placing the strong phrase in last position Pater willingly dispenses with or, we may say, subverts, because the two following subject phrases do not at once establish their relationship to the verb and object, but instead trail rather mysteriously and indeterminately after. Such examples truly show Pater writing English "as a learned language." Indeed, as Gerald Monsman has pointed out, Pater's "complicated syntax, threatening always to break the cognitive sequence, resembles the highly inflected structure of the classical languages, which permits a more arbitrary order of words" (Monsman, *Pater's Art*, p. 37). Pater, writing in the most inflectionless of all European languages, must remedy the loss of inflections by resorting to punctuation marks. For as G. P. Marsh had written,

> the use of commas, semicolons and brackets, supplies the place of inflections, and enables us to introduce, without danger of equivocation, qualifications, illustrations and parenthetical limitations, which, with our English syntax, would render a long period almost unintelligible, unless members were divided by marks of punctuation. (Marsh, *Lectures*, p. 414)

Punctuation marks, then, are the stigmata of written vernacular languages like English, marking the "fall" from perfectly consequent classical Latin and Greek style that Marsh describes so glowingly (Marsh, *Lectures*, pp. 407-12). And so too are Pater's elaborate and involuted periods the sign of written language, dependent as they are not simply upon punctuation but upon the regularity and easy legibility of the printed page.

If written language forms the enabling condition of Pater's "arbitrary" syntactical order, his syntax arises from his architectural sense of prose that steadily "foresees the end in the beginning and never loses sight of it," foresees, that is, the end of the sentence, the death to thought, the period of the period. For Pater's prose is always too conscious of its own end, too restlessly intent upon displaying itself as a verbal arabesque or measuring itself out as a length of written language ("the ornamental word, the figure, the accessory form or colour or reference") to be truly called "static." But in this effort, which in *Marius the Epicurean* is described with grammarians' terms for written language ("to perpetuate 'what is so *transitive*'. . . . to arrest certain *clauses* of experience"), we also discover the stylistic equivalent to Marius's ethic of receptivity, "that elaborate and lifelong education of his receptive powers . . . of preparing himself toward possible further revelation some day—towards some ampler vision" (Pater, *Marius*, 2:219). Hence Pater's characteristic preference for adjectives in the comparative degree ("ampler . . . further"), a preference he will pursue, as Christopher Ricks has shown, even to the point of misquoting his sources. For where superlatives establish "a climax, a completion, and outcome," the comparative degree, as Ricks points out, implies "an endless process and a 'tension of nerve.' "[31] Like his use of proleptic reference or his lingeringly elucidated qualifications, Pater's comparatives keep potentiality more multitudinously open to some "ampler vision" beyond.

In the aesthetic of delay as enacted in Pater's later writing, there are the first unmistakable hints of a stylistic revolution, something oddly registered in George Saintsbury's contemporary defense of Pater's style, in which, he protested, there was not to be discovered "the least sacrifice of the phrase to the word, of the clause to the phrase, of the sentence to the clause."[32] The very energy of denial here serves to alert us that Pater is being defended against some charge of subversion; and so he is, for Saintsbury is anticipating in the most precise manner the terms that Paul Bourget, and following him, Friedrich Nietzsche, would use in the 1880s to define Decadence. Havelock Ellis made Bourget's definition available to English readers

[31] Christopher Ricks, "Pater, Arnold and Misquotation," *Times Literary Supplement* (25 November 1977), p. 1384.
[32] George Saintsbury, "Modern English Prose," *Fortnightly Review* 25 o.s., 19 n.s. (February 1876): 257.

in 1889: "A style of decadence is one in which the unity of
the book is decomposed to give place to the independence
of the page, in which the page is decomposed to give place
to the independence of the phrase, and the phrase to give
place to the independence of the word."[33] Bourget's definition of Decadent style proceeds analogically from his so-
ciological analysis: in Bourget's view, a mature society
verges on anarchy when the individual energy of its members becomes exaggerated and insubordinate, threatening
the whole. "A similar law," he concludes, "governs the development and decadence of that other organism which we
call language." Bourget's pseudo-Darwinian vocabulary
of "laws" and "organism" takes on its full significance only
when we see that it represents no contrived metaphorical
application of Darwinian hypotheses to language. Rather,
as August Schleicher had argued, just the reverse: language provided a founding analogy for and confirmation of
Darwinian biology. Even though, as we have seen, the organic model for language was decisively set aside by the
Neogrammarians, the new and abiding sense of the independence of linguistic elements, which the organic model
was first devised to express, and which, of course, the Neogrammarians themselves had firmly upheld, here intensifies Bourget's uneasy sense of impending anarchy in style.

---

[33] Havelock Ellis, "A Note on Paul Bourget," in *Views and Reviews: A Selection of Uncollected Articles 1884-1932*, First and second series (Boston
and New York: Houghton Mifflin, 1932), p. 52. In *Der Fall Wagner* [1888],
Nietzsche paraphrased Bourget: "the word becomes sovereign and leaps out
of the sentence, the sentence reaches out and obscures the meaning of the
page, and the page comes to life at the expense of the whole—the whole is no
longer a whole." See Walter Kaufman, *Nietzsche: Philosopher, Psychologist,
Antichrist*, 4th ed. (Princeton: Princeton University Press, 1974), p. 73.
That Bourget and Nietzsche alike owe a debt to Désiré Nisard for this idea
of the "Decadent" subordination of whole to parts is argued in J. Kamerbeek,
" 'Style de Décadence,' " *Revue de Littérature Comparée* 39 (1965): 268-86.

This was the same vocabulary of organic disruption that Arthur Symons, in his influential article "The Decadent Movement in Literature" (1893), was to use to describe French Decadent writing. Though Symons specifically exempts Pater's style from the "violent" syntactical experimentation of the Goncourt brothers, he readily assimilates Pater's writing to Mallarmé's impeded poetic line with its radical syntactical license and its "depravation": "It is, indeed, in part a reversion to Latin phraseology, to the Latin construction, and it has made, of the clear and flowing French language, something irregular, unquiet, expressive, with sudden surprising felicities, with nervous starts and lapses, with new capacities for the exact noting of sensation."[34] Mallarmé, as Henri Mitterand reminds us, patterned his inverted and disrupted word order on the examples he found in English and, it may be, in Pater.[35] And Mallarmé, at once teacher and student of the English language, perceived in English the same rich but heterogeneous linguistic resources that Pater had called archaisms and neologies: "Par sa Grammaire . . . marche vers quelque point futur du Langage et se replonge aussi dans le passé, même très ancien et mêlé aux débuts sacrés du Langage, l'Anglais: Langue Contemporaine peut-être par excellence, elle qui accuse le double caractère de l'époque, rétrospectif et avancé."[36]

[34] Arthur Symons, "The Decadent Movement in Literature," *Harper's New Monthly Magazine* 87 (November 1893): 862. Cf. John Earle, *English Prose: Its Elements, History, and Usage* (London: Smith, Elder, 1890), p. 284: "The Latin cast of diction still has its votaries, and in our day it is most ably represented by the artistic pen of Mr. Walter Pater. His writings afford a frequent taste of the peculiar genius of the Latin sentence so far as it can be assimilated with English Prose."

[35] See Henri Mitterand, "De l'écriture artiste au style décadent," *Wissenschaftliche Zeitschrift der Humboldt-Universität zu Berlin* 18 (1969): 617-23.

[36] Stéphane Mallarmé, *Les mots anglais*, in *Oeuvres complètes*, ed. Henri Mondor et G. Jean-Aubry (Paris: Gallimard, 1945), p. 1053.

An unquiet sense of the linguistic autonomy of certain kinds of literary writing is thus what motivates Saintsbury's response to Pater. For despite his protestations, Pater's sentences *are* subtly insubordinate to their paragraphs. Even if we did not know that Pater's habitual unit of composition was the sentence rather than the paragraph, we would detect their persistently asserted "independence." So too, we are likely to notice in "Style" what David DeLaura has pointed out, namely, that despite Pater's repeated emphasis in that essay upon the indissolubility of form and content, Pater's own presentation of this theme constantly verges itself upon dissolution: "[T]he drift of Pater's reiterated reflections on form and matter, thought and word, is atomic, fractionary, a matter of this or that expressive unit, far more than the development or growth of an entire work from a unitary Coleridgean germ."[37] The tendency of Decadence, Nietzsche wrote, is ever towards an "anarchy of atoms." Pater's prose style never quite yields itself to this last release from the linear. But so often atomic, fractionary, it registers the allure of the Heraclitian flux.

Pater's program of stylistic Euphuism, then, his promotion and enactment of an aesthetic of delay, must ultimately issue in the demand not only for a new kind of writing but for a new kind of writer, the contemporary author as "erudite artist" (Pater, *Marius*, 1:56), and as "scholar" (Pater, "Style," p. 12). The linguistic medium itself and the scientific nature of language study both require the writer to be a scholar, whose art is "summed up in the observance of those rejections demanded by the nature of his medium, the material he must use" (Pater, "Style," p. 13).

[37] David DeLaura, *Hebrew and Hellene in Victorian England: Newman, Arnold and Pater* (Austin and London: University of Texas Press, 1969), p. 332.

Scholarship consists in science and good taste, and these concern themselves respectively with "the essential qualities of language" and with "its aptitudes for contingent ornamentation." As Pater's contrast of "essential" and "contingent" is meant to suggest, the scientific analysis—its history, its laws—is of primary importance to the literary artist, for science will penetrate, as mere "good taste" will not, to a true understanding of the linguistic medium.

Pater's scholar-artist is no mere aestheticizing philologist, however, but a writer who brings to his artistic work the pertinacity of observation and the breadth of historical knowledge that philologists bring to their tasks. Thus the scholar-artist will recognize as a matter of acquired knowledge, and not of simple untutored intuition, all the uncodified little "laws" of literary language, "those affinities, avoidances, those mere preferences, of his language, which through the associations of literary history have become a part of its nature, prescribing many a neology, many a license, many a gipsy phrase which might present itself as actually expressive" (Pater, "Style," p. 13). Nor is the scholar-artist a pedant. His broad historical view (for the scholar is "nothing without the historic sense") will save him from the parochialism and uncouth prescriptivism of the amateur grammarians: "he will be no authority for correctnesses which, limiting freedom of utterance, were yet but accidents in their origin; as if one vowed not to say '*its*,' which ought to have been in Shakespeare; 'his' and 'hers,' for inanimate objects, being but a barbarous and really inexpressive survival" (Pater, "Style," p. 16). At the same time, the scholar-artist is no complaisant latitudinarian in matters of linguistic "freedom," no enthusiastic advocate of "the rights of the *proletariate* of speech." He will ever "resist a constant tendency on the part of the majority of those who use them to efface the distinctions of language, the facility of writers often reinforcing in this respect the work of the vulgar. . . . and will show no favour to short-cuts, or hackneyed illustration, or an affectation of learning designed for the unlearned" (Pater, "Style," p. 13).

This is the revolutionary moment in Pater's stylistic and aesthetic program, for, having taken over from scientific philology without protest a notion of literary English as a dead language, he now repudiates its other main assumption, the identification of linguistic reality with living speech. Pater's whole effort in *Marius* and in "Style" has been to enrich a dialect he found newly impoverished of its authority, that is, to defend an idea of written language accepted at its lowered philological estimate *as* an "artificial" dialect. But having granted this much, Pater in quiet triumph grants no more. The living authority for this artificial dialect can never reside in the mass of speaking men. It resides instead in scholars: "That living authority which language needs lies, in truth, in its scholars, who recognizing always that every language possesses a genius, a very fastidious genius, of its own, expand at once and purify its very elements, which must needs change along with the changing thought of living people" (Pater, "Style," p. 5). So powerful is Pater's desire to reserve a last authority to the literary elite that he assimilates to it even that democratizing champion of "the real language of men": Wordsworth himself, declares Pater, wrote "with the tact of a scholar" (Pater, "Style," p. 15).

The scholar-artist prepares himself for his task by observing those chastening exercises of will and expression Pater so cherished: "Self-restraint, skilful economy of means [here Pater is appealing etymologically, with Newman and the Tractarians, to the patristic notion of οἰκογο-μία or judicious handling], *ascêsis*" (Pater, "Style," p. 17). Pater is offering to Victorians a modern version of Marius's "sacred service" and Flavian's patriotic "chivalry" to the mother tongue. And the modern scholar-artist's reward for such *ascêsis* or self-curtailment, Pater promises, will be to find in literature, that is to say, in literature written according to the scholarly ideal that he himself follows, "a sort of cloistral refuge, from a certain vulgarity in the actual world. A perfect poem like *Lycidas*, a perfect fiction like *Esmond*, the perfect handling of a theory like Newman's *Idea of a University*, has for [scholars] something of the uses of a religious 'retreat' " (Pater, "Style," p. 18).

The "retreat," however, will be for the select rather than for the solitary, for there always remains a danger of solecism for the scholar-artist. Solecism, that "subjectivity, the mere caprice, of the individual, which must soon transform it into mannerism" (Pater, "Style," p. 36), is the equivalent in the realm of literary expression to Paterian solipsism, that nightmare of "each mind keeping as a solitary prisoner its own dream of a world." But the scholar-artist's awareness of his scholarly audience will preserve him from solecism: "[T]here is . . . for every lineament of the vision within, the one word, the one acceptable word, recognisable by the sensitive, by others, 'who have intelligence' in the matter, as absolutely as ever anything can be in the evanescent and delicate region of human language" (Pater, "Style," p. 36). For in addressing "the sensitive" and those " 'who have intelligence' in the matter," the scholar-artist will assure that the artificial dialect he fashions remains an accessible language and not an incommunicable idiolect. Yet even more than this, in addressing "the scholarly," he joins an elite that has been charged with duties that set them apart from the mass of speaking men, but that at the same time constitute them as a sort of priestly brotherhood.

At just this point, obviously, we are dealing with Pater's

inheritance from Coleridge. Pater, with other Victorians, and with Matthew Arnold especially, shares in "that inexhaustible discontent, languor, and home-sickness, that endless regret" (Pater, "Coleridge," p. 104) that Coleridge, as Pater saw, had so fully embodied. Pater himself seemingly resigns without a discernible pang the passion for the absolute that Coleridge had so hectically prosecuted, and that Arnold soberly maintained; and this dissent unmistakably divides Pater from Coleridge. Nonetheless, Pater could still identify his own heterodoxy and his fondness for elaborate long sentences and for strange words with Coleridge's own: "To note the recondite associations of words, old or new . . . to recover the interest of older writers who had a phraseology of their own—this was a vein of inquiry allied to his undoubted gift of tracking out and analysing curious modes of thought" (Pater, "Coleridge," p. 82). And from Coleridge, Pater derived his opinion that a good style must not evacuate all difficulty for its readers, that to "really strenuous minds there is a pleasurable stimulus in the challenge for a continuous effort on their part" (Pater, "Style," p. 17).

Yet to see Coleridge as the figure looming in the immediate background of Pater's argument here is simultaneously to measure the transformation of those ideals of *lingua communis* and national clerisy that were Coleridge's great legacy to Victorian thought. What has become of Coleridge's *lingua communis* in Pater's hands? Pater has defended its basis in written language, and specifically in the higher modes of literature, against the philologically authorized claims of the spoken idiom. At the same time, Pater has allowed, in the interests of "heterogeneity," the inclusion of certain expressive terms from the popular idiom. But precisely as Pater's new *lingua communis* extends its reach into the widening vocabularies of science, the professions, and the spoken vernacular, does it become less held and less understood in common.

Thus Coleridge's *lingua communis* is transformed into nothing other than the dialect of Pater's new clerisy of scholars "writing for the scholarly." There is no "permanent, nationalized, learned order" in Pater, only a learned order that is sequestered, almost fugitive, living in voluntary asceticism at the margins or in the interstices of national life. Recognizable only to each other and virtually unacknowledged by all others, Pater's clerisy express their influence entirely through their literary style. Through a distinguished style writers may still exert "a kind of religious influence" (Pater, "Style," p. 26), but this is a power drastically diminished from that of Carlyle's "perpetual priesthood" or Arnold's ideal "community of spiritual authority." Even more significant, Pater's scholarly clerisy verges upon a secret alienation, not simply from the mass of speaking men, whose "voice" is too hurried and importunate to find expression in a "learned language," but from the official culture now become too attentive to that importunate new voice. It is at this point that Pater's chivalric, sacred, ritual service to the national language begins to lose its patriotic coloring and first offers itself as a secret language, a code for conspirators, or simply a self-expressive idiolect. It is at this point, in short, that Euphuism becomes Decadence.

❦ ❦

Euphuism has long been identified with either a decayed literary power or a feverishly immature appetite for stylistic novelty, and Pater's defense of Euphuism thus took its place at the end of a long line of Victorian discussions of Euphuism, a debate that had ranged over the works of

Carlyle and Dickens as well as the Spasmodics, and included denunciations of Ruskin as well as George Meredith.[38] Pater's defense of Euphuism is important, not because it succeeded for very long in redefining Euphuism, but simply because it was a *defense*. Even if the difficulty of defending Euphuism by name persuaded Pater to drop the name when he argued for eclecticism in "Style," his defense continued to shape the fin de siècle debate over literary Decadence. Specifically, Pater's curious praise of Tennyson ("How illustrative of monosyllabic effect, of sonorous Latin, of the phraseology of science, of metaphysic, of colloquialism even ... what a fine fastidious scholarship throughout!") was to authorize J. C. Collins's discussion of Tennyson's "euphuistic" and "artificial" style, the discussion that became the occasion in the early 1890s for the debate over literary Decadence.

Like Pater, Collins saw in Tennyson not simply the familiar poet and philosopher beloved of all Victorian reading circles, but an "antiquarian and scholar" as well.[39] Collins identified Tennyson with a certain class of poets arising in all literatures "at a certain point in their development" (Collins, *Illustrations*, p. 2). If this ominous phrase did not signal to Victorians Collins's drift, his characterization of Tennyson's work as "essentially imitative and reflective," full of poems that are "not direct studies

---

[38] See, for example, [Henry Morley], "Euphuism," *Quarterly Review* 109 (April 1861): 350-83; Richard F. Weymouth, "On Euphuism," *Transactions of the Philological Society* (1870-72): 1-17; Mowbray Morris, "An Alexandrian Age," *Macmillan's Monthly Magazine* 55 (November 1886): 361-67. John M. Robertson in "Concerning Preciosity," *Yellow Book* 13 (April 1897): 79-106 gives a Paterian account of preciosity or Euphuism ("an assertion of individual or special personality as against the common usage of talk").

[39] J. C. Collins, *Illustrations of Tennyson* (London: Chatto and Windus, 1891), p. 23.

from simple nature, but studies from nature interpreted by art" (Collins, *Illustrations*, pp. 2, 5) clearly should have done so. For Collins continued to stress the Alexandrian element in Tennyson's work, his "subtly elaborated diction," his epithets "pregnant with recondite significance," and his habit of affecting "archaisms and the revival or adoption of obsolete or provincial words" (Collins, *Illustrations*, pp. 9, 14, 18). Collins, that is to say, is attentive to the rich linguistic texture of Tennyson's poetry, a texture given its richness in part, as we have seen, by the philological influences of Tennyson's Trinity College, Cambridge in the 1830s and 1840s. Like many other Victorians, Collins associated this Alexandrian linguistic and philological self-consciousness with decadence. Unlike his contemporaries, however, Collins *declared* that "these peculiarities in the style of Nonnus and Tennyson . . . are characteristic of all literatures in their decadence" (Collins, *Illustrations*, p. 12), and his assumption that Tennyson's poetry was in this sense decadent precipitated a critical storm.

To rescue the beloved Poet Laureate from the charge of decadence, critics struggled to define literary Decadence anew. Richard Le Gallienne, for example, now defined it as "the euphuistic expression of isolated observations," so that he could reassure his readers that for Collins to "speak of decadence . . . in connection with such poets as Virgil and Lord Tennyson . . . is mere anarchy."[40] In the matter of literary Decadence, it should be said, Le Gallienne himself was half publicist, half prosecutor, for at times he adopted aggressively "Decadent" poetic themes, only to

[40] Richard Le Gallienne, "Considerations Suggested by Mr. Churton Collins' *Illustrations of Tennyson*," *Century Guild Hobby Horse* 7 (1892): 81. For a fuller discussion of Le Gallienne, see R.K.R. Thornton, *The Decadent Dilemma* (London: Edward Arnold, 1983), pp. 43-50.

damn them later. But Le Gallienne's attack upon Collins, and later upon a famous collection of poems by one of Wilde's protégés, *Silverpoints* (1893) by John Gray, would then prompt a far abler critic, Arthur Symons, to write a serious defense of Decadence as a movement. Le Gallienne's own discussion of Decadence is predictably confused and confusing, compounded as it is from a Paterian aesthetic sensibility and an unconquerable sentimentality, with the resulting lump leavened by Le Gallienne's commercially prudent moralism.

The significance of Le Gallienne's remarks, rather, is the way he moralizes the elements of Pater's ideal eclectic style while at the same time exaggerating or misrepresenting their relations. In Le Gallienne's hands, that is to say, Euphuism has lost all the subtle shades of its Paterian redefinition. Thus alliteration and onomatopoeia, for example, are no longer part of its repertoire, and the "unique word" is no longer part of its care. Instead, Euphuism is crudely taken to be the "antithesis" of slang, while "slang" represents Le Gallienne's vulgarization of "neologies," one of the constituent elements in Pater's Euphuism. Le Gallienne doubtless reached this caricature of Paterian Euphuism with the help of Wilde who, as we shall see, appropriated Paterian stylistic ideas to describe the famous "poisonous book" in *The Picture of Dorian Gray* (1890, expanded version 1891) as possessing a "curious jewelled style, vivid and obscure at once, full of *argot* and of archaisms, of technical expressions and of elaborate paraphrases."[41]

Argot and archaism—Wilde's phrase would be taken over in turn by Max Beerbohm in his wittily unapologetic

---

[41] Oscar Wilde, *The Picture of Dorian Gray*, ed. Isobel Murray (London: Oxford University Press, 1974), p. 125.

apologia to the *Yellow Book* in July 1894.[42] Reinforced by Le Gallienne's "euphuism and slang," this capsule definition of literary Decadence represents a perhaps inevitable simplification of Pater's complex and linguistically informed ideal of eclectic style. Yet in this diminution and trivialization of Pater lies one of the characteristic motives of fin de siècle Decadence: its impulse towards burlesque and parody, most often self-parody. Pater had in effect proposed a new style for literary artists composing in the postphilological moment, the moment when written language is accepted at its philological estimate as linguistically artificial and inauthentic. The parodic mode of Victorian literary Decadence, granting the philological estimate but deflating Pater's exquisite stylistic rationale of it into a mere slogan, delights at the same time in showing how complete a world can be fashioned out of mere archaisms and argot.

Aubrey Beardsley's unfinished pornographic travesty, *The Story of Venus and Tannhäuser* (written 1895-1896, published 1907) gives the fullest expression to this mode of Victorian Decadence. The deflationary pressure of Beardsley's tale is irresistible as it reduces, first of all, the high-art theme ennobled in Wagner's opera and Swinburne's "Laus Veneris" to an occasion for pornographic variations, and then turns around to deflate the tumescent pretensions of pornography as well. For Beardsley cheerfully admits that his hero utterly lacks the "Gargantuan facility" required of the typical erotic hero; his Tannhäuser is frankly relieved when, after a mere hour or so of sexual dalliance, Venus is taken off his hands by more indefatigable revelers.[43]

[42] Max Beerbohm, "A Letter to the Editor," *Yellow Book* 2 (July 1894): 284.

[43] Aubrey Beardsley, *The Story of Venus and Tannhäuser or Under the*

The mock-heroic reductionism of Beardsley's tale is intent, not simply on reducing all behavior to sexual behavior—the premise of pornography—but on revealing all behavior, including sex, as play. Hence the childish good nature and playfulness that suffuse Beardsley's diminutive, matinal underworld of feasts and concerts, breakfasts and romps. Hence the change from Swinburne's tragic sexual stigma in "Laus Veneris" ("her neck,/ Kissed over close, wears yet a purple speck/ Wherein the pained blood falters and goes out;/ Soft, and stung softly—fairer for a fleck"[44]) to Beardsley's painted vignettes and silhouettes that "showed through a white silk stocking like a sumptuous bruise" (Beardsley, *Venus and Tannhäuser*, p. 37). Where Swinburne's lines appeal to a Baudelairean *reversement* of categories in which pain is pleasure and bruises are beauties, Beardsley invokes this tortured Sadesque consciousness only to overthrow it in its turn. Beardsley's "sumptuous bruise" is no fleshly mark of sexual obsession, inflicted in the desperate hope of becoming one with the beloved. Beardsley's bruise, like the "exquisite august disease" mentioned as well, is merely one decorative motif among many others, such as "fans of big living moths stuck upon mounts of silver sticks," "masks of green velvet that make the face look trebly powdered," "sleeves cut into the shapes of apocryphal animals," and "delightful little moustaches dyed in purples and bright greens" (Beardsley, *Venus and Tannhäuser*, pp. 36-37).

Beardsley's parodic mode of Decadence thus appropri-

Hill, ed. Robert Oresko (London: Academy; New York: St. Martin's, 1974), p. 55. This edition is based on the 1907 version printed by Leonard Smithers, with two interpolations in Chapter 7 from Beardsley's expurgated *Under the Hill* text in *Savoy* 1 (April 1896).

[44] A. C. Swinburne, "Laus Veneris," in *The Complete Works of Algernon Charles Swinburne*, ed. Edmund Gosse and T. J. Wise, 20 vols. (London: William Heinemann, 1925), 1:46.

ates many of the familiar devices and techniques of what may be called antinomian or apocalyptic Decadence—the extended catalogues of exotica, the insistent adjectivalism, the digression as stylistic arabesque, the heterogeneity of diction—in order laughingly to subvert the strict categories of good and evil, beauty and horror upon which antinomian Decadence depends. The parodic mode nonetheless participates fully in the linguistic self-consciousness of literary Decadence, for Beardsley's world, no less than Pater's, is a world of written language: *Venus and Tannhäuser* is filled with references to obscure books, many of them, as Stanley Weintraub has demonstrated, non-existent.[45] So too, Beardsley's is a textual world, inscribed and superinscribed with decorative motifs—in which, for example, pearls embroidered over a blood-red slipper may be worn over a white silk stocking drawn over a leg painted over with black silhouettes. The ubiquitous decorative motifs, moreover, are to be "read" as texts, for the inhabitants of Venus's underworld all amuse themselves by "finding a delightful meaning in the fall of festoon, turn of twig and twist of branch. . . . [or] what thing was intended by a certain arrangement of roses" (Beardsley, *Venus and Tannhäuser*, p. 41).

Beardsley's *Venus and Tannhäuser* in this sense represents the apotheosis of linguistic self-consciousness, a world so entirely fashioned out of archaisms and argot, so fully conceded to be artificial, that Beardsley's curiously campy patois soon seems in this sunny underworld of agreeably insatiable appetites to be nothing more than the ordinary language of an everyday world. Hence the persistent catachrestical impulse to link surprising adjectives

[45] Stanley Weintraub, *Beardsley: A Biography* (New York: Braziller, 1967), p. 167.

to unsuitable nouns, so that laughter is "atrocious," curls are "intelligent," voices are "slender," and breasts are "malicious." And hence Beardsley's tendency, also noted by Weintraub, to introduce unitalicized foreign, usually French, words—coiffeur, chevelure, cassolettes, fardeuse, bandeaux—and use them matter-of-factly, as if they were proper English.

The complex, silken tension of Pater's style loosens here in Beardsley's hands, for breasts are called "malicious" not out of any long-meditated etymological motive but simply for the sake of surprise or pleasurable variation. Where Pater's etymologizing implied a deeper connection or coherence between word and idea, Beardsley's catechresis dispenses with such notions of ideal fitness in the name of free linguistic play. Where Pater, attending to the historical "laws" or customs of linguistic usage, declines to modify "laughter" with "atrocious," Beardsley, perceiving the synchronic independence of language from all customs except irreducibly syntactic ones, blithely couples the two words. Beardsley avails himself of the new linguistic freedom bestowed by linguistic science upon writers and indeed all users of language, the freedom to throw over, as the poet John Gray said, "the tyranny of the grammar book; to use the word that best conveys the impression desired, although such have not the sanction of custom."[46]

Venus and Tannhäuser thus presents a world entirely unconcerned with Pater's careful, scholarly "affinities, avoidances, those mere preferences" of language. The incessant, indiscriminate sexual coupling in *Venus and Tannhäuser*, like its incessant decorative motive, expresses instead a world of complete linguistic independence,

[46] John Gray ["Translator's Note"], in Louis Couperus, *Ecstasy* [1892], quoted in Ruth Z. Temple, "The Other Choice: The Worlds of John Gray, Poet and Priest," *Bulletin of Research in the Humanities* 84 (1981): 53.

where, restrained only by the inherent structural limitations of sexual and linguistic forms, everything may modify everything else. In the same way, the disappearance in Beardsley's prose of Pater's italics and quotation marks means that the sharper friction that Pater maintained between foreign and home language is smoothed away. In Beardsley's hands, Pater's eclectic style no longer lingers to display itself as heterogeneous and artificial (artificial, that is, as compared to an absent but competing dialect). Instead, Beardsley's wholly artificial world—where masks imitate *powdered* faces, and false moustaches are dyed bright *green*—is homogenously linguistic: it shows the way the world looks when it is perceived to be wholly made out of language.

Yet even as Beardsley's style liberates itself from the more deliberate processes of Pater's Euphuism, it belongs at last to the artificial idiom of literary Decadence. This is what Haldane Macfall sees, for instance, in his denunciation of Beardsley's writing: "He uses his native tongue as if it were obsolete, a dead language—he is more concerned with dead words than with live. . . . In short, he is a hopeless decadent in art."[47] By now, Macfall's equation of literary Decadence with a "dead language" has become a critical commonplace, but what vitality it retains is due to an implicit metaphor, the idea that Decadent language was "dead" due to some sort of linguistic corruption or disease, which in turn derives from the assumption that language constituted an "organism" potentially subject to "disease" or "degeneration," an idea we have seen to be familiar to Victorians from the linguistic work of August Schleicher and Max Müller.[48] So, too, did Theophile Gau-

[47] Haldane Macfall, *Aubrey Beardsley: The Man and His Work* (London: John Lane, 1928), pp. 80, 83.
[48] Cf. also E. R. Lankester, *Degeneration: A Chapter in Darwinism* (Lon-

tier adopt the organicist linguistic vocabulary when in 1868 he called Baudelaire's style "gamy and marbled with corruption" (*le style tacheté et faisandé*), the image describing external corruption rather than internal morbidity.[49] J.-K. Huysmans specifically identifies putrefaction with disease when, in *A Rebours* (1884), he characterizes Baudelaire's and Mallarmé's writing as showing "the decadence of a literature attacked by incurable organic disease . . . exhausted by the excess of grammatical subtlety."[50] Here the assumption is that an element inside language—in Mallarmé's case, the element of syntax—can corrupt and weaken language from within.

Another governing assumption in Macfall's equation of Decadence and "dead language" is that languages become dead languages through an excess of "learning." The French had not overlooked this aspect of Decadence; Gautier, for example, observed that Decadent style was "an ingenious complicated style, full of shades and of research,

---

don: Macmillan, 1880), pp. 74-75: "[Degeneration in language] includes two very distinct things; the one is degeneration of grammatical form, the other degeneration of the language as an instrument of thought. The former is a far commoner phenomenon than the latter, and, in fact, whilst actually degenerating so far as grammatic complexity is concerned, a language may be at the same time becoming more and more serviceable, or more and more perfect as an organ. The decay of useless inflexions and the consequent simplification of language may be compared to the specialization of the one toe of the primitively five-toed foot of the horse. . . . Degeneration, in the proper sense of the word, so far as it applies to language, would seem to mean simply a decay or diversion of literary taste and of literary production in the race to which such language may be appropriate."

[49] Theophile Gautier, "Charles Baudelaire," in Baudelaire, *Les Fleurs du mal* (Paris: Calmann-Lévy, [1925]), p. xvi: "la langue marbrée déjà des verdeurs de la décomposition et comme faisandée du bas-empire romain. . . ."

[50] J.-K. Huysmans, *Against the Grain* (New York: Dover, 1969), pp. 186-87. Huysmans's stress on the heterogeneity and expressiveness of the Decadent Latin of Petronius and Apuleius, and the stylistic resemblance of these authors to modern French Romantic writers, closely resembles Pater's portrayal of Euphuism in *Marius the Epicurean*.

constantly pushing back the boundaries of speech, borrowing from all the technical vocabularies" (Gautier,
"Baudelaire," p. xvi). But the emphasis on learning as disease is much more marked in English than in French Decadence, thanks to the separate history of English Romanticism with its Wordsworthian stress on spoken rural
dialects and its apparent hostility to more elaborate figures
of rhetoric. The association of Decadence and learning
arises explicitly, for instance, in Matthew Arnold's observation that "one of the signs of the Decadence of a literature, one of the factors of its decadent condition indeed, is
this—that new authors attach themselves to the poetic
expression the founders of a literature have flowered into,
which may be *learned* by a sensitive person, to the neglect
of an inward poetic life," and the equation surfaces as well
in Arthur Symons's remark of 1897 that what "Decadence, in literature, really means is that learned corruption
of language by which style ceases to be organic, and becomes, in the pursuit of some new expressiveness or
beauty, deliberately abnormal."[51] But the association of
learning and Decadence is implicit in Lionel Johnson's
opinion that Decadence consists in refinement, after-
thought, and reflection, and it colors Symons's own stress
in his "Decadent Movement in Literature" article on the

[51] Matthew Arnold, *Letters of Matthew Arnold to Arthur Hugh Clough*, ed.
Howard Forster Lowry (London: Oxford University Press, 1932), p. 64.
Arthur Symons, "A Note Upon George Meredith," in *Studies in Prose and
Verse* (New York: E. P. Dutton, 1922), p. 149: "Like Carlyle, but even
more than Carlyle, Meredith is in the true, wide sense, as no other English
writer of the present time can be said to be, a Decadent. The word Decadent
has been narrowed, in France and England, to a mere label upon a particular
school of very recent writers. . . . Meredith's style is as self-conscious as Mallarmé's." Cf. also p. 143: " 'Let writers find time to write English more as a
learned language,' said Pater; but Meredith has always written English as if
it were a learned language. . . . he has invented a whole vocabulary which has
no resemblance with the spoken language."

"qualities that mark the end of great periods, the qualities that we find in the Greek, the Latin, decadence: an intense self-consciousness, a restless curiosity in research, an over-subtilizing refinement upon refinement, a spiritual and moral perversity."[52]

The great exemplar of a language "dead" through internal "organic" failure as well as external "learned" corruption is, of course, late Latin. As we have seen, late Latin provided an analogue for nineteenth-century literary Decadence that had been persistently invoked ever since Désiré Nisard's *Etudes de moeurs et de critique sur les poètes latins de la décadence* (1834). The appeal of late Latin to French writers lay chiefly in the model of stylistic freedom that its "degenerated" linguistic structures seemed to offer to a generation oppressed by the tyranny of the alexandrine and the rectitude of French classicism generally. Hence Baudelaire's note to his Latin poem "Franciscae meae laudes" in *Les Fleurs du mal* (1857): "Ne semble-t-il pas, au lecteur, comme à moi, que la langue de la dernière décadence latine . . . est singulièrement propre à exprimer la passion telle que l'a comprise et sentie le monde poétique moderne? . . . Dans cette merveilleuse langage, le solécisme et le barbarisme me paraissent rendre les négligences forcées d'une passion qui s'oublie et se moque des règles."[53] The vogue for late Latin that Baudelaire began was continued in France with Huysmans's *A Rebours* and Remy de Gourmont's *Latin Mystique* (1892).

Similarly in England, as we have seen in the case of Pa-

---

[52] Lionel Johnson, "A Note Upon the Practice and Theory of Verse at the Present Time Obtaining in France," *Century Guild Hobby Horse* 6 (1891): 64; Symons, "Decadent Movement," 859-60. R.K.R. Thornton says that Symons likely derived much of his notion of classical Decadence from Johnson.

[53] Baudelaire, "Franciscae Meae Laudes," *Les Fleurs du mal*, p. 99.

ter, late Latin was valued for its peculiarly "modern" expressiveness. Pater's portrayal of Apuleian Euphuism and the "sonorous organ-music of medieval Latin" was influential among the younger generation of writers who followed him. George Moore, for instance, followed Pater's account almost slavishly in his novel *A Mere Accident* (1887), where his hero John Norton describes the school of Apuleius and Cornelius Fronto as "a school pre-occupied above all things by form; obsolete words set in a new setting, modern words introduced into old cadences to freshen with a bright delightful varnish, in a word, a language under visible sign of decay . . . yet how full of dim idea and evanescent music—a sort of Indian summer, a season of dependency that looked back on the splendours of Augustan yesterdays—an autumn forest."[54] So too, J. A. Symonds indulged in an ultra-Paterian evocation of the Latin of the Vulgate Bible:

> Jerome clad the Roman strength of speech with Asiatic pomp, bent its imperial stiffness to Greek subtlety, drew from its iron chords the melodies of Syrian lyres and harping hallelujahs of apocalyptic ecstasy. . . . Like the chords of penetential psalms, chanted by male voices in the gloom of cathedral choirs, the deep reverberations of these weighty Latin words go rolling through the cavernous aisles of the mysterious mediaeval period. . . . Like the breaking of an alabaster box of precious ointment, like the tossing up of heavy-perfumed censers; so the penetrating odours of this prose, artless in style, oppressive in passionate suggestion, float abroad through all the convents and the churches of the centuries to come, laden with languors

[54] George Moore, *A Mere Accident* (London: Vizetelly, 1887), p. 38.

of mystic love, pregnant with poetry undreamed of on the banks of the Tiber or Ilissus.[55]

In Moore and Symonds and other writers as well, we encounter the feeling that Latin in its cosmopolitan heterogeneity expresses a distinctively modern sensibility, as well as a sense that late Latin, in its linguistic "decay" and its "apocalyptic" ambitions, offers a vehicle for antinomian resistance to established norms: as Moore's John Norton says, "Cosmopolitan Hellenism forces and breaks down the bars of classical traditions, and, weary of restrictions, these writers first sought personal satisfaction, and then addressed themselves to scholars rather than the people" (Moore, *A Mere Accident*, p. 37).

Despite Pater's encouragement of such attitudes, he and those who wrote in his stylistic mode were not the only hierophants of the fin de siècle cult of style. For Pater's influence was balanced by that of other late-Victorian writers, not least of whom was R. L. Stevenson, whose essays, "On Some Technical Elements of Style in Literature" (1885) and "A College Magazine" (1887) constituted a virtual instruction manual for ambitious younger stylists.

[55] J. A. Symonds, "Notes on Style," in *Essays, Speculative and Suggestive*, 2 vols. (London: Chapman and Hall, 1890), 1:289-91. This passage seems to be indebted to Pater's depiction of "a wild, convulsed sensuousness in the poetry of the Middle Age" in Pater's review of William Morris's poetry [1868], largely reprinted as "Aesthetic Poetry" in the first edition of *Appreciations* [1889]. Phyllis Grosskurth, *John Addington Symonds: A Biography* (London: Longmans, 1964), p. 157, depicts the relations between Pater and Symonds (who was a year younger) as "waspishly antagonistic," noting that "Pater is said to have referred habitually to Symonds as 'poor Symonds.' . . . [Symonds wrote of Pater to a friend]: 'There is a kind of Death clinging to the man, who makes his Music (but heavens! how sweet that is!) a little faint & sickly. His view of life gives me the creeps, as old women say. I am sure it is a ghastly sham; & that live by it or no as he may do, his utterance of the theory of the world has in it a wormy-hollow-voiced seductiveness of a fiend.' "

Thus, for instance, Arthur Machen's *The Hill of Dreams*
(composed 1895-1897, published 1907) combines both
Stevensonian and Paterian elements of the fin de siècle cult
of style, and in doing so emerges as a parable of what may
be called antinomian Decadence. Machen tells the story of
Lucian Taylor (whose Latinate name is itself Paterian), a
poor but aspiring Welsh youth who, after a profound but
unspecified sensual experience near the ruins of an old Roman camp (the "hill of dreams" of Machen's title), devotes
himself to the life of literature. Specifically, Lucian devotes
himself to enshrining his love for a simple village girl in a
talismanic book:

> [He] copied and recopied the manuscript nine times
> before he wrote it out fairly in a little book which he
> made himself of a skin of creamy vellum. In his mania
> for acquirements that should be entirely useless he
> had gained some skill in illumination, or limning as he
> preferred to call it, always choosing the obscurer word
> as the obscurer arts. First he set himself to the severe
> practice of the text; he spent many hours and days of
> toil in struggling to fashion the serried columns of
> black letter, writing and re-writing till he could shape
> the massive character with firm true hand. He cut his
> quills with the patience of a monk in the scripto-
> rium.[56]

Writing his love poetry gives Lucian deep sensual pleasure: "There were phrases that stung and tingled as he
wrote them, and sonorous words poured out in ecstasy and
rapture, as in some of the old litanies"; and so does hiding
the meaning of his love poetry, as Lucian "hugged the
thought that a great part of what he had invented was in

[56] Arthur Machen, *The Hill of Dreams* (London: Richards, 1954), p. 90.

the true sense of the word occult: page after page might have been read aloud to the uninitiated without betraying the inner meaning" (Machen, *Hill*, p. 90).

In such moments of ecstasy begins the transformation of the book into an actual object of worship. To adorn the book as object Lucian studies books of medieval architecture, seeking his ornamental designs, as if in a private reinvention of Art Nouveau, in "the poisonous growth of great water-plants, and the parasite twining of honeysuckle and briony" (Machen, *Hill*, p. 93). And in a macabre ritual of bibliophilic worship, he then makes himself a bed of brambles and reads his book upon it ("as he turned over page after page, and saw the raised gold of the majuscules glow and flame in the candlelight, he pressed the thorns into his flesh" [Machen, *Hill*, pp. 294-95]). At this point it becomes clear that Lucian worships, not the pedestrian Annie, but the fetishistic book itself: "At such moments he tasted in all its acute savour the joy of physical pain; and after two or three experiences of such delights he altered his book, making a curious sign in vermilion on the margin of the passages where he was to inflict on himself this sweet torture" (Machen, *Hill*, p. 95). As its masochistic fervor increases, Lucian's devotion to the book comes to parody not only the mortifications of religious life, but Pater's notion of literary martyrdom as well:

He was covered with scars, and those that healed during the day were torn open afresh at night; the pale olive skin was red with the angry marks of blood, and the graceful form of the young man appeared like the body of a tortured martyr. He grew thinner and thinner every day, for he ate but little; the skin was stretched on the bones of his face, and the black eyes burnt in dark purple hollows. His relations noticed that he was not looking well. (Machen, *Hill*, pp. 95-96)

Lucian's initiation into the cult of style leads in its next stage to the "vale of Avallaunius," an imaginary Roman world he enters through a power of imaginative projection so intense it borders on hallucination, the world of *Marius the Epicurean* with all the history and philosophy left out: "The boys who served brought the wine in dull red jars that struck a charming note against their white robes. They poured out the violet and purple and golden wine with calm sweet faces as if they were assisting in the mysteries, without any sign that they heard the strange words that flashed from side to side" (Machen, *Hill*, p. 124). Yet as the insistent chromatic adjectivalism suggests, this is really Pater's prose as registered by Wilde. We see in Lucian's aesthetic opinions Wilde's characteristic habit of appropriating, exaggerating, and hence "coarsening" Pater's thought. Thus Pater's remark in "Style" that *Lycidas* represents "a perfect poem" here becomes "*Lycidas* . . . the most perfect piece of pure literature in existence," while Lucian, in an imitation of Wildean critical verve, abuses the elegaic subject of *Lycidas* as "some wholly uninteresting and unimportant Mr. King" (Machen, *Hill*, p. 127).

We should scarcely need Machen's acknowledgement that *The Picture of Dorian Gray* influenced the writing of *The Hill of Dreams*,[57] for Wilde's influence is everywhere evident, as in Machen's exotic inventories ("Some cups were of a troubled and clotted red, with alternating blotches of dark and light, some were variegated with white and yellow stains" [Machen, *Hill*, p. 125]), in the newly ominous atmosphere now surrounding such Pater-

[57] Aidan Reynolds and William Charlton, *Arthur Machen: A Short Account of His Life and Work* (London: Richards, 1963), p. 59.

ian words as "curious" and "strange," and above all in Lucian's hostility to utilitarian assumptions about literature:

> The rich sound of the voices impressed him above all things, and he saw that words have a far higher reason than the utilitarian office of imparting a man's thought. The common notion that language and linked words are important only as a means of expression he found a little ridiculous; as if electricity were to be studied solely with the view of [sending telegrams] to people, and all its other properties left unexplored, neglected. (Machen, *Hill*, p. 126)

This rejection of the "common" idea of language leads Lucian to see language as independent of logic and indeed thought itself: "Here lay hidden the secret of the sensuous art of literature; it was the secret of suggestion, the art of causing delicious sensation by the use of words" (Machen, *Hill*, p. 126). Such an anti-representational aesthetic insistently recalls Mallarmé's Symbolist dictum, "Suggérer: voilà le rêve," for Machen here seems to be appealing to a realm of alogical, non-discursive experience that words cannot imitate or represent so much as magically invoke.

The theme of Machen's tale has now become its hero's descent into stylism, in the third and last stage of which we witness the terminal effects of his obsessional pursuit of literary style. Lucian moves to London, rents a room and begins to write "the work":

> He had fallen into the habit of always using this phrase "the work" to denote the adventure of literature; it had grown in his mind to all the austere and grave significance of "the great work" on the lips of the alchemists; it included every trifling and laborious page and the vague magnificent fancies that sometimes

hovered before him. All else had become mere by-play, unimportant, trivial; the work was the end, and the means and the food of his life—it raised him up in the morning to renew the struggle, it was the symbol which charmed him as he lay down at night. (Machen, *Hill*, p. 162)

Dissatisfied with the bald effects of writing addressed to the corporeal ear ("the loud insistent music of 'never more' " [Machen, *Hill*, p. 155]), he sets himself Stevensonian tasks of sedulous imitation: "He tried to imitate this art, to summon even the faint shadow of the great effect, rewriting a page of Hawthorne, experimenting and changing an epithet here and there, noting how sometimes the alteration of a trifling word would plunge a whole scene into darkness, as if one of those blood-red fires had instantly been extinguished" (Machen, *Hill*, p. 160). At last, one morning, after a night besieged by nightmare and somehow presided over by the image of a small blue-black bottle, Lucian realizes his elusive Paterian ideal: "He was astonished that morning at his own fortune and facility; he succeeded in covering a page of ruled paper wholly to his satisfaction, and the sentences, when he read them out, appeared to suggest a weird elusive chanting, exquisite but almost imperceptible, like the echo of the plainsong reverberated from the vault of a monastic church" (Machen, *Hill*, p. 156).

Yet even in this moment of intensely private triumph, we understand that its cost has been terrible Flaubertian paralysis in "seeking the phrase" and Mallarméan horror before the appalling whiteness of the page. Beyond the "anguish of the empty page" (Machen, *Hill*, p. 162), Lucian has been willing to "endure the austerities of a monk in a severe cloister, to suffer cold, to be hungry, to be lonely and friendless, to forbear all the consolation of friendly speech" (Machen, *Hill*, p. 178). The "martyr-dom" to style has meant subsisting solely on green tea and black tobacco. Moreover, as he shuns all "common" com-municative notions of language, Lucian becomes es-tranged from his fellows, "an alien and a stranger amongst citizens" (Machen, *Hill*, p. 178). This, he tells himself, is simply the result of the "hatred of the barbarian for the maker" (Machen, *Hill*, p. 179), but in his moments of des-titution and despair, he imagines he will at last "leave his retreat and go forth to perish at [the barbarians'] hands, so that he might at least die in company, and hear the sound of speech before death" (Machen, *Hill*, p. 179). Lucian, who has daily struggled with his own written language as if it were an *other*, endowed with an independent, resisting existence, has now become as silent as his own white page: "Lucian felt most keenly that in his case there was a double curse; he was as isolated as Keats, and as inarticulate as his reviewers. The consolation of the work had failed him, and he was suspended in the void between two worlds" (Machen, *Hill*, p. 179). As the echo of Arnold's "Stanzas from the Grand Chartreuse" ("Wandering between two worlds, one dead,/ The other powerless to be born") im-plies, the cult of the literary work, like the orthodox cult of the Bible on which it is modelled, is doomed to fail without revealing what faith could possibly succeed it.

The Hill of Dreams ends in a sexual Black Sabbath, the apocalypse of a waking nightmare, as that sensuousness of language that Lucian had earlier repressed with the help of gorse boughs, or had imaginatively sublimed away into a supersensuous parallel realm of ineffable suggestion, now rises up to claim him as its victim. He dies a misera-ble, Chattertonian death. Only then, in a sort of trick end-ing, do we learn that Lucian's writing—the few pages that with their elusive exquisite chanting quality have ever satisfied him—are in fact gibberish: Lucian has all the while been under the spell of laudanum taken from a small blue-black bottle. Thus does Machen's tale portray the dead end of the cult of style. Just as Pater's ideals of Euphuism and the priestly band of scholars represent a privatized, attenuated version of Coleridge's *lingua communis* and clerisy, so Machen's story represents in its turn a last unconscious parodic diminution of Pater. For the implicit distance between artist and "barbarians" has become an overt and immediately threatening hostility, while the audience of fellow "scholars" has fallen completely away. Lucian's life of self-curtailment before the implacable page has been existential solipsism. And solipsism has led to the most extreme form of stylistic solecism—a language so perfected in its private symbolism that it will no longer yield its meaning even to the select few, but only to the unique reader, Lucian himself.

The deepest implications of Machen's vision of sensuous language are evaded, in a sense, when at the last he reveals Lucian's experience of artistic persecution as an opium dream; but no evasion can disguise that sense of the autonomy—so often the evil autonomy—of written language he had learned from Wilde, as Wilde had learned it from Pater: "Words! . . . they seemed to be able to give a plastic form to formless things. . . . Mere words! Was there anything so real as words?"[58] This sense of language as possessing an independent life is everywhere in fin de siècle literature: in, for example, the frequently parodied emphasis on symbolism and the symbolic dimension of ordinary

---

[58] Wilde, *Dorian Gray*, p. 19. Isobel Murray notes in the Introduction to *Dorian Gray* that this passage derives from Pater's unfinished novel *Gaston de Latour* [1888] in which it is said of Ronsard's odes, "Never before had words, single words, meant so much" (p. xii).

language, as when Prince Zaleski, M. P. Shiel's Decadent detective, says, "[In] the shape of a cloud, the pitch of a thrush's note, the *nuance* of a sea-shell you would find, had you only insight *enough*, inductive and deductive cunning *enough*, not only a meaning, but, I am convinced, a quite endless significance"; or when Earl Lavender, John Davidson's satiric Stevensonian adventurer whose very name enacts the point (Lavender being a corruption of his "real" name, L'Avenir) declares, "There is not a vein upon a leaf, not a scratch upon a pebble, not a name above a shop, not a torn word on a scrap of paper, without a message for me, and I am in despair because I cannot read the meaning here. The 'Razor and Hen.' "[59]

Literary Decadence in its apocalyptic mode invariably portrays this independent linguistic life as something mysterious, disruptive, evil, or, to use Wordsworth's term, as "a counter-spirit, unremittingly and noiselessly at work to derange, to subvert, to lay waste, to vitiate and to dissolve," which explains, for instance, the recurrence in Decadent literature of such tropes as the unutterability *topos*, the familiar convention that asserts the total inadequacy of language to express what is meant. In Machen's tale *The Great God Pan* (1894), a handwritten account of an evil woman's seductions is offered to one character:

> Austin took the manuscript, but never read it. Opening the neat pages at haphazard his eye was caught by

---

[59] M. P. Shiel, "The Stone of the Edmundsbury Monks," in *Prince Zaleski* (London: John Lane, 1895), p. 78; John Davidson, *A Full and True Account of the Wonderful Mission of Earl Lavender* (London: Ward and Downey, 1895), p. 250. Earl Lavender is puzzled by a public house sign: "The Razor and Hen." The meaning of the sign is shown, rather laboriously, to be the history of the sign: when upon the death of the publican his daughter inherits the public house ("The Hen and Chickens"), she marries a barber and changes the sign.

a word and a phrase that followed it; and, sick at heart, with white lips and a cold sweat pouring like water from his temples, he flung the paper down. "Take it away, Villiers, never speak of this again. Are you made of stone, man? . . . I will not read it; I should never sleep again."[60]

Machen made use of the unutterability *topos* so frequently in this tale that reviewers complained about it, but within the story it operates thematically to associate written language itself with the literally "unspeakable" phenomena of primeval physical horror: "such awful, unspeakable elements enthroned as it were, and triumphant in human flesh" (Machen, *Pan*, p. 29).

Similarly, Lord Alfred Douglas's famous poem "Two Loves" in effect appropriates the unutterability *topos* in order to invert it. The down-cast youth who upon being asked his name answers, "I am the love who dare not speak its name" seems to be repressing, as Machen repressed, language too horrible to be borne by mortal ear or eye. Yet this is not so. For we already know what the sad youth's name is: he has already said, "My name is Love," and has been rebuked for saying so by his cheerful companion. What is truly unmentionable or unspeakable about the downcast youth's name, then, is not its Sodomic difference from, but rather its full identity with, the name of the buoyant youth who so unwillingly accompanies him and whose task it is to fill the hearts of boy and girl with heterosexual flame. What it is impermissible to say is that *both* youths bear the name "Love." Thus the fearsome power of language here resides, not in its abominations, but in its ordinary words.

An identical sense of linguistic autonomy, of written or

---

[60] Arthur Machen, *The Great God Pan* (London: John Lane, 1894), p. 92.

literary language possessing a dangerous life of its own, explains the rhetoric of secrecy in such a work as Wilde's "The Portrait of Mr. W. H." (published 1889, expanded version 1893). Psychological explanations of Wilde's work normally trace his penchant for secrets in his works to the psychopathology of his sexual identity—to the secret, so imperfectly kept and disastrously revealed, of his homosexual life. But the rhetoric of secrecy in "Mr. W. H."—"mystery," "hidden," "secret," "key," "lock," "reveal," and above all "strange"—has a purely literary meaning. Applied to such works as Shakespeare's Sonnets and Ficino's translation of Plato, this rhetoric describes the autonomous life of literary language, hinting at the dangerous effect such language can have on human life and consciousness. In "Mr. W. H." the lure of solving the "secret" of Shakespeare's Sonnets tempts the three chief characters to intervene in Shakespeare's text. The narrator, for instance, decides to rearrange the sequence of the Sonnets in order better to "reveal" the hidden story of Shakespeare's love for the boy-actor Willie Hughes. But the effect of this meddling with literary language is fatal to the narrator's two friends Cyril and Erskine. Although the narrator is ultimately able to disengage himself from an obsessive interest in the autonomous linguistic world of Shakespeare's art, the very energies that compose this world seemingly turn upon the other two intruders. For like the very syntactic elements of Decadent style itself ("the page is decomposed to give place to the independence of the phrase, and the phrase to give place to the independence of the word"), Cyril and Erskine in their early excitement and subsequent deaths are first discomposed and then decomposed by the "secret" of the text.

The full implications of Decadent linguistic anxiety converge most obviously in the fin de siècle notion of the "fatal book," something anticipated in "The Picture of Mr. W. H.," when Wilde traces to Shakespeare's Sonnets the deaths of Cyril and Erskine, but finally something more complex and, properly understood, more terrible. The fatal book *is* fatal, that is to say, not because of its power to kill outright, but because of its power decisively to change an individual life. This is the power that Pater himself depicts in the famous Chapter 5 of *Marius the Epicurean* ("The Golden Book"), when he shows the profound literary and personal influence of Apuleius's *Golden Ass* upon Marius and Flavian. And this is the power that Pater's Gaston de Latour feels after reading Ronsard's Odes or that Duke Carl of Rosenmold experiences after finding the *Ars versificandi* of Conrad Celtes. Often, Gerald Monsman has noted, "in Pater's description of the development of his characters, a literary discovery is suddenly the textual prelude to their maturer manhood" (Monsman, *Pater's Art*, p. 116). Literary texts in Pater seem to preside over or indeed produce a climacteric of mental and physical change in their readers.

This power of linguistic autonomy becomes in a precise sense Decadent, however, only when portrayed as a poisonous or seducing power, as when George Moore treats the fatal power of specific books as a sexually seductive presence, making explicit what Machen had left unsaid in *The Hill of Dreams* when Lucian is thrilled by "the sensuous art of literature . . . the art of causing delicious sensation by the use of words." In *Confessions of a Young Man* (1888), Moore describes his own conversion to the divine delights of the flesh as a result of reading Gautier's *Mademoiselle de Maupin*. In describing Gautier's gospel of sensuality ("the Word that has become so inexpressibly a part of me. . . . Great was my conversion . . . so great was my conversion,"[61] Moore's antinomian inversion of conventional religious language is far less startling than his assertion that he was persuaded to this new life of sensualism by the sexual seductiveness of Gautier's literary style: "Who has not been, unless perhaps some musty old pedant, thrilled and driven to pleasure by the action of a book that penetrates to and speaks to you of your most present and most intimate emotions. This is of course pure sensualism. . . . But there are affinities in literature corresponding to, and very analogous to, sexual affinities—the same unreasoned attractions, the same pleasures, the same lassitudes" (Moore, *Confessions*, p. 99).

The power of language to seduce its readers in a specifically sexual sense lies as well behind Moore's enrollment of *Marius the Epicurean* in the roster of seducing books, his insistence upon the coincident sympathies and effects of *Marius* and *Maupin*: "[W]hen a few adventitious points of difference be forgotten, it is interesting to note how firm is the alliance, and how cognate and co-equal the sympathies on which it is based; the same glad worship of the visible world, and the same incurable belief that the beauty of material things is sufficient for all the needs of life. Mr. Pater can join hands with Gautier saying—*je trouve la terre aussi belle que le ciel, et je pense que la correction de la forme est la vertu*" (Moore, *Confessions*, p. 166). Moore's readers cannot escape the conclusion that Pater, like Gautier, converts his readers to a gospel of visible beauty through a sexual seductiveness of style.

In this manner does Moore strip away the hesitating scruples, the exquisite qualifications of Pater's prose style, single-mindedly identifying the fugitive effects and eva-

[61] George Moore, *Confessions of a Young Man*, ed. Susan Dick (Montreal and London: McGill-Queen's University Press, 1972), p. 79.

sive conduct of that style—"all those lurking half-mean-
ings and that evanescent suggestion," as he called them
(Moore, *Confessions*, p. 166)—with an implicitly homo-
erotic mode of seduction, the teasing, fleeting allure of "the
love that dare not speak its name." Pater, who doubtless
would have preferred being thought a "musty old pedant"
by Moore, attempted to evade his disciple's impression of
his own "sensualism" in his essay "Style," taking over
Moore's notion of "sense-judgment" or "sensualism" in literature and transforming it into the idea of "soul in style,"
a brilliant attempt to make Moore's aggressive appropriation of religious language ("the Word," "my conversion")
yield up its antinomian heat as it becomes in his own essay
a mild invocation of "theological interests" (Pater,
"Style," p. 25).

In one sense, Pater's great essay on style may be read as
an attempt to protect himself from the full implications of
Moore's notion of the book as seducer by sublimating the
metaphor into something less throbbingly fleshly. Indeed,
so firm is Pater's revision of Moore's "sensualism" that we
are invited to read the following sentences as if Pater wrote
them with Moore uppermost in mind: "There are some to
whom nothing has any real interest, or real meaning, except as operative in a given person; and it is they who best
appreciate the quality of soul in literary art. They seem to
know a *person*, in a book, and make way by intuition" (Pater, "Style," p. 27). If this is meant as a mild rebuke to
Moore, it is a qualified one, and qualified here with praise.
For insofar as Moore's coarse reductionism deserves a
check, his keen responsiveness to literary style at the same
time merits praise. Yet however keen, mere intuitionism
about style and its relationship to an author's sexual identity is finally inadequate, and so must be reminded of its
limits. Readers like Moore, that is to say, must be told that

although they thus enjoy the completeness of a personal information, it is still a characteristic of soul, in this sense of the word, that it does but suggest what can never be uttered, not as being different from, or more obscure than, what actually gets said, but as containing that plenary substance of which there is only one phase or facet in what is there expressed. (Pater, "Style," p. 27)

That plenary substance. The occult phrase lies at the center of a stylistic labyrinth of quintessentially Paterian qualification ("not as being different from, or more obscure than"), negative or concessive definition ("never . . . not"; "but . . . only"), synonymic multiplication ("phase or facet") and impalpable clausal nouns ("what can never be uttered . . . what actually gets said . . . of which there is only one phase . . . what is there expressed"). As we have seen, these are the linguistic organs of Pater's ideal of receptivity, the ideal Marius had pursued in "that elaborate and lifelong education of his receptive powers." In their apparent imprecision and their postponement of cognitive closure, they keep the plenitude of significance open and crude exclusivity at bay. Such stylistic structures are designed precisely to guard and guarantee the mysterious potentiality—what in *Marius* Pater was fond of calling the "mysticity"—of stylistic power from such violating eyes or intuitions as Moore's.

Even as Pater struggles to evade the uncomfortable implications of Moore's view of his style, however, there remains in his writing an irreducibly sensuous element, one of which Pater's own doctrine of "soul in style" will scarcely allow him to divest himself. For it is, paradoxically, the sensuous element that allows "profane" writers like Pater to exercise "a kind of religious influence" (Pater,

"Style," p. 26). As Pater's own terms suggest, the paradox is rooted in his own relation to the theological sense of language he is invoking. For Pater, as David DeLaura has convincingly shown, composed in the intellectual and stylistic penumbra of J. H. Newman: the essay "Style" was surely written with Newman's "Literature" open before him.[62] Pater's sense of an inspiriting "soul" in style, a stylistic "force" that can be apprehended as a living "person" derives from Newman's famous definition of literature as the *personal* use or exercise of language. Literature is personal, in Newman's view, because it proceeds, as breath and speech proceed, from "some one given individual," and it is "proper" to that individual "in the same sense as his voice, his air, his countenance, his carriage, and his action, are personal" (Newman, "Literature," pp. 238, 239). In a writer of genius, literary style is quite simply "the faithful expression of his intense personality"; it is, for Newman, "his personal presence" (Newman, "Literature," pp. 241, 250).

Yet Newman's idea of style draws at such moments directly on a theological explanation of language and the world, and from this Pater's similar notion of style as the expression of intense personality is forever excluded. Newman could confidently assert the perfect incarnation of "intense personality" in style because the simultaneous union in secular writers of thought and word was implicitly guaranteed by the divine Logos of the Gospel of St. John.

[62] DeLaura, *Hebrew and Hellene*, p. 334: "That Pater had Newman's lecture at his elbow while composing the essay on 'Style' is scarcely to be questioned." For the contemporary Victorian opinion that Newman continued the stylistic mode of the Anglican liturgy and Prayer Book, see J. C. Shairp, *Aspects of Poetry* [1881], pp. 443-44: "There are hundreds of passages in Cardinal Newman's writings, which, for graceful rhythm and perfect melody, may be placed side by side with the most soothing harmonies of the Prayer Book."

But Pater, a "profane" writer, could find no such sanction there. Nor could he seek authority in the new gospel of comparative philology, for as we have seen, the linguistic science that had begun by sweeping aside J. P. Süßmilch's argument for the divine origin of language had ended by dismissing Max Müller's secularized pseudo-scientific equivalent to it. Insofar as linguistic scientists remained interested at all in the question of the origin of language (and in France the Société de linguistique urged them to abandon this interest), they had come generally to agree that words in their primary signification derived from sense impressions. Thus did matters return to where they had stood at the beginning of the nineteenth century, when Horne Tooke clamorously proclaimed the sensuous or material basis of language: truth was merely what a man *troweth*. The connection between word and concept was no longer to be thought of as necessary and ideal but simply arbitrary and sensuous: "the spirit" did but mean "the breath."

The dark and troubling vision of the fatal book as it was to haunt fin de siècle writing, then, originates in that profane "soul in style" that Pater could never quite free from the sensuous materiality of language, and that thus becomes itself the ghost of linguistic materiality. Like the "dark angel" of Lionel Johnson's famous poem, it is the false companion, the "dark Paraclete"—is, in short, the unholy spirit or inverted logos known by its "whisper in the gloom,/ The hinting tone, the haunting laugh." This stylistic effect of "intense personality" unconsecrated by ideality is what George Moore read as a seducing presence in the works of Gautier and Pater, a counterspirit that inhabited certain poisonous books: "Books are like individuals; you know at once if they are going to create a sense within the sense, to fever, to madden you in blood and brain" (Moore, *Confessions*, p. 76). The most famous of these fatal books is the "poisonous" book, with its yellow cover, soiled pages, and curious jewelled style of archaism and argot, that Lord Henry Wotton gives the ageless hero of Wilde's *Picture of Dorian Gray*, allowing Wilde with his tale to answer George Moore's remark in *Confessions* that "I know of no story of the good or evil influence awakened by the chance reading of a book, the chain of consequences so far-reaching, so intensely dramatic" (Moore, *Confessions*, p. 80). As research has shown, Wilde unmistakably modelled his fatal book upon elements in Huysmans's *A Rebours*, Pater's "Conclusion," *Marius*, and *Gaston de Latour*, as well as several more fugitive works (from which Wilde permitted himself to borrow with more generosity).[63]

In Wilde's tale, the poisonous book functions as Lord Henry's surrogate, and under its tutelage Dorian becomes an exquisite connoisseur of evil: "Things that he had dimly dreamed of were suddenly made real to him. Things of which he had never dreamed were gradually revealed" (Wilde, *Dorian*, p. 125). Dorian, the antinomian descendant of Pater's characters, has been roused by a book to "maturer manhood." Specifically, Lord Henry's fatal book opens the *history* of sin to Dorian's eyes, for the book's young Parisian hero attempts "to realize in the nineteenth century all the passions and modes of thought that belonged to every century except his own, and to sum up, as it were, in himself the various moods through which the

[63] See Murray, "Introduction" to *The Picture of Dorian Gray*, pp. vii-xxviii. Wilde's notion of corruption through books may have been colored by non-literary sources as well: Wilde first met Swinburne at Lord Houghton's, whose extensive library of erotica and pornography was notorious. Houghton had introduced Swinburne (at the latter's insistence) to the works of Sade.

world-spirit had ever passed" (Wilde, *Dorian*, p. 125). Just as Dorian sees in the young Parisian hero "a kind of prefiguring type of himself," so the fatal book shows him whole centuries of prefiguring types—murderous Renaissance princes and before them, the wonderful line of decadent Roman Emperors: Tiberius, Domitian, Nero, and finally the transvestite Elagabalus who "painted his face with colours, and plied the distaff among the women" (Wilde, *Dorian*, p. 145).

It is not simply that Dorian later imitates in his own life the historical episodes of vice he reads about, but that under the influence of its curious jewelled style he perceives his own life in the "artificial" terms of the fatal book: his life seems to him to be simply a mosaic of sins and sensations, a subtly cadenced dream. The fatal book, that is to say, supplies the implicit pattern for the exotic experiments with music, embroidery, and precious gems Dorian conducts in Chapter 11, and these then become the models for Dorian's continuing experiments in "life." More significantly, the effect of the fatal book, both as Dorian himself experiences reading it and as we see its influence on his life, is to collapse time: hours pass unheeded as Dorian reads, and "years" pass as we read of his reading. Lord Henry's book is fatal precisely because its language achieves Flavian's Euphuistic ideal: artificially to arrest "what is so transitive":

> The mere cadence of the sentences, the subtle monotony of their music, so full as it was of complex refrains and movements elaborately repeated, produced in the mind of the lad, as he passed from chapter to chapter, a form of reverie, a malady of dreaming, that made him unconscious of the falling day and creeping shadows. (Wilde, *Dorian*, p. 126)

Lord Henry's poisonous gift to Dorian in *The Picture of Dorian Gray* may ultimately be taken as the emblem of the fatal book in fin de siècle writing because it is less a sexual seducer than a subtler instrument of the cerebral lechery that Mario Praz in *The Romantic Agony* has seen to be the Decadent extreme of normal sexuality. For in the tale Lord Henry, as Wilde tells us, never does a wrong thing, and this is because he never really acts at all; his corruptions are Decadent because wholly cerebral. As was perhaps inevitable, however, the fatal book *topos* was soon vulgarized as its sexuality was unveiled. If in Machen's *Hill of Dreams* the fatal book is an inverted Bible, in *Dorian Gray* it is, implicitly at least, a bible of inversion. This aspect of the fatal book becomes yet more explicit in such a work as Eric Stenbock's *Studies in Death* (1894), for example, where in one story the vampire Count Vardalek is said alone to understand "certain curious mystical books" and uses the books as a pretext to prey upon (for Stenbock is using vampirism as a code for homosexual seduction) the toothsome youth Gabryel.[64] By the time of Compton MacKenzie's *Sinister Street* (1913), the fatal book is nothing more than an absurd prop in an obligatory scene of pulp fiction:

> [S]hall I not buy you a book—some exquisite book full of strange perfumes and passionate courtly gestures? . . . Shall I buy you Mademoiselle de Maupin, so that all her rococo soul may dance with gilded limbs across your vision? Or shall I buy you A Rebours, and teach you to live? And yet I think neither would suit you perfectly. So here is a volume of Pater—Imaginary Portraits. You will like to read of Denys l'Aux-

[64] Eric Stenbock, "The True Story of a Vampire," in *Studies in Death: Romantic Tales* (London: David Nutt, 1894), p. 135.

errois. One day I myself will write an imaginary portrait of you, wherein your secret, sidelong smile will reveal to the world the whole art of youth.[65]

Wilde's sense of autonomous language, bestowed on him by that new philology that, in the famous dictum of his former teacher Max Müller, was to insist that thought is bred of words, not words of thought,[66] is in its way the central theme of *Dorian Gray*; "it is simply expression . . . ," he says there, that gives reality to things." It was perhaps not until Wilde's *Salome* (written in French 1891, published in English 1894), in its vision of a world created and utterly disrupted by the powers of autonomous language, that this sense was to become overtly apocalyptic: "And now the moon has become as blood," Herod cries out in an anguish of foreboding over the "word" he has given Salome. And yet its apocalyptic undertones had been throughout implicit in the very notion of Decadence, for without any logos to unify reality, the world at any moment can be undone with a word. The search for a substitute logos, for a new "volume paramount" expressive of the post-philological moment, was to be hectically pursued in the fin de siècle. As Mallarmé said that the age sought to bring forth a "sacred book," and D'Annunzio hoped for "some ideal book of modern prose," Yeats, looking backward long after, would recall that "some of us thought that book near towards the end of last century."[67]

[65] Compton MacKenzie, *Sinister Street*, 2 vols. (London: Martin Secker, 1913), 1:278.
[66] Cf. Oscar Wilde, "The Critic as Artist" [1891], in Ellmann, p. 359: "There is no mode of action, nor form of emotion, that we do not share with the lower animals. It is only by language that we rise above them, or above each other—by language, which is the parent, and not the child of thought." Wilde attended Müller's lectures while he was at Oxford in the mid-1870s.
[67] W. B. Yeats, *Autobiography* (New York: Macmillan, 1965), p. 210.

Yeats's brilliant portrait of the "Tragic Generation" in his *Autobiography* has made Pater's *Marius the Epicurean*, perhaps irrevocably, the sacred, fatal book of the Victorian fin de siècle, a book, like the other fatal books, that seduces less by overt doctrine than by the covert insinuations of its stylistic grace:

> [I]t still seemed to me, as I think it seemed to us all, the only great prose in modern English, and yet I began to wonder if it, or the attitude of mind of which it was the noblest expression, had not caused the disaster of my friends. It taught us to walk upon a rope, tightly stretched through serene air, and we were left to keep our feet upon a swaying rope in a storm. Pater had made us learned. . . . (Yeats, *Autobiography*, p. 201)

Fatal or not, Pater's book, born out of a cultural anxiety introduced with the new scientific philology, written in the hope of achieving victory through an acquiescence in the vision of autonomous language conjured into being by linguistic science, had set in motion the forces that converged in literary Decadence.

IV

Disembodied Voices

A voice on the winds,
A voice by the waters,
Wanders and cries. . . .
—JOHNSON,
"To Morfydd"

Literary Decadence, representing a moment when the linguistic artificiality and autonomy of written language are mirrored in a mode of curious stylistic opacity, was no more than a short-lived moment in the literary history of the Victorian fin de siècle. For literary Decadence figures simply as one among a number of competing experimental and traditional modes of writing during the 1890s, and even those writers who stand most plainly in the Aestheticist line that stems from Pater—Ernest Dowson, Lionel Johnson, Arthur Symons, and the young W. B. Yeats— are to be described only partially or punitively with the term "Decadent." Yet clearly, our very uneasiness with the term arises from the genuine complexity of the literary situation in which these inheriting Aestheticist writers found themselves. Thus, even though none of them writes as a consistently or programmatically Decadent writer, each of them writes with an uneasy awareness of the Decadent mode; the specifically Decadent portrayal of written language as an artificial and usurping power shapes their artistic choices as they struggle to claim Pater's inheritance without incurring Pater's limitations. For Decadence in the English literary experience always represents less a

175

program than a perception about the materiality and autonomy of its own linguistic medium. Literary Decadence, one might say, is Romanticism demoralized by philology, and though the mood of demoralization soon passes in the Victorian fin de siècle, the perception of the linguistic nature of written language remains to exert a constant pressure on literary practice.

To understand the situation of the inheriting Aestheticist writers of the 1890s, then, is to perceive how circumscribed they were by the two great Aestheticist writers who preceded them, namely, Pater and Swinburne. As we have seen, it was Pater's genuine achievement in *Marius the Epicurean* and the later works to win a rich yet linguistically permissible idiom from the discredited verbal medium left to him by nineteenth-century scientific philology. Pater's literary inheritors of the 1890s, however, found themselves left with artistic choices more limited still. For Pater's great example of written language accepted and deployed as an admittedly artificial dialect lay ever before them, at once seductive and yet resistantly inimitable.[1] The elaborate language of *Marius* was to come to represent for them an outer limit on what English written as a classical language could do.

Equally inhibiting to the Aestheticist writers of the 1890s, though posing an opposite sort of limitation altogether, was the tragicomic example of Swinburne. For Swinburne, too, had grown up as an artist under the postphilological dispensation: Max Müller had been one of

---

[1] Cf. Oscar Wilde, "Mr. Pater's Last Volume" [i.e. Pater's *Appreciations*], in *The Artist as Critic: Critical Writings of Oscar Wilde*, ed. Richard Ellmann (New York: Random House, 1968), p. 234: "[In] Mr. Pater, as in Cardinal Newman, we find the union of personality with perfection. He has no rival in his own sphere, and he has escaped disciples. And this, not because he has not been imitated, but because in art so fine as his there is something that, in its essence, is inimitable."

Swinburne's examiners before he left Oxford without taking a degree. Faced, like Pater, with a newly limited range
of linguistically allowable models for literary language,
Swinburne had chosen song over written language. Indeed, there could be no appeal for Swinburne to any ideal
of written language like Pater's. For in Swinburne's view
the language of the book implicitly derived its power from
the Bible, and the Bible is always for Swinburne the type
of repressive authority. Instead, the Bible and all the "volumes paramount" that live in the shadow of its spurious
authority must be overthrown. Hence all the persistent in-
versions of the Bible in Swinburne's poetry, as when, for
example, he calls Gautier's *Mademoiselle de Maupin* "the
holy writ of beauty."[2] And hence all Swinburne's catachrestical applications of Biblical diction and imagery, as
when in "The Masque of Queen Bersabe" his hieratic presentation of twenty-two fatal women mocks the intermi-
nable genealogical sequences of the Old Testament.

Instead of the written language of the book, then, Swinburne adhered to an earlier model of poetic song, by which
the human voice participated materially in the true essence
of things, their physical sounds: "The heavens that murmur, the sounds that shine,/ The stars that sing and the
loves that thunder,/ The music burning at heart like
wine," as Swinburne says in "The Triumph of Time."[3]
Clearly there is in this view no evasion of the linguistic
conditions of language, for Swinburne gives spoken language privilege over written. Nor is there any overt com-

[2] A. C. Swinburne, "Sonnet (With a Copy of *Mademoiselle de Maupin*),"
in *The Complete Works of Algernon Charles Swinburne*, ed. Edmund Gosse
and T. J. Wise, 20 vols. (London: William Heinemann, 1925), 3:60.

[3] A. C. Swinburne, "The Triumph of Time" [1866], in *Complete Works*
1:180. For Swinburne's belief that the essence of things is the sounds they
make, see David G. Riede, *Swinburne: A Study of Romantic Mythmaking*
(Charlottesville: University of Virginia Press, 1978), pp. 73-76.

promise with what Swinburne despised as the bankrupted religious doctrines of spiritual transcendence. Rather, in Swinburne's appeal to a notion of sound as constituting the essence or "soul" of things, there is a striking echo of his old Oxford examiner Max Müller and Müller's peculiar theory of "phonetic types" ("There is a law which runs through nearly the whole of nature, that everything which is struck rings. Each substance has its peculiar ring").

The poetic consequences of Swinburne's pursuit of pure sound have variously enchanted and bored generations of his readers. So successfully did he realize the elemental sonic nature of things, particularly through his brilliant onomatopoeic technique, that to many readers Swinburne seemed to speak simply *as* those elements, "with the breath of the wind and wave . . . [in] an absolute surrender of his own personality," as Oscar Wilde was to remark in a review.[4] Wilde and Yeats, however, disapproved vehemently of this surrender of personality. Although Swinburne had in effect won back legitimacy and permanence for poetic speech conceived of as elemental sound, in the later works in which this achievement reaches its fullest expression he simply forfeited the admiration of the Aestheticist writers who succeeded him. Thus it was just as Swinburne attained to a genuinely new mode of literary language—language that was elementally "unliterary" while yet seamlessly incorporating into its own suave medium whole passages from the literary past—that he lost the attention of those writers who most wondered how literature could reassert its claims in a post-philological age.

If the deadeningly uniform sublimities of Swinburne's later poetry alienated the Aestheticist writers of the 1890s,

[4] Oscar Wilde, "Mr. Swinburne's Last Volume" [i.e. *Poems and Ballads*, Third Series, 1889), in Ellmann, p. 148.

who unrepentantly preferred the inspiriting poems of Swinburne's first collection of *Poems and Ballads* (1866) to the vatic mythopoeia of "On the Cliffs" (e.g. "Love's priestess, mad with pain and joy of song,/ Song's priestess, mad with joy and pain of love"), their reaction to Pater was much more ambivalent. For though many of Pater's own students and followers turned against his ideal of ascetic Euphuism, they did so almost reluctantly, without overt "Philistine" rejection. Even the most famous public protest against Pater's style, namely Max Beerbohm's, is notable for its accommodative spirit, for a parodic yet persistent admiration that is instructive because it characterizes the response of so many of Pater's other heirs.

Less than eighteen months after Pater's death, Beerbohm wrote in the *Pageant* (1896): "Not that even in those more decadent days of my childhood [i.e. 1890] did I admire the man as a stylist. Even then I was angry that he should treat English as a dead language, bored by that sedulous ritual wherewith he laid out every sentence as in shroud—hanging, like a widower, long over its marmoreal beauty or ever he could lay it at length in his book, its sepulchre. From that laden air, the so cadaverous murmur of that sanctuary, I would hook it at the beck of any jade."[5] This is, as R.K.R. Thornton has pointed out, criticism and parody at once. For even as Beerbohm deflates Decadent style by treating the commonplace equation of Decadent style and Latin literally ("a dead language"), he catches the elusive, hesitating rhythm of Pater's periods, his archaisms ("or ever he could"), and Pater's trick of delaying the end of the sentence with appositional phrases ("in his book, its sepulchre"). Indeed, as John Felstiner has ar-

---

[5] Max Beerbohm, "Be It Cosiness" [later titled "Diminuendo"], in *Aesthetes and Decadents of the 1890s: An Anthology of British Poetry and Prose*, ed. Karl Beckson, rev. ed. (Chicago: Academy Press, 1981), p. 67.

gued, it may be truer to say that Beerbohm's parody *is* his criticism, is an equivocating critical mode that allows Beerbohm to participate (at a safe satiric distance) in attractive imaginative worlds that might otherwise overwhelm him. For revealingly, Beerbohm's attempt at accommodation through parody intensifies whenever he deals with artists like Pater and Wilde and Henry James who make large claims for artistic autonomy. As Felstiner points out, "Beerbohm only partly dissociated himself from these claims, having it both ways in the fin-de-siècle issue of art for art's sake. He made fun of Wilde for dismissing morals from art, but took over from him the literary genres least capable of a direct, moral vision of life— fairy tale, fantasy, paradoxical essay."[6]

This is precisely the equivocal response we meet in the *Pageant* essay when Beerbohm dismisses Pater's cult of intense experience in favor of the pawky domesticities of London's suburbia. Because he savors suburban banality with exquisite Paterian attention ("the asbestos in my grate will put forth its blossoms of flame") expressed in Paterian dying-fall prose ("In summer cool syrups will come for me from the grocer's shop"), Beerbohm preserves in transfigured form the aesthetic values he seemingly attacks. For Beerbohm's decision to retreat from Paterian "pulsations" to a chastened life "exempt from all outer disturbance" is *itself* Paterian. So too, Beerbohm's *faux-naïf* interest in the rich multiform existence of the Prince of Wales ("He has hunted elephants through the jungles of India, boar through the forests of Austria, pigs over the plains of Massachusetts") participates, albeit at a parodic

[6] John Felstiner, "Max Beerbohm and the Wings of Henry James," in *The Surprise of Excellence: Modern Essays on Max Beerbohm*, ed. J. G. Riewald (Hamden, Conn.; Archon, 1974), pp. 197-98. See also R.K.R. Thornton, *The Decadent Dilemma* (London: Edward Arnold, 1983), pp. 56-57.

distance, in the Paterian ideal of imaginative receptivity. Finally, no less Paterian if less kindly is Beerbohm's manner when he regards that "small, thick, rock-faced man" who is Pater himself—and with a graceful tremor of aesthetic distaste dismisses even Pater for wearing "gloves of *bright* dog-skin" (Beerbohm, "Be It Cosiness," p. 67).

Beerbohm's parody thus combines most overtly the competing strains of admiration and resistance that colored the reactions of Pater's other inheritors. Even Pater's most reverential followers, Lionel Johnson and Ernest Dowson, who, unlike Wilde and Beerbohm, eschewed parodying Pater, felt the tug of divided loyalties as they struggled to reconcile the inheritance of ascetic Euphuism with a desire to return to the voice. For the reaction against Pater's linguistically problematic "dead language" coincided in the 1890s with a "renaissance of romance," with a neo-Wordsworthian demand for a model of literary language once again based upon the voice, the speaking voice now recognized in all its linguistic legitimacy. The fin de siècle ballad revival, the attraction to pastoral, the animus against Parnassian metrical forms and what Yeats was to call "rhetoric," the interest not simply in spoken language but in non-standard idioms—all these participate in Wordsworth's revolutionary aesthetic.

This return to the voice, however, was no simple matter. Even those writers who called for it most emphatically, poets like William Sharp, for instance, soon found themselves in difficulties. It was one thing to sneer at the elaborate forms of the written tradition and boldly announce the new age of the authenticating voice:

> There are those among us who would prefer a dextrously turned triolet to such apparently uncouth measures as "Thomas the Rhymer," or the ballad of

"Clerk Saunders": who would rather listen to the
drawing-room music of the Villanelle than to the wild
harp-playing by the mill dams o' Binnorie or the
sough of the night-wind o'er drumly Annan Water.
But the heyday of the merely literary poet is on the
wane: we are all tired of pseudo-classicism, pseudo-
mediaevalism, pseudo-aestheticism.[7]

But it was quite another to find the real language of men
that could supply the passionate syntax and revivifying
diction that was needed. Sharp in his Romantic primitiv-
ism had turned against what J. A. Symonds called the
"mental ear,"[8] and so did he abandon the imaginative complexity and richness that Pater had incorporated into his
ideal of stylistic Euphuism. Instead, Sharp relied upon
"the old-fashioned 'ear' which was good enough guide
even for the unsophisticated person who wrote 'Hamlet'
and 'Macbeth' " (Sharp, "Dedicatory Introduction," p.
viii). And this homely organ directed him to what Sharp
imagined to be the riches of the Scottish dialect tradition:
"The weet saut wind is blawing/ Upon the misty shore;/
As like a stormy snawing. . . ." In fact, of course, Sharp
had merely fallen upon the factitious and by now fairly
shopworn glamour of literary Scots. And this, in Sharp's
hands at least, was not enough. As Wilde remarked imperturbably of Sharp's work, "Even 'drumly,' an adjective of

[7] William Sharp, "Dedicatory Introduction," *Romantic Ballads and Poems
of Phantasy* (London: Walter Scott, 1888), p. vii.

[8] J. A. Symonds, "A Comparison of Elizabethan with Victorian Poetry,"
Fortnightly Review 51 o.s., 45 n.s. (January 1889): 69: "In this later age a
poet allows himself far wider scope of treatment when he writes a song. He
does not think of the music of voice or viol, but of that harmony which intel-
lectually sounds in the ears of the soul. The result is a wealthier and fuller
symphony, reaching the imaginative sense not upon the path of musical
sound, but appealing to the mental ear and also to that 'inward eye which is
the bliss of solitude.' "

which Mr. Sharp is so fond that he uses it both in prose and verse, seems to me to be hardly an adequate basis for a new romantic movement."[9]

Yet what *was* to be its basis? Wilde himself conceded that "if this [literary] Renaissance is to be a vital, living thing, it must have its linguistic side," for he assumed with Pater that it was style that regenerated the artistic medium, not just new subjects: "Just as the spiritual development of music, and the artistic development of painting, have always been accompanied, if not occasioned, by the discovery of some new instrument or some fresh medium, so, in the case of any important literary movement, half of its strength resides in its language. If it does not bring with it a rich and novel mode of expression, it is doomed either to sterility or to imitation. Dialect, archaisms, and the like, will not do" (Wilde, "A Note," p. 99). Wilde's own answer to the linguistic question is highly instructive, for it presents in an extreme form the fin de siècle effort to accommodate Pater while returning to the voice.

Like Beerbohm, Wilde turned against his master's later style. Though he confessed that Pater's *Studies in the History of the Renaissance* became and remained for him a "golden book," Wilde, reviewing Pater's *Appreciations* (1889), discerned a change in Pater's later writing, a change he considered a falling off, a sort of stylistic congestion or petrification:

> In 1868 we find Mr. Pater writing with the same exquisite care for words, with the same studied music, with the same temper, and something of the same mode of treatment. But, as he goes on, the architec-

[9] Oscar Wilde, "A Note on Some Modern Poets [an 1888 review of W. E. Henley's *Book of Verses* and Sharp's *Romantic Ballads and Poems of Phantasy*]," in Ellmann, p. 100.

ture of the style becomes richer and more complex, the epithet more precise and intellectual. Occasionally one may be inclined to think that there is, here and there, a sentence which is somewhat long, and possibly, if one may venture to say so, a little heavy and cumbersome in movement. (Wilde, "Pater's Last Volume," p. 231)

A few months later, in "The Critic as Artist," Wilde spoke his opinion less hesitantly: "Even the work of Mr. Pater, who is, on the whole, the most perfect master of English prose now creating amongst us, is often far more like a piece of mosaic than a passage in music, and seems, here and there, to lack the true rhythmical life of words and the fine freedom and richness of effect that such rhythmical life produces."[10]

Wilde set Pater's individual stylistic fall against the background of a larger decadence: the petrification of the speaking voice by print:

Since the introduction of printing, and the fatal development of the habit of reading amongst the middle and lower classes of this country, there has been a tendency in literature to appeal more and more to the eye, and less and less to the ear which is really the sense which, from the standpoint of pure art, it should seek to please, and by whose canons of pleasure it should abide always. . . . We, in fact, have made writing a definite mode of composition, and have treated it as a form of elaborate design. . . . Yes: writing has done much harm to writers. (Wilde, "Critic as Artist," pp. 350-51)

In Pater's later work, devoted as it was to rarified etymologizing and elaborate excursions from a central theme,

---

[10] Oscar Wilde, "The Critic as Artist," in Ellmann, p. 351.

Wilde detected a disposition to compose for the printed page, the only medium through which such complex effects could be comprehended or made visible. Yet though such prose satisfied the desire for variation and "visual" arabesque, it alienated the ear. Wilde's answer to the problem posed by Pater's later style was simple: "We must return to the voice. That must be our test . . ." (Wilde, "Critic as Artist," p. 351). At the same time, Wilde was unwilling to resign the richness of Pater's Euphuistic ideal for the sake of mere colloquial ease. Instead, the ideal Wilde sought—"a language different from that of actual use, a language full of resonant music and sweet rhythm, made stately by solemn cadence, or made delicate by fanciful rhyme, jewelled with wonderful words, and enriched with lofty diction"[11]—was to be scaled to the capacities of the speaking voice. Whatever the speaking voice could accommodate, literary style might also attempt.

As Wilde conceived them, these capacities were generous. At Oxford he had heard Pater's slow drawl and Ruskin's melodious voice,[12] and he had learned much from their modes of speech. Wilde then experimented with his own speech to test the limits of what could be perfectly said with neither affectation nor the lame gait of ordinary talk. Hence Yeats's astonishment when he first heard Wilde "talking with perfect sentences, as if he had written them all overnight with labour and yet all spontaneous."

[11] Oscar E. Wilde, "The Decay of Lying," in Ellmann, p. 302. Wilde is characterizing the language of Renaissance drama before "Life . . . shattered the perfection of the form."

[12] Max Müller in *Auld Lang Syne*, First series (New York: Charles Scribner's Sons, 1898), p. 147, said that Ruskin was one of those who "seemed to take a real delight in building up their sentences, even in familiar conversation, so as to make each deliverance a work of art." Another auditor said Ruskin's voice was "more intensely spiritual, more subduedly passionate, more thrilling than any voice I ever heard." Quoted in John Ruskin, *Letters to M[ary] G[ladstone] and H. G.* ([London]: privately printed, 1903), p. 13.

Yeats knew that the artificiality of Wilde's speech arose from the deliberation and the perfect rounding of his sentences, yet Wilde's slow, carefully modulated cadence always "sounded natural to my ears." Other auditors, entranced, moved to tears, have testified to the extraordinary power and beauty of Wilde's talk, especially in his spoken parables or *contes parlés*, when he spoke less to converse than, like Lord Henry Wotton in *The Picture of Dorian Gray*, to create.[13] This is the "genius" Wilde spent upon his life, when he reserved merely his "talent" for his works. It was only when Wilde ceased to speak his tales and elaborated them in print that his style—as Yeats and Robert Ross and André Gide all agreed—stiffened into artifice.[14]

Clearly, Wilde's solution to the post-philological problem of language solves some major difficulties, for in his *contes parlés* (and virtually all Wilde's published tales were *contes parlés* first), he restored language to its authentic spoken form without the loss either of richness or of "in-

---

[13] It was common for Wilde's listeners to compare his performances to Lord Henry's in *Dorian Gray*, Chapter 3: "He played with the idea, and grew wilful; tossed it into the air and transformed it; let it escape and recaptured it; made it iridescent with fancy, and winged it with paradox. The praise of folly, as he went on, soared into a philosophy, and Philosophy herself became young. . . ."

[14] See Léon Guillot de Saix, "Le Dormeur Éveillé," in *Le Chant du Cygne: Contes Parlés d'Oscar Wilde* (Paris: Mercure de France, 1942; reprinted New York: Garland, 1976), pp. 34-36. Cf. Yeats, *Autobiography*, p. 190: "Wilde published that story [i.e. "The Doer of Good"] a little later, but spoiled it with the verbal decoration of his epoch, and I have to repeat it to myself as I first heard it, before I can see its terrible beauty." Yeats's phrase will perhaps remind readers most immediately of the tolling refrain of his "Easter 1916": "All changed, changed utterly:/ A terrible beauty is born." But the phrase ultimately derives from the catachrestical impulse in Decadent writing we have already noticed. Like Beardsley's "malicious breasts" and Theodore Wratislaw's "murderous hair," Yeats's "terrible beauty" looks back to the "sweet shames" and all the other catachrestical compounds of Swinburne.

tense personality." Yet just as obviously the costs of this solution are correspondingly great, for Wilde's performative ideal of language requires both enormous, self-depleting skill and an entire assent to the evanescence and final extinction of the spoken work of art. There is in this view of art and the artist as self-consuming artifacts much modernist agonism, though it is an agonism as yet untainted by modernist self-pity. Literature was for Wilde the greatest of the arts precisely because, as G. E. Lessing had said, it existed as a series of articulated tones in time, and thus could treat of time and change:

> The statue is concentrated to one moment of perfection. The image stained upon the canvas possesses no spiritual element of growth or change. If they know nothing of death, it is because they know little of life, for the secrets of life and death belong to those, and those only, whom the sequence of time affects. . . . It is Literature that shows us the body in its swiftness and the soul in its unrest. (Wilde, "Critic as Artist," p. 363)

That literature, perfected as elaborate speech, might pass away from the artist or with the artist always mattered far less to Wilde than that art be continually called into existence *by* the artist: "Understand that there are two worlds: the one that is without one's speaking about it: it's called the real world because there's no need to talk about it in order to see it. And the other is the world of art: that's the one which has to be talked about because it would not exist otherwise."[15] In Wilde's own talk, in the monologual dialogues of the great critical essays, in the passionate solilo-

---

[15] André Gide, *Oscar Wilde*, p. 18, quoted in Aatos Ojala, *Aestheticism and Oscar Wilde*, 2 vols. (Helsinki: Suomalaisen Tiedeakatemian Toimituksia, 1955), 2:40.

quies of Salome and Herod, the artist pronounces the all-creating word to speak a new world into being. In Wilde, that is to say, the Romantic secularization of the Christian religious myth of the Logos finds its unabashedly extreme statement.

Like Pater's ascetic Euphuism, Wilde's ideal of "beautiful style" derives its authority from the intense personality of the artist. This authority, however, must be repeatedly enacted or enunciated through speech, for as we have seen, it cannot according to Wilde be secured or made permanent through the petrifactions of written language. If the artistic personality is conceived of as anything less than infinite, Wilde's performative mode is thus quite literally self-exhausting. Wilde's own trials and imprisonment were to suggest (with a certain melodramatic vividness) some of the constraints upon the performing self. Yet even before Wilde's catastrophe, the limits upon the speaking voice had become clear to the younger poets of the Rhymers' Club.

❦ ❦

Chief among the Rhymers' Club poets caught between the claims of the speaking voice and those of Pater's stylistic Euphuism is Lionel Johnson, who was at once the theorist and theologian of that most untheoretical and heterodox group. Johnson was famous for his own form of Wildean performance, yet the differences between Johnson's imaginary conversations with the great and Wilde's *contes parlés* are significant, and they illustrate the fin de siècle attempt to accommodate in some poetic form the competing idioms of contemporary speech and the elaborate language of the written tradition. Johnson invented conversations with such eminent men as Newman and Gladstone, and quoted them so impressively, according to Yeats, that no one who heard them ever doubted their authenticity: "He never altered a detail of speech, and would quote what he invented for Gladstone or Newman for years, without amplification or amendment, with what seemed a scholar's accuracy" (Yeats, *Autobiography*, p. 203). Where Wilde freely improvised from moment to moment, Johnson adhered to an invisible and pre-existent "text." What so persuaded listeners like Yeats was less the polish of these repeated conversations than their "casual accidental character." Newman's fictitious greeting to Johnson—"I have always considered the profession of a man of letters a third order of the priesthood!"—seemed precisely the sort of remark that Newman might make in such a situation to a younger man. At least those like Yeats and Johnson, full of late-Romantic assumptions about the high vocation of poetry, were persuaded it was so.

Through such phantasmagoria as these ghostly conversations with the great, Yeats said, Johnson's "philosophy of life found its expression" (Yeats, *Autobiography*, p. 204), by which Yeats meant that through such forms Johnson could impose his values of "ritual" and "hierarchy" upon chaotic life, and enter into seemingly direct communication with figures of authority—in the case of Newman and Gladstone, with living representatives of sacred and secular power. Even more significant, however, is that Johnson's relationship with these figures of traditional authority is *conversational*. Yeats, with his self-confessedly provincial view of literary London, attributed Johnson's imaginary conversations to Johnson's half-conscious desire to retain some tie to the great world he had by the aesthetic vow of poverty renounced. But it is perhaps truer to say that these ghostly conversations represent, and represent perfectly, the intimate and immediate nature of Johnson's relationship to literary tradition. For aesthetically, Johnson's imaginary conversations belong, not to Wilde's emergent modernist mode of the existential performance, but to the tradition of the literary genre perfected by Walter Savage Landor: the imaginary conversation, a tradition of exquisite yet unostentatious scholarship proportioned to the human voice. To continue the imaginary conversation as an oral genre was for Johnson both to insist upon the living nature of literary tradition and to insert oneself within it.

Literature was for Johnson, as Ian Fletcher has pointed out, one of a series of sustaining institutions that drew his piety and allegiance; Winchester, Oxford, the Catholic Church, and Ireland were the others.[16] And in literary matters Johnson was a classicist; that is, he held to the classical standard of Matthew Arnold and Thomas Gray with its emphasis, as Fletcher has said, "on sanity, proportion and *ordonnance*" and its habit, "so frequent in Latin verse, particularly after Pontanus—of silently assuming the phrases, sometimes the sentences even, of earlier writers" (Fletcher, *Johnson*, p. lx). This, as we have said, is the habit of Swinburne and not of Pater, whose style always betrays an anxiety about impinging influences and about its own originality—an anxiety, as Walter J. Ong has argued, that arises from the experience of language as a written, specifically a printed form, and from the corollary sense of a literary work as a unit in itself, set off from other works and ideally independent of all outside influence.[17] Where Pater registers, even telegraphs, other writers' in-

[16] See the "Introduction" to *The Collected Poems of Lionel Johnson*, ed. Ian Fletcher, 2nd rev. ed. (New York: Garland, 1982), pp. xvii-xix. All quotations of Johnson's poetry are from this edition.

[17] See Walter J. Ong, *Orality and Literacy: The Technologizing of the Word* (London and New York: Methuen, 1982), p. 133.

fluence upon his own work through his punctuation, tone, and syntactic emphasis, Johnson appropriates and incorporates silently and invisibly.

Johnson's appropriations are thus acts of filial piety to the classical, which is also to say, the conversational tradition in poetry. One of the normative standards of literary classicism is the measure of what may be properly said between persons of sensibility and refinement. Johnson's own "conversations" with literature were catholic, observing no distinction between past and present, Latin and English, spoken and written. "He would have been content always writing Latin, I think," declared Ezra Pound, "but failing that he set himself the task of bringing into English all that he could of the fineness of Latinity. He wrote an English that had grown out of Latin."[18] So too, Pound observed, the "speech of books" was to Johnson as immediate and persuasive as the speech of men. And Yeats recalled being ridiculed by Johnson for "consider[ing] words made to be read, less natural than words made to be spoken" (Yeats, *Autobiography*, p. 205).

This invisible tradition of civilized speech is the source of the predominantly aural values in Johnson's poetry, and sanctions his omission there of visual imagery or color. Indeed, visual images in Johnson are usually associated with what is confused, as when he says "that Old World is best:/ Ours, a witless palimpsest" (Johnson, "Vigils," p. 64), or still more, with what is disturbingly sensuous or evil, as when the speaker of "The Dark Angel" tells his unholy antagonist, "The ardour of red flame is thine" (Johnson, "The Dark Angel," p. 53). Johnson accommodates the world's visual splendor most comfortably only when it is

[18] Ezra Pound, "Preface," in *The Poetical Works of Lionel Johnson* (London: Elkin Mathews, 1915), p. viii.

broken or somehow diminished, as in the lines "the flame/
Of delicate poppies, rich and frail, became/ Wan dying
weed" (Johnson, "Harvest," p. 80), or in "Red wreckage
of the rose,/ Over a gusty lawn" (Johnson, "In England,"
p. 30), where the alliteration and the abstract noun both
mute the visual force of the image; or when visual imagery
or color is redeemed by some religious use, as in "To a Passionist," where an uneasy poise is struck between the
speaker's sensuous delight in "the dawn/ Red with the
sun, and with the pure dew pearled," and his religious apprehension of the passion-flowers embroidered on the
priest's vestment, "Purple they bloom, the splendour of a
King:/ Crimson they bleed, the sacrament of Death"
(Johnson, "To a Passionist," p. 54). Even the innocent
sensuousness of childhood is recalled in primarily non-vis-
ual terms:

> Stronger than remembered looks,
> Nearer than old written words,
> Cling the old loved fragrances
> . . . .
> From rich wilding mignonette,
> Clustered heliotrope, and wet
> Meadows, O fair years of yore!
> (Johnson, "Incense I," p. 136)

It is as if Johnson perceived some slight vulgarity in the
overtly visual, a vulgarity of aesthetic representation given
"the shadowy nature of the world" (Johnson, "In a Work-
house," p. 147).

Johnson continues his imaginary conversation with the
literary tradition in his poems, where books are portrayed
less as treasured objects than as living personages or
voices. In "Plato in London," for example, "the old and
comely page" quickly dissolves to become "This converse

with a treasured sage" (Johnson, "Plato in London," p. 6). So too, Johnson hails the works of Goldsmith, Richardson, Lamb, Gray, and other cherished authors not as things, but as "dead friends," "great ghosts," and "Dear, human books,/ With kindly voices, winning looks!" (Johnson, "Oxford Nights," p. 67). In such poems the conversation of books creates a safe inner space of warmth and order against an encircling outer chaos: "Without, a world of noise and cold:/ Here, the soft burning of the fire" (Johnson, "Plato in London," p. 7), or, less menacingly because the setting is Oxford, "Without, an world of winds at play:/ Within, I hear what dead friends say" (Johnson, "Oxford Nights," p. 67). The great ghosts and kindly voices of literature keep at bay the "surging cries" and "tumultuary gales" outside the speaker's room, even as they diminish his own inner turmoil, "Till weariness and things unkind/ Seem but a vain and passing wind" (Johnson, "Oxford Nights," p. 68).

Yet it is even more common for Johnson to elide the difference between inner and outer, and to identify literary voices with the elemental forces themselves. So, for example, the "mighty music" of the Brontë sisters' literary works, music that "storms our heart," is identified with the moorland winds of their native district. Just so, their Celtic name Brontë "that sounds of Greece" (i.e. resembles the Greek word for thunder) is identified with thunderous "Passion, that clears the air for peace" (Johnson, "Brontë," p. 70). Johnson invites the winds to encircle and enter the Haworth church where Emily is buried as if to prepare with preliminary thunder that sheltered space for peace: "let each wind/ Cry round the silent house of sleep:/ And there let breaths of heather find/ Entrance." At the same time, Johnson merges the actual breaths of heather with the imagined, but similarly elemental, breath of Charlotte Brontë's fictional characters, "Creatures of thine, our perfect friends:/ Filled with imperishable breath,/ Give thee back life, that never ends"—an echo of the proud boast of Swinburne's Sappho.

The theme recurs in Johnson's poem "Hawthorne," where the American author's "haunting voice borne over the waste sea" is said to have learned "That music, which is sorrow's perfect breath" from the western winds of passage (Johnson, "Hawthorne," pp. 34, 35). The westerliness of the winds, in turn, allows Johnson's poetic speaker to identify them with the Hesperian gales and climes of classical literature; this is why the speaker can bestow the unlikely adjective "mild" upon Hawthorne's Massachusetts fields, and imagine Hawthorne in those fields calmed by "old" winds and touched with "aërial grace" (Johnson, Hawthorne," p. 35). In much the same way, the westerly winds that bring—indeed, that *are*—Hawthorne's literary voice fill the speaker's own world with a significance it otherwise would not have had. Johnson's speaker can persuade himself that the "pensive loneliness" he himself feels in the "dark woodlands" is not simply a projection of his own inward emotion on outward phenomena, but is rather an objective aspect of an elementally and aesthetically unified nature: "Thy voice," he tells Hawthorne, "and voices of the sounding sea,/Stir in the branches." In late-Romantic poetry, that is to say, the "something more deeply interfused" in nature is usually Art.

Hence, too, the iterated "haunting" and "chaunting" rhymes in Johnson's poetry. The deliberate, Pre-Raphaelite archaism of "chaunting" links present songs to those of the past, while the aural union of "chaunting" and "haunting" merges immaterial song with the natural, or as the poem addressed to "The Bells" suggests, the supernatural elements:

> Could we lay hold upon your haunts,
>   The birthplace of your chaunts:
> Were we in dreamland, deathland, then?
>   We, sad and wondering men?
> (Johnson, "The Bells," p. 89)

As Johnson suggests in another poem, the haunt or land where one may indeed listen to "the chaunting air," that is, the "Land, where music is not born,/ For music is eternal there," is simple heaven (Johnson, "Saint Columba," p. 88). The earthly equivalent to Heaven is, for Johnson at least, the lands of the Celtic West, whose westerly winds are, once again, Hesperian: "thou in the mild West,/ Who wouldst thy children upon earth suffice/ For Paradise, and pure Hesperian rest" (Johnson, "Ireland," p. 93). The winds and air of these lands, their invisible, imperishable elements, are identified with the powers of aesthetic and spiritual order: "Voices of Celtic singers and Celtic Saints/ Live on the ancient air" (Johnson, "Wales," p. 79). In Ireland, Wales, and Cornwall, the inner voice or breath of art and the outer winds of nature merge into a single inspiration:

> And yet great spirits ride thy winds: thy ways
> Are haunted and enchanted evermore.
> Thy children hear the voices of old days
> In music of the sea upon thy shore,
> In falling of the waters from thine hills,
>   In whispers of thy trees:
> A glory from the things eternal fills
> Their eyes, and at high noon thy people sees
> Visions, and wonderful is all the air.
> (Johnson, "Ireland," p. 96)

Johnson even suggests that this breathing elemental unity of western voice and western wind coheres beyond ra-

195

tional explanation. Although Gaelic, the quintessential "voice" of these western lands, yearly fails as a language, eroded by forgetfulness, Johnson portrays the language nonetheless making music in its decline as enduring as the music of wind and sea upon rock cliff:

> Like music by the desolate Land's End
>   Mournful forgetfulness hath broken:
> No more words kindred to the winds are spoken,
> Where upon iron cliffs whole seas expend
> That strength, whereof the unalterable token
> Remains wild music, even to the world's end.
>   (Johnson, "Celtic Speech," p. 38)

The elemental unity between inner voice and outer wind, is, however, much more difficult for Johnson to sustain once his imagination leaves the Celtic, Hesperian West. Like Swinburne's, Johnson's identification of human voice and elemental winds appeals to a Pythagorean notion of an underlying ordering music within all existence. Johnson can appeal as well to the Christian belief in the Logos, so that when such individual human voices as those of Tennyson and Ernest Renan fail, the natural elemental world is still heard to breathe with a rational inspiration:

> From out two golden mouths, the marvellous
>   breath,
> France! may not charm thee more; nor, England!
>   thee:
> Only between two silences of death
> Sounds the vast voice of the unquiet sea:
> While moving on the waters God is heard,
> Eternal Spirit with Eternal Word.
>   (Johnson, "Renan and Tennyson," p. 141)

But away from the West, the elemental unity of wind and voice loses coherence as the forces of modernity and unbelief confuse and disrupt—disrupt even in the safe haven of traditional Oxford:

> Here, beneath the carven spires,
> We have dreams, revolts, desires:
> Here each ancient, haunted Hall
> Holds its Brocken carnival;
> Where Philosophy attires
> All her forms, to suit us all.
>
> . . . .
>
> *Man is dust: The soul a breath:*
> *Who knows aught?* Each fair Lie saith.
> (Johnson, "Vigils," p. 64)

The disruptive forces of unbelief are associated with "vehement" winds, a word Johnson uses frequently with an active sense of its etymological meaning, "lacking mind." Like the "Red Wind from out of the East" (i.e. from England), such winds scorch and wither "Hesperian peace" (Johnson, "The Red Wind," p. 86). In moments of energy and confidence, Johnson sees such forces as part of God's apocalyptic plan. Vehement winds are the natural outward equivalent to the principle of inward antagonism we meet in "The Dark Angel": what such winds do "is what God saith." At these moments Shelley's vehement, revolutionary wind and the inspiriting wrath of the "Lord God of Hosts" (Johnson, "The Coming of War," p. 40) seem to be one and the same, and Johnson greets them both with apocalyptic ardor: "Liberty! for the end is come:/ The end, that shall begin new earth,/ And end the old Heavens" (Johnson, "Dawn of Revolution," p. 107). Even when the winds of change shake the Church itself, when "The Saints in golden vesture shake before the gale;/

The glorious windows shake, where still they dwell enshrined" (Johnson, "The Church of a Dream," p. 65), Johnson is triumphantly content; for as the paralleling of outer gales of autumn and inner clouds of incense in the poem suggests, their inspiration is the same. Such winds and clouds merely hasten the desired apocalyptic end, "the end of all" (Johnson, "A Cornish Night," p. 24).[19]

Yet at other moments, when the inspiriting wind fails, the inward correspondent breeze fails too: "I grow tired in a pause of wind:/ The clouds drag, the worn flowers are still" (Johnson, "Dawn of Revolution," p. 107). These, of course, are Johnson's most famous moments, the ones Yeats prized, the moments when the personal voice, chastened but unchilled by its austere conventions of speech, speaks of its personal emotion. The poems of such moments, poems like "To Morfydd" and "Mystic and Cavalier," are for the most part confessional only in the root meaning of the word: they "speak"or "utter" with a disembodied voice that knows itself both to be unassimilated by the natural elements—*Oh! what are the winds?/ And what are the waters? Mine are your eyes*! (Johnson, "To Morfydd," p. 6)—and unhoused by human tradition: "Desolate and forlorn,/ We hunger against hope for that lost heritage" (Johnson, "The Age of a Dream," p. 66). At such times Johnson's scholarly conventions of diction, rhyme, and even punctuation supply a last frail connection to the

---

[19] As Ian Fletcher points out, the anomalous details given about the mass in "The Church of a Dream" (e.g. it is celebrated with incense, as in a solemn High Mass, but with only one priest, as in a Low Mass) suggest that Johnson is imagining the Church in a time when it has "once again become a secret cult either through indifference or persecution" (Fletcher, *Johnson*, p. 297). Cf. also Harold Bloom, *Yeats* (London and Oxford: Oxford University Press, 1970), p. 44: "The gale, in Johnson's poem, is derived from the autumnal wind of Shelley, the nineteenth century's emblem of revolutionary change."

classical tradition of civilized speech; they restrain the disembodied voice from dissolution into the merely personal. So, for example, Johnson's idiosyncratic use of colons to punctuate his poetic line permits a formal pause without either the break imposed by the full stop or the loose accumulation of phrases allowed by the comma. Instead, the phrases preceding and following the colon are brought into formal yet fluid relationship, as in a logical or mathematical ratio.

In the same way, Johnson's preference for polysyllabic, dactylically stressed nouns and adjectives—"verity," "majesty," "immemorial," "vesperal"—and his habit of inverting such adjectives after their referent nouns allows him to portray the ceremonial dignities of the past as fading and insubstantial in the present. Thus, for example, when the single ancient priest of "The Church of a Dream" murmurs "holy Latin immemorial," the inverted adjective conveys something of the ritual elaboration of his speech. And when Johnson, inverting and anastrophically separating adjective from noun, says that to the priest suffice "Melancholy remembrances and vesperal," he suggests something of the pale attentuation of tradition in an autumnal age, when believing men have faded into memories, and qualities no longer seem to inhere in their substances but float apart from them, immaterial.

Like Johnson's fondness for slightly jarring assonances—e.g. "years of yore," "pure pearls," "far fair Gaelic places," "Child of wilds and fields,"—his preferred formalities of address and verbal arrangement create an expressive tension between the traditional and the idiosyncratic. So, for example, in "Mystic and Cavalier," the confession "I am one of those, who fall" is framed by the formal or Biblical "Go from me" and concluded with the gravely courteous anastrophe "Dear my friend" (Johnson,

"Mystic and Cavalier," p. 24). And even within the central confession itself, the pedantically placed comma—"I am one of those, who fall"—bestows a noble cadence upon this admission of personal decadence.

As Yeats realized, Johnson's characterizing moment as a poet occurs when the poetic voice of civilized speech addresses a world that has just then slipped from its traditional moorings in faith and place. Johnson's moment is thus by its very nature brief, for formal elegies over lost order cannot long continue without either lapsing into self-parody—Ezra Pound's choice in "Hugh Selwyn Mauberley"—or admitting base elements of the new incoherence—T. S. Eliot's choice in "The Waste Land." In Johnson's "To Morfydd" and "Mystic and Cavalier," the disembodied voice still speaks in the formal mode made possible by an ordered cosmos, but it addresses elemental forces blent by cosmic disorder and "blind with gloom" (Johnson, "Oxford Nights," p. 66). Thus in "To Morfydd" it is impossible to tell whether the "voice on the winds" is Morfydd or Morfydd's lover; indeed, the voice we hear insists upon the identity of the two, repeating, *"Mine are your eyes!"* And in "Mystic and Cavalier," the speaker's eyes, the skies, and the crystal ball of fortune-telling are mixed into a single shifting image in which it is as difficult to distinguish human from object from element as it is to decipher what each or all may mean: "Seek with thine eyes to pierce this crystal sphere:/ Canst read a fate there, prosperous and clear?" (Johnson, "Mystic and Cavalier," p. 25).

Thus what had been elemental unity and clarity in Johnson's poems of place and faith becomes in "Mystic and Cavalier" confusion and obscurity: "Only the mists, only the weeping clouds:/ Dimness, and airy shrouds." When the "annulling clouds" (Johnson, "Incense I," p.

135), the "clouds of doom" (Johnson, "Mystic and Cavalier," p. 24) descend, they can be dispersed only by action
from without: "When the cold winds and airs of portent
sweep,/ My spirit may have sleep" (Johnson, "Mystic and
Cavalier," p. 25). This action Johnson's poetic speaker
seeks to initiate by addressing those forces in a noble apostrophe: "O rich and sounding voices of the air! (Johnson,
"Mystic and Cavalier," p. 25). He does so because to apos-
trophize such forces is necessarily not to create them but to
call upon them as already constituted and existent, just as
to pronounce the sublime "O" of apostrophe is declaredly
to embody the poetic tradition and the spirit of poesy itself.[20]

Only homeless modern poets must create out of thin air,
and though Johnson manifestly inhabits their situation, he
steadfastly refuses to join their number. Although chaos
and personal dissolution approach, Johnson's formal conventions of speech concede nothing to the "annulling
clouds," but instead remake them through the animating
ritual of classical rhetoric into something at once fine, traditional, and human:

> O rich and sounding voices of the air!
> Interpreters and prophets of despair:
> Priests of a fearful sacrament! I come
> To make with you mine home.
> (Johnson, "Mystic and
Cavalier," p. 25)

If Johnson's reiterated apostrophes to "You chivalries of
air, unreconciled/ To the warm breathing world!" (Johnson, "A Cornish Night," p. 22) seem at times to be ad-

[20] See Jonathan Culler, "Apostrophe," in *The Pursuit of Signs: Semiotics,
Literature, Deconstruction* (Ithaca: Cornell University Press, 1981), pp.
142-43.

dressed to powers of the air darker and more damned than the Hesperian winds, yet even these represent an ordering force ("Yet, what thou dost, is what God saith") that with its streaming, directed motion rescues consciousness, as Pater's linear idea of history rescued consciousness, from mere flux and "clouds of doom."

When Johnson recited such poems as "Mystic and Cavalier" and "By the Statue of King Charles at Charing Cross," the effect, Yeats remembered, was like hearing a great speech: here were purity, dignity, and intense personality, all alive in a single utterance. Wilde's injunction—"We must return to the voice. That must be our test"—became a house rule at the Rhymers' Club. Or at least so Yeats remembered it: "[T]hat we read out our poems, and thought that they could be so tested, was a definition of our aims" (Yeats, *Autobiography*, p. 200). This "delight in poetry that was, before all else, speech or song" was the reason, Yeats decided, that Francis Thompson, who prized the "elaborate verse" of the written tradition, never returned to the Rhymers' Club after his first visit; as Thompson himself said in his poem "The Singer Saith of His Song," "The touches of man's modern speech/ Perplex her unacquainted tongue."[21] At the same time, it was because Johnson and Dowson alike recited "perfect song, though song for the speaking voice," songs that therefore could "hold the attention of a fitting audience like a good play or good conversation," that Yeats wished to have their poems written down in the first *Book of the Rhymers' Club*, "to hold them in my hand" (Yeats, *Autobiography*, p. 200) and so arrest the terrible evanescence of speech.

Like Johnson, Ernest Dowson felt the pull of compet-

---

[21] Francis Thompson, "The Singer Saith of His Song," *The Poems of Francis Thompson* (London and New York: Oxford University Press, 1937), p. 350.

ing allegiances. But in Dowson's work the tension between the written tradition and the speaking voice operates within an already diminished scope. Dowson's poetry,
we may say, stands in relation to Johnson's much in the
way Keats's does to Shelley's: sensuousness is embodied
rather than etherealized, delight in poetic tradition is
newly discovered rather than ingrained, passion is personal rather than generously political. Where Johnson is
pre-eminently the poet of night and wind, of laurels
"gleaming to the gusty air" (Johnson, "Summer Storm,"
p. 33) and voices "Crying from roseless lands" (Johnson,
"In England," p. 28), Dowson is the poet of roses, dreams,
and rest:

> In music I have no consolation,
>   No roses are pale enough for me;
> The sound of the waters of separation
>   Surpasseth roses and melody.[22]

Where Johnson's seawinds cry, Dowson's merely sigh, for
his sea is landlocked and inanimate, an expansive Styx.
Dowson's is no less literary a sea than Johnson's, but it is
always a classical or, as here, a Biblical body of water, not
a restlessly Celtic one.

So too, Dowson's learning, while not superficial, rests
more on the surface of his poetry—in his long Latin titles
and his obvious verbal borrowings from Pater and Swinburne—whereas Johnson's learning is ingrained, invisible. Hence Dowson's scholarship always measures the distance between his poetic speakers and a nobler, more
active poetic tradition. His speakers say, in the accents of
Horace, "I am not what I was under good Cynara's reign"

---

[22] Ernest Dowson, "Exile," *The Poems of Ernest Dowson*, ed. Ernest Longaker (Philadelphia: University of Pennsylvania Press, 1962), p. 61. All subsequent citations are from this edition.

(*non sum qualis eram bonae sub regno Cynarae*), and the distance remarked is more than that between the speaker's early innocence and later experience; it marks a cultural distance as well. Between the guiltless pleasures of Horace or Propertius and this poetic speaker's oppressed consciousness ("I am desolate and sick of an old passion") has fallen the shadow of the sickness unto death and the old passion of Christ. Dowson, that is, here rehearses the great theme of Swinburne, his favorite poet, in *Poems and Ballads*, First series.

Yet if Swinburne struggled to cast off the interdicting Christian shadow and live unoppressed in pagan sunlight and sea, Dowson clearly does not: regret and resignation are his distinctive notes. No less passive is Dowson's attitude toward his poetic medium: "After all with all our labours of the file and chisel we cannot approach [the Latin poets] in this our gross tongue."[23] What Dowson achieves as a poet is reached through parsimony[24] rather than expropriation. There is in this parsimony something of Pater's *ascêsis* and "economy," for Paterian self-curtailment is an ideal that appealed to Dowson in both prose and verse.[25] But Dowson's parsimoniousness reaches further

---

[23] *The Letters of Ernest Dowson*, ed. Desmond Flower and Henry Maas (Rutherford, N.J.: Fairleigh Dickinson University Press, 1967), p. 181.

[24] Cf. Arthur Symons, "Ernest Dowson" [1900], in *The Poems of Ernest Dowson* (New York: Dodd, Mead, 1924; reprinted St. Clair Shores, Mich.: Scholarly Press, 1979), p. xxiv: "He was Latin by all his affinities, and that very quality of slightness, of parsimony almost in his dealings with life and the substance of art, connects him with the artists of Latin races, who have always been so fastidious in their rejection of mere nature, when it comes too nakedly or too clamorously into sight and hearing, and so gratefully content with a few choice things faultlessly done."

[25] Cf. Ernest Dowson, "Apple Blossom in Brittany," in *The Stories of Ernest Dowson*, ed. Mark Longaker (London: W. H. Allen, 1949), p. 107: "He had renounced, but he had triumphed; for it seemed to him always against the sordid facts of life, a protest against the vulgarity of instinct, the tyranny of institutions."

back, to the Pre-Raphaelites, whose poetic simplifications, as Yeats said of Rossetti, verged upon an apocalyptic reductionism:

> [T]hroughout his work one feels that he loved form and colour for themselves and apart from what they represent. One feels sometimes that he desired a world of essences, of unmixed powers, of impossible purities. It is as though the Last Judgment had already begun in his mind and that the essences and powers, which the Divine Hand had mixed into one another to make the loam of life, fell asunder at his touch.[26]

Dowson's sense of an ending lacks Lionel Johnson's keen apocalyptic edge. In Dowson's poetry, extinction is personal rather than cultural or historical, and even then death is not all that conclusive. The weary speakers who in life "sit and wait/ For the dropt curtain and the closing gate" (Dowson, "Dregs," p. 123) may find themselves after death loitering in precincts equally weary, in "Hollow Lands" (Dowson, "A Last Word," p. 138) bordering Swinburne's classical underworld on one side and the wastelands of T. S. Eliot's Hollow Men on the other. But if Dowson's pursuit of impossible purities is not apocalyptic or world-disintegrating, it is world-contracting; that is, Dowson reduces the "real" multitudinous Tennysonian world to a simpler sphere of roses, wine, desire, and death.

Dowson achieves this effect by severely limiting what we may call his verbal palette, and by frequent repetition of lines, half-lines, and words, most notably in the poetic forms like the villanelle, where repetition is, as it were, written into the form. Dowson's "wine, women and song" are thus not so much synecdochical of a larger world as,

---

[26] W. B. Yeats, "The Happiest of the Poets [i.e. William Morris]" [1902], in *Essays and Introductions* (New York: Collier, 1968), p. 53.

along with a few other master-words—"vanity," "child," "gray," "roses," "tired," "weep"—constitutive of the only world there is. Indeed, we may say of Dowson what Geoffrey Hartman has said of Valéry, namely, that his reduction of poetic symbols to a very few confers upon them the power of abstract variables whose meaning resides in a system—a system, moreover, that is largely indifferent to the usual responsibilities of representation.[27]

Dowson further simplifies his poetic world by adopting a narrow tonal range and largely undifferentiated poetic *personae*. If his speakers' characteristic tone of neutral disillusion owes a good deal to that "center of indifference," Swinburne's "Garden of Proserpine," it owes much as well to Rossetti in Rossetti's less intense moments, in, for example, "The One Hope": "When vain desire at last and vain regret/ Go hand in hand to death, and all is vain" or even more strikingly, in "The Woodspurge":

> The wind flapped loose, the wind was still,
> Shaken out dead from tree and hill:
> I had walked on at the wind's will,—
> I sat now, for the wind was still.[28]

This, it is fair to say, and not Verlaine's nervy, half-hysterical "Spleen" (which Dowson translated for *Decorations* [1899]), is the true source of Dowson's own poem entitled "Spleen":

> I was not sorrowful, I could not weep,
> And all my memories were put to sleep.

---

[27] Geoffrey Hartman, *The Unmediated Vision: An Interpretation of Wordsworth, Hopkins, Rilke and Valéry* (New Haven: Yale University Press, 1954), pp. 162-63.

[28] Dante Gabriel Rossetti, "The One Hope," *The Poetical Works of Dante Gabriel Rossetti* (New York: Thomas Y. Crowell, n.d.), p. 276; "The Woodspurge," p. 150.

I watched the river grow more white and strange,
All day till evening I watched it change.
                                    (Dowson, "Spleen," p. 62)

For here is the same flat parataxis, the emotional quietism,
verging in Dowson's poem upon emotional autism. Rossetti's poem represents a "belated" rewriting of Wordsworth's nature poetry in which the wisdom that Wordsworth found in "the meanest flower that blows" has been
reduced to a benumbed botanical observation:

> From perfect grief there need not be
> Wisdom or even memory:
> One thing then learnt remains to me,—
> The woodspurge has a cup of three.
> (Rossetti, "The Woodspurge," p. 150)

Dowson, in much the same way, rewrites Rossetti; for in
"Spleen" there is neither wisdom nor even "the one thing
then learnt," merely an almost imperceptible revolution of
mood, a change as imperceptible as the turn of a long gray
day into a gray night. Thus although the poem ends by exactly reversing its beginning—"And left me sorrowful, inclined to weep,/ With all my memories that could not
sleep"—its point is that the new mood and old are the
same. Dowson, in short, reduces Wordsworth's "wise passiveness" to passiveness.

Dowson's poetic reductionism made his poems seem experimental after the manner of (or at least what was ac-
counted the manner of) Verlaine, with Verlaine's famous
dictum "De la musique avant tout chose." "[M]y latest
versicles," Dowson wrote one friend, "[are] the merest
'symbolism,' almost too slight for criticism! It's an attempt
at mere sound verse, with scarcely the shadow of a sense in
it: or hardly that so much as a vague Verlainesque emo-

tion."[29] Though Dowson is probably referring in his letter to the inferior "Vanitas," his experimental "sound verse" is better illustrated by "A Coronal," in which the iterated lines, "Violets and leaves of vine/ We gather and entwine" (Dowson, "A Coronal," p. 40), expressive as they are of the Aestheticist "P.V.F." ideal of melic language,[30] "entwine" or bind together through sound lines that have little syntactic or thematic connection to one another.

Paralleling this prosodic emphasis on "mere sound" over sense is Dowson's persistent thematic emphasis on silence and the inefficacy of words. As Richard Benvenuto has observed, these themes are central to Dowson's work and are closely related to his poems of sequestered life, poems such as "Nuns of the Perpetual Adoration," "Carthusians," and "To One in Bedlam."[31] Dowson's poems of

---

[29] Dowson, a letter sent to Victor Plarr, 20 March 1891, in *Letters*, p. 189. Cf. Lionel Johnson, "A Note Upon the Practice and Theory of Verse at the Present Time Obtaining in France," *Century Guild Hobby Horse* 6 (1891): 65-66: "M. Verlaine is now well known, and advanced in years: his poetry is musical to the verge of actual sound, in which meaning is of no value. Not that it is indeed so, with him: but mere melody could scarce go farther yet remain intelligible." Cf. also John Gray's poem "Sound" written about this time, which, as Gray noted later, "is about *Sound*, not about *Music*, quite a different thing. To me it is the high praise of monotony, love of sound for its own sake," in *Sound* (London: privately printed for A.J.A. Symons, 1926), unpaginated.

[30] This heavily alliterative and self-consciously mellifluous mode of writing was largely influenced by R. L. Stevenson. Cf. Gleeson White's "imaginary letter" to R.L.S. in *Letters to Eminent Hands* (Derby: Frank Murray, 1892), p. 52: "You started the search for the buried P.V.F., and turned us from treasure hunts in the Pacific to alphabetical explorations in prose. . . . If by untoward accident we heard the ancient liturgy of the Church, it was no longer a sequence of stately cadences but a rich deposit of buried P.V.F.; if we tried to read or listen to Shakespeare, the '*purple*, perfumed sails' set us tracking syllables, running after the sound and letting the sense take care of itself."

[31] See Richard Benvenuto, "The Function of Language in the Poetry of Ernest Dowson," *English Literature in Transition* 21 (1978): 158-67.

conventual life look backwards to the devotional poems of
Christina Rossetti; and his "Carthusians," in its portrayal
of the "sweeter service of the most dolorous Cross" (Dowson, "Carthusians," p. 108), forms an interesting contrast
to Matthew Arnold's "Stanzas from the Grand Chartreuse," with its picture of the almost savage severities of
the Carthusian rule. In the same way, the poems of Dowson that present the superiority of gesture over words,
poems such as "Terre Promise":

> Ah might it be, that just by touch of hand,
> Of speaking silence, shall the barrier fall;
> And she shall pass, with no vain words at all,
> But droop into my arms, and understand!
>   (Dowson, "Terre Promise," p. 73)

look backwards to Dowson's beloved Meredith, who explored the inadequacy of language in prose.[32]

Yet Benvenuto is surely right to argue that Dowson's
praise of silence and his disillusionment with language
represent a new and significant moment in Victorian poetry, a moment of reassessment and divided loyalties. As
we have said, Dowson, like Johnson, continues in his loy-
alty to Pater (as his letters bear abundant witness), but the
specific influence of Pater's ascetic Euphuism upon Dowson's poetry is distinctly muted, more a matter, as R.K.R.
Thornton has shown, of poem titles (e.g. "Amor Umbra-
tilis," "Ad Domnulam Suam") than any thoroughgoing
application of prose principles to poetry.[33] Here and there

[32] For this aspect of Meredith, see Gillian Beer, *"One of Our Conquerors":
Language and Music,"* in *Meredith Now: Some Critical Essays*, ed. Ian
Fletcher (London: Routledge Kegan Paul, 1971), pp. 265-80; and Michael
Sprinker, " 'The Intricate Evasions of As': Meredith's Theory of Figure,"
Victorian Newsletter No. 53 (Spring 1978): 9-12.

[33] See Thornton, *Decadent Dilemma*, pp. 91-92.

in Dowson we find a Paterian consciousness of etymology, as in such lines as "the altar . . . illustrious with light" (Dowson, "Benedictio Domini," p. 54) or "some ulterior land" (Dowson, "Vanitas," p. 60), but in general Dowson declines to mine the hidden riches of words, to purify the words of the tribe.

Instead, it is the space between words that interests Dowson stylistically, just as it is the idea of silence purifying words that interests him thematically:

> Be no word spoken;
>   Weep nothing: let a pale
> Silence, unbroken
>   Silence prevail!
> Prithee, be no word spoken,
>   Lest I fail!
>   (Dowson, "O Mors, Quam Amara
>   Est Memoria Homini Pacem Ha-
>   benti In Substantiis Suis," p. 63)

Arthur Symons said of this poem, "surely the music of silence speaks, if it has ever spoken. The words seem to tremble back into the silence which their whisper has interrupted" (Symons, "Dowson," p. xxvi). And indeed, the lines do not simply praise silence, they enact its blessing, its relief from painful speech. The short choked phrases, as if gasped out, yearn to return to silence. The halting effort of Dowson's speech, with its repeated words, its long pause reluctantly broken into by the final hurried anapest ("Lest I fail!") represents all that silence is not. In this way, Dowson can "represent" silence without talking too much about it, the error Lionel Johnson could not quite avoid in his poem "The Precept of Silence."

Dowson's concern with the spaces between words, especially with the placement of the caesura, is largely what gives his best poems their colloquial quality as "songs for the speaking voice." In the alexandrines of his most famous poem, for example, the constantly shifting caesura produces the seemingly spontaneous inflections of a speaker constantly swerving between memory and exculpation:

> Last night, ah, yesternight, betwixt her lips and
>   mine
> There fell thy shadow, Cynara! thy breath was shed
> Upon my soul between the kisses and the wine;
> And I was desolate and sick of an old passion,
>   Yea, I was desolate and bowed my head:
> I have been faithful to thee, Cynara! in my fashion.
>   (Dowson, "Non Sum Qualis Eram Bonae
>   Sub Regno Cynarae," p. 58)

In the same way, the repeated words and phrases ("I was desolate," "roses, roses") and the skillfully inserted interjections convey the sense of a speaker, drunk with remorse as much as wine, at the penultimate moment before such eloquence ("ah, yesternight!") turns maudlin.

Dowson thus suppresses a dramatic situation that Browning or Rossetti would have made explicit: the classically educated speaker remembers his nobler self amidst the low surroundings of his fallen life. It is this implicit dramatic situation, of course, that unifies or explains the speaker's diction, split as it is between such elevated phrases as "when the feast is finished and the lamps expire" and the demotic, pathetically iterated qualification "in my fashion." At the same time, because Dowson has stripped away all the stage props of the dramatic monologue, it is only through the stylistic effects of the speaker's language—the self-aggrandizing grandiloquence, say, of "Flung roses, roses riotously with the throng"—that we can discern anything of the dramatic circumstances of his speech. By simultaneously loosening rhythm while compressing vocabulary, Dowson has made the lyric and the dramatic modes converge in a single contemporary speaking voice, a feat of style that instructed Eliot when he came to write "The Love Song of J. Alfred Prufrock."

As the very success of Dowson's poem makes clear, however, such elaborate language as "ah yesternight! betwixt her lips and mine" now requires some additional sanction. Dowson, as we have seen, gives such language a dramatic justification; in effect he guarantees the intensity and sincerity of his high literary diction by invoking a demotic realm (e.g. "her bought red mouth") that is the reverse of high or "literary." But as with Johnson's poetry, this is a poetic moment of necessarily limited duration: the cultured voice cannot long speak from the midst of an authenticating sordor before it lapses into bathos or self-parody. Dowson therefore strengthens his speakers' position by implicitly identifying their marginal world with the romantic criminal world of Villon and Swinburne and Wilde.[34] Hence, for example, the family resemblance between Dowson's "Yvonne of Brittany" and Swinburne's "In an Orchard." In that poem, Dowson's lover, unlike Swinburne's, does not actually murder his mistress, but he

[34] For an explanation that traces Dowson's portrayal of the artist as criminal to Schopenhauerian philosophy, see Chris Snodgrass, "Ernest Dowson's Aesthetics of Contamination," *English Literature in Transition* 26 (1983): 162-74. The Pre-Raphaelite rehabilitation of Villon—"Student, Poet and Housebreaker," in R. L. Stevenson's phrase—was carried out by Swinburne, Rossetti, and John Payne and was continued by Wilde. Verlaine, chronicler of *poètes maudits*, was considered himself a *poète maudit* because of his criminal experiences, and hence was seen as the lineal descendant of Villon. Cf. John Gray, "The Modern Actor," *Albemarle* 2 (July 1892): 20: "François Villon was lashed and imprisoned and condemned to death. He who bears to-day the tradition of Villon's song lies at this moment sick and hungry and naked."

is responsible for her death (his seduction of her in the orchard brings on a fatal chill). Moreover, the speaker's criminality clearly buoys his speech, lifting it above the usual sort of lament for a dead mistress as the speaker swings along, carelessly addressing his lost love:

> In your mother's apple-orchard
> It is grown too dark to stray,
> There is none to chide you, Yvonne!
> You are over far away.
> There is dew on your grave grass, Yvonne!
> But your feet it shall not wet:
> No, you never remember, Yvonne!
> And I shall soon forget.
> (Dowson, "Yvonne of Brittany," p. 53)

In "Yvonne of Brittany," Dowson in effect braces conventional Victorian poetic diction ("The dear trees lavishing/ Rain of their starry blossoms/ To make you a coronet") with the bravado of a criminal speaker. Elsewhere he controls the received diction through radical simplification by limiting himself to a world of roses, wine, and death. And in a few poems, such as "Non Sum Qualis Eram," "Benedictio Domini," and "To One in Bedlam," he tempers the richness of the high literary tradition with the impoverished but authentic sordor of literary naturalism. But plainly, these are the shifts of a poet reduced to a handful of poetic alternatives as he attempts to preserve out of the written tradition something rich, yet sayable, for the speaking voice.

❧ ❧ ❧

If we detect in the poetry of Johnson and Dowson a weakening rationale for the elaborate language of the high written tradition, we see the movement away from that tradition dramatically accelerate in the work of Arthur Symons. Like his two Oxford-educated colleagues in the Rhymers' Club, Symons was a devoted admirer of Pater, but unlike Johnson and Dowson, he responded most deeply to the "sensational" rather than the "ascetic" Pater, the Pater of the "Conclusion" to *The Renaissance* rather than the Pater of *Marius the Epicurean*. "That book of *Studies in the Renaissance*, even with the rest of Pater to choose from," Symons reflected, "seems to me sometimes to be the most beautiful book of prose in our literature. Nothing in it is left to inspiration: but it is all inspired."[35]

In pursuing the Paterian quest after exquisite, fleeting sensations, however, Symons was quickly drawn into the clamorous, sensual world of the London music-halls, a visceral world far removed from Pater's "religious retreat" for scholar-artists, indeed, a world contiguous to the overtly vernacular realm of such "Counter-Decadent" poets as W. E. Henley, Rudyard Kipling, and John Davidson. In rendering that world, Symons came to adopt a stylistic mode removed from Pater's self-consciously linear Euphuism; he adopted a "primitive" mode focussed on gesture, a mode we now recognize as one of the heralds of literary modernism.

In his famous 1893 essay, Symons described the ideal of literary Decadence as "a disembodied voice, and yet the voice of a human soul,"[36] and the phrase describes fin de siècle linguistic self-consciousness as it floated between the artificial dialect of literature and the "barbaric yawp"

[35] Arthur Symons, "Walter Pater" [1896], in *Strangeness and Beauty: An Anthology of Aesthetic Criticism 1840-1910*, ed. Eric Warner and Graham Hough, 2 vols. (Cambridge and London: Cambridge University Press, 1983), 2:216-17.

[36] Arthur Symons, "The Decadent Movement in Literature," *Harper's New Monthly Magazine* 87 (November 1893): 867.

of vernacular speech. Symons's poetic career indicates his own fascination with the ideal of a disembodied voice, for his first volume, *Days and Nights* (1889), filled with extended Browningesque dramatic monologues, gave way to *Silhouettes* (1892; 2nd rev. ed. 1896) and *London Nights* (1895; 2nd ed. 1897), both full of rapid impressionistic sketches. In these later volumes, and particularly in *London Nights*, Symons omits details of setting and characterization, much as Dowson does in "Non Sum Qualis Eram." Symons's characteristic speaking voice is "disembodied" because it has no history and no story to tell; it has detached itself from the larger, objective relationships of place or faith or literary tradition, the attachments Lionel Johnson seeks out in his poetry to substantiate the speaking voice. Nor, though they do express some slight aesthetic preferences, do Symons's poetic speakers maintain "opinions," those perniciously discursive impurities that Yeats so objected to in Victorian poetry.

Instead, Symons's speakers, as Michael J. O'Neal has described, register in a characteristically simple and idiomatic syntax their own perceptual and cognitive processes, registering them seemingly as they occur.[37] Symons's focus upon such primary sense impressions and the intensity of his attention to them typically results in a poem of sensory fragments, a poem such as "Pastel":

> The light of our cigarettes
> Went and came in the gloom:
> It was dark in the little room.
>
> Dark, and then, in the dark,
> Sudden, a flash, a glow
> And a hand and a ring I know.

[37] See Michael J. O'Neal, "The Syntactic Style of Arthur Symons," *Language and Style* 15 (1982): 208-18.

> And then, through the dark, a flush
> Ruddy and vague, the grace—
> A rose—of her lyric face.[38]

The syntax here is paratactic, demotic, and only slightly skewed from natural word order ("went and came") so as to follow the sequence of impressions. At the same time, the voice that is registering its sense impressions is also seeking to construe their meaning—not their larger symbolic significance, but their import as compounds of sense data, as Lockean complex ideas. This process of construal moves from fairly rudimentary deductions ("It was dark in the little room") to a brief but genuinely aesthetic perception ("—A rose—"),[39] a perception as fleeting as the physical phenomena—the struck match, the flame—that supplied the conditions for vision. In O'Neal's words, Symons's poem "recapitulates the process of articulating a highly subjective, even primitive, perception in a syntax that does not point to relations among things, but that relies on contiguity; the syntax preserves . . . the simultaneity of datum and meaning" (O'Neal, "Syntactic Style," p. 211).

What is most interesting about the poem, however, is the way Symons's suppression of discursive detail combines with his attention to sense data to produce a quasi-Symbolist "estrangement" or *Verfremdung* of the poetic object. To be sure, the details Symons does include are telling ones in the manner of Henry James, for the shared cigarettes (a "shocking" period note, as R.K.R. Thornton points out) and the shared darkness indicate the relation-

---

[38] Arthur Symons, "Pastel," *Silhouettes*, 2nd rev. ed. (London: Leonard Smithers, 1896), p. 11.

[39] Symons emphasized the moment of aesthetic perception when he revised the poem for his *Collected Works* (1924) by repunctuating it as: "(A rose!) of her lyric face."

ship between the man and woman can only be an illicit sexual one. But other details are omitted with the rapid selectivity of the artistic medium to which the poem's title alludes: we see the effect of the match ("a flash, a glow"), not the match itself. In consequence, what in other hands would have been (and indeed elsewhere in Symons's poetry is)[40] a rather deliberately sordid scene of prostitute and client is here rendered at once lyrical and strange. In recognizing in the darkness "a hand and a ring I know," the speaker recognizes in another sense that he does *not* know the being whose suddenly illuminated, glowing face in this moment so surprises him with its strange ("ruddy and vague") beauty.

Symons's primitive poetic syntax is, we may say, the deep structure underlying his characteristic thematic concerns: artifice, light love, vagrant moods. That is, his syntax makes more casual the random contiguities of artificial and natural, innocent and sophisticated, and most of all, male and female ("And still beside me, through the heat/ Of this September night, I feel/ Her body's warmth upon the sheet" [Symons, "Leves Amores II," p. 45]) that earned Symons such notoriety and critical abuse during the middle nineties. Symons defended his thematic choices in the prefaces to the revised editions of *Silhouettes* and *London Nights* as he sought to combat "the curious fallacy by which there is supposed to be something inher-

---

[40] Cf. Theodore Wratislaw's "A Summer Night": "As bathed in sweat and feigning love we lay/ Embraced beneath the jet of feeble light," in *Caprices* (London: Gay and Bird, 1893), p. 25; and Arthur Symons's own "Leves Amores II," in *London Nights* (London: Leonard Smithers, 1897), p. 45:

> And still I see her profile lift
>   Its tiresome line above the hair,
> That streams, a dark and tumbled drift,
>   Across the pillow that I share.

ently wrong in artistic work which deals frankly and lightly with the very real charm of the light emotions and the more fleeting sensations."[41] Symons's defense is obviously part of the earlier Art for Art's Sake campaign for artistic freedom of subject and treatment. Yet we detect in Symons's restatement of the case not simply the alluring arguments of his master Pater, but also the self-reflexiveness and diminution so characteristic of fin de siècle treatments of inherited themes:

> The moods of men! There I find my subject, there the region over which art rules; and whatever has once been a mood of mine, though it has been no more than a ripple on the sea, and had no longer than that ripple's duration, I claim the right to render, if I can, in verse; and I claim, from my critics and my readers, the primary understanding, that a mood is after all but a mood, a ripple on the sea, and perhaps with no longer than that ripple's duration.[42]

Symons's last few words clearly catch the phrasing of Pater's famous "your moments as they pass, and simply for those moments' sake." At the same time, he takes Pater's version of the grand humanist dictum *nihil humanum mihi alienum puto*: "Everything that has occupied man, for any length of time, is worthy of our study," and narrows it to apply to the most evanescent and idiosyncratic of mental states ("what ever has once been mood of mine . . . I claim the right to render"). So too, he converts Pater's philosophical analogy ("a tremulous wisp constantly reforming itself on the stream") to a specific observation in a specific

[41] Symons, "Preface: Being a Word on Behalf of Patchouli," *Silhouettes*, p. xiv.

[42] Symons, "Preface," *London Nights*, p. xv.

place and time ("here on these weedy rocks of Rosses Point, where the grey sea passes me continually"); and in so doing Symons suggests that his defense of a poetry of moods is itself the result of a mood.

Symons defends the artistic importance of the trivial partly for Wildean reasons: such paradoxes usefully unsettle the anaesthetic middle classes. Yet Symons was also convinced that moods and physical sensations represented a fresh subject for contemporary poets faced with the exhaustion of traditional themes. The personal note in verse—"[o]ne might call it personal romance, the romance of oneself"—was, he declared (in the accents of Arnold), "the one thing worth doing, the one thing left to be done."[43] This is why Symons responded so enthusiastically to the poetry of W. E. Henley; for Henley, particularly in his free verse sequence of poems "In Hospital" (drawn from his experiences as a patient and amputee in the Royal Edinburgh Infirmary) conveyed the "ache and throb of the body in its long nights on a tumbled bed," and for Symons there could be nothing more uniquely "personal" than physical sensations:

> You are carried in a basket,
>   Like a carcase from the shambles,
>   To the theatre, a cockpit
>   Where they stretch you on a table.
>
> Then they bid you close your eyelids,
>   And they mask you with a napkin,
>   And the anaesthetic reaches
>   Hot and subtle through your being.

[43] Arthur Symons, "Mr. Henley's Poetry," *Fortnightly Review* 58 o.s., 52 n.s. (August 1892): 188.

And you gasp and reel and shudder
In a rushing, swaying rapture,
While the voices at your elbow
Fade—receding—fainter—farther.

Lights about you shower and tumble,
And your blood seems crystallising—
Edged and vibrant, yet within you
Racked and hurried back and forward.[44]

Such lines, Symons felt, approached the achievement of Verlaine; in them the "disembodied voice" enacts its radical detachment by scrupulously observing the pangs and throes of its own body.

Henley's was a "poetry made out of personal sensations, poetry which is half physiological, poetry which is pathological," in short, a "poetry of the disagreeable" (Symons, "Henley's Poetry," p. 186). Like Whistler's transformations of riverside fireworks displays or Degas's rendering of ballet rehearsals, Henley's "In Hospital" casually dispenses with the genteel concern over "the dignity of the subject." Even more, such poetry declared itself to be part of what John Addington Symonds, thinking of Walt Whitman, called "Democratic Art," an art "free in its choice of style, free in its choice of subject; an art which has recovered sobriety after the delirium of romantic revolution; but which retains from that reactionary movement one precious principle—that nothing in nature or in man is unpoetical, if treated by a mind which feels its poetry and can interpret it."[45] Thus, although Symons's stress on "moods, sensations, caprices" derives from Pater and Pa-

[44] W. E. Henley, "Operation" [first four of six stanzas], *A Book of Verses* (London: David Nutt, 1888), p. 7.

[45] J. A. Symonds, "Democratic Art," in *Essays, Speculative and Suggestive*, 2 vols. (London: Chapman and Hall, 1890), 2:33-34.

ter's ideal of a cultivated elite, it quickly leads, thanks to Symons's emphasis upon physical and above all sexual sensations, to the "democracy of the body," that recognition of the common experience of all flesh.

Symons, to be sure, was himself far from being an aesthetic democrat, but his emphasis on common pleasures, especially those of the music-hall, aligns his work with that of Henley, Kipling and, most of all, his Rhymers' Club colleague John Davidson. Davidson's work forms an interesting contrast to Symons's, for both men felt the special claims of a "poetry of the disagreeable," and in particular both recognized in disagreeable modern cities like London a significant test of poetic authenticity, as Symons said, a "test of poetry which professes to be modern—capacity for dealing with London, with what one sees or might see there, indoors and out" (Symons, "Henley's Poetry," p. 184). This was the test that Henley's poetic sequence "London Voluntaries," with its "sense of the poetry of cities, the romance of what lies beneath our eyes, if we only have the vision and the point of view," had so successfully passed.

Symons found London charged with "romance" not least because it was the thrilling venue for his own sexual adventures; his poetic speakers see London's "villainous music-halls" and "little rooms" brimming with a special, if at times factitiously lurid glamour. But a number of Symons's admittedly less interesting poems belong to a commoner fin de siècle poetic mode, a mode we may call urban pastoral.[46] Some of this poetry achieves a *frisson* of Bau-

---

[46] William B. Thesing distinguishes three poetic approaches adopted by poets in the 1890s who dealt with London: (1) *vers de société*, (2) the cult of artifice and impressionism, (3) the celebration of urban energy. See *The London Muse: Victorian Poetic Responses to the City* (Athens, Ga.: University of Georgia Press, 1982), pp. 147-99.

delairean "strangeness" by importing anomalously rural elements into urban settings, as in Wilde's "Symphony in Yellow": "An omnibus across the bridge/ Crawls like a yellow butterfly," or Le Gallienne's "A Ballad of London": "Like dragonflies, the hansoms hover,/ With jewelled eyes." At times the re-vision of London as a pastoral world is overt, as in Symons's "In Kensington Gardens," where a bucolic exuberance lacks only an oaten pipe: "Love and the Spring and Kensington Gardens:/ Hey for the heart's delight." At other times the pastoral premise is more suppressed, as in Herbert Horne's "Paradise Walk," where a blithe rhythm out of Herrick transforms a girl in a slum street:

> She is living in Paradise Walk,
> With the dirt and the noise of the street;
> And heaven flies up, if she talk,
> With Paradise down at her feet.
>
> She laughs through a summer of curls;
> She moves in a garden of grace:
> Her glance is a treasure of pearls,
> How saved from the deeps of her face!
>
> And the magical reach of her thigh
> Is the measure, with which God began
> To build up the peace of the sky,
> And fashion the pleasures of man.[47]

Davidson, too, took up the mode of urban pastoral in his Stevensonian prose satire *Earl Lavender*, and more obviously in his two volumes of *Fleet Street Eclogues* (1893, 1896) where, seemingly, he met the implied challenge in

---

[47] Herbert Horne, "Paradise Walk" [first three of four stanzas], *Diversi Colores* (London: privately printed, 1891), p. 23.

E. B. Browning's line from *Aurora Leigh*, "And Camelot
to minstrels seemed as flat/ As Fleet Street to our poets,"[48]
by treating the seasonal cycle of joys and sorrows among
hack journalists: "We review and report and invent:/ In
drivel our virtue is spent."[49] Interestingly, though Davidson's poetry elsewhere shows the clear impress of Decadent diction (e.g. "Swinging incense in the shade/ The honeysuckle's chandelier," or "Scales of pearly cloud inlay/
North and south the turquoise sky"),[50] he typically does
not employ this vocabulary of artifice to describe London.
Instead, his journalist swains flee London as often as they
can; and even when they are in their city taverns pent,
they are more likely to celebrate the genuinely pastoral
English countryside or the English yeoman than the
"iron lilies of the Strand" found in ironic urban pastoral.

This may be because Davidson found his own poetic
premise of an idyllic Fleet Street a little too ghastly to pursue. Himself as hopeless an inhabitant of Grub Street as
any character in his friend George Gissing's fiction,
Davidson shared the conviction of one of his embittered
speakers that

> Who reads the daily press,
> His soul's lost here and now;

[48] E. B. Browning, *Aurora Leigh*, in *The Complete Works of Elizabeth Bar-
rett Browning*, ed. Charlotte Porter and Helen A. Clarke, 6 vols. (New York:
Thomas Y. Crowell, 1900), 5:7.

[49] John Davidson, "New Year's Day," *Fleet Street Eclogues* (London:
Elkin Mathews and John Lane, 1893), p. 7.

[50] John Davidson, "Summer," *Ballads and Songs* (London: John Lane;
Boston: Copeland and Day, 1894), p. 118; "Holiday at Hampton Court,"
The Last Ballad and Other Poems (London and New York: John Lane,
1899), p. 124. For Davidson's stylistic affinities with literary Decadence, see
Andrew Turnbull, "Introduction" to *The Poems of John Davidson*, 2 vols.
(Edinburgh and London: Scottish Academic Press, 1973), 1:xxiii.

Who writes for it is less
Than the beast that tugs a plow.
(Davidson, "New Year's Day,"

p. 9)

Yet for all his contempt of journalism, Davidson despised
even more the "prismatic cloud" that the high literary tradition had interposed between men and the unlovely reality of their lives. Burns, Blake, Wordsworth—only a handful of poets had seen things truly. All the rest "saw men as
trees walking; Tennyson and Browning are Shakespear-
ian. The prismatic cloud that Shakespeare hung out between poets and the world!"[51] The impressionist poetic vision of urban pastoralists like Wilde was thus merely
another billow in the deceiving cloud, another flounce in
the stifling bed-curtains of "culture."

Davidson's hostility to high culture was at times vehement, and was to become inveterate. It gives some of his
better-known poems their proletarian tang and hence
their special interest for literary modernism. Like Symons
and Yeats, Davidson came to London as a provincial out-
sider; unlike them, however, he remained one. Davidson
antagonized Yeats by insisting that the Rhymers lacked
"blood and guts," and declared in the same key some years
later that literature was "a matter of sinew and sperm."[52]
He saw in delicate, laborious, discriminating taste, Yeats
said acidly, "an effeminate pedantry, and would, when
that mood was on him, delight in all that seemed healthy,
popular, and bustling" (Yeats, *Autobiography*, p. 211).
This is the mood Davidson gave vent to in *Smith: A Tragic
Farce* (1886), when one of his characters declares:

[51] John Davidson, *A Rosary* (London: Grant Richards, 1903), p. 37.
[52] Davidson, in a letter sent to Grant Richards in 1904, quoted in J. Benjamin Townsend, *John Davidson: Poet of Armageddon* (New Haven: Yale
University Press, 1961), p. 355.

> Let [the poet] address the street:
> No subtle essences, ethereal tones
> For senses sick, bed-ridden in the down
> Of culture and its stifling curtains.[53]

And some years later Davidson treated the democratization of poetry as having been accomplished: "Poetry has been democratized. Nothing could prevent that. The songs are of the highways and the byways. . . . The poet is in the street, the hospital (Davidson, *Rosary*, pp. 35-36). By this time Davidson had entered his sour and tormented period as a disregarded Nietzschean prophet, years that finished with his suicide in 1909. Neither his materialist belief in poetry ("Poetry is Matter become vocal, a blind force without judgment")[54] nor in the poet-prophet could sustain him, though it did goad him to renew his attack upon the effeminate ethereal culture of Arnold and Pater: "[T]he vaunted sweetness and light of the ineffective apostle of culture are like a faded rose in a charnel-house, a flash of moonshine on the Dead Sea" (Davidson, *Rosary*, p. 35), a stance that was to earn him the lasting admiration of his Scots countryman and inheritor Hugh MacDiarmid.

For all his contempt of journalism, Davidson paradoxically credited newspapers with tearing away the prismatic cloud from poets' eyes: "The newspaper is one of the most potent factors in moulding the character of contemporary poetry. Perhaps it was first of all the newspaper that couched [i.e. removed the cataracts from] the eyes of poetry." It is a measure of Davidson's self-preoccupation that he should so ignore the contribution of Victorian fiction writers, from Dickens to Arthur Morrison, to this

[53] John Davidson, *Smith: A Tragic Farce*, in *Plays* (London: Elkin Mathews and John Lane, 1894), p. 229.

[54] John Davidson, "On Poetry" [1905], in *Poems of John Davidson*, 2:532.

changed view of the city and its marginal classes: "It was the newspapers that brought about what may be called an order of Pre-Shakespeareanism. It was in the newspapers that Thomas Hood found the "Song of the Shirt"—in its place the most important English poem of the nineteenth century" (Davidson, *Rosary*, pp. 36-37). Stylistically, Davidson's own efforts in this poetic line ("I see the loafer-burnished wall;/ I see the rotting match-girl whine")[55] owe considerably more to the example of William Blake than to the *Daily Telegraph* or the *Pall Mall Gazette*, though something of the unveiled, prosaic "Pre-Shakespeareanism" he hoped for from the influence of newspapers on poetry may be seen in a stanza of Francis Adams's "Dublin at Dawn," written after the Phoenix Park murders:

> This is a conquered city;
> It speaks of war not peace;
> And that's one of the English soldiers
> The English call "police."[56]

Adams's stanza is much more likely, however, to remind us of the traditional street-ballad, and thus will perhaps remind us that the ballad and the ballad stanza, rather than any hybridized poetic forms based on journalistic models, became the most serviceable vehicle in the 1890s for the poetic plain-spokenness that Davidson was calling for. Indeed, Davidson himself adopted the ballad for the poem that has proved his most influential, "Thirty Bob a Week," not least because the ballad could accommodate the vernacular speech of the urban lower classes. Though he later

[55] John Davidson, "St. George's Day," *A Second Series of Fleet Street Eclogues* (London: John Lane; New York: Dodd, Mead, 1896), p. 81.
[56] Francis Adams, "Dublin at Dawn," *Songs of the Army of the Night*, ed. H. S. Salt, 3rd ed. (London: William Reeves, 1894), p. 48.

turned against the ballad for being *too* popular, during a
brief period in the nineties Davidson prized the ballad for
its straightforwardness and factual immediacy; indeed,
Davidson often sounded a good deal like the rugged Scots
character in Charles Kingsley's *Alton Locke* (1850) who
tells the struggling poet, "Ay, Shelley's gran'; always
gran'; but Fact is grander."[57] Davidson in his ballads thus
chooses a different speaking voice from those chosen by
Yeats and William Sharp in theirs, but his choice of the
ballad, like theirs, reflects the fin de siècle return to the
voice: "People began to imitate old ballads," as Yeats recalled years later, "because an old ballad is never rhetorical. I think of *A Shropshire Lad*, of certain poems by
Hardy, of Kipling's *Saint Helena Lullaby*, and his *The
Looking-Glass*."[58]

The ballad, moreover, tended to raise to visibility the
linguistic or philological concerns that so often lay just beneath the surface of late-Victorian poetry. Sharp, as we
have seen, wished to root the ballad in a rural or (even better because more remote and uncompromised by modernity) a regional vernacular. Yet the very feature in regional
dialect poetry that appealed to poets like Sharp—its melancholy remoteness from the forms of modern life—inevitably made it less suitable as a mode for renovating poetic
language. Such regional dialects appealed to Sharp for the
same reason they appealed to Thomas Hardy: they were
dying out, the last whispers of ancient and vanishing races.

[57] Charles Kingsley, *Alton Locke, Tailor and Poet*, quoted in Thesing, *London Muse*, p. 37.

[58] W. B. Yeats, "Modern Poetry: A Broadcast" [1936], in *Essays and Introductions*, p. 497. Housman's character as a vernacular poet was recognized virtually from the first. Cf. William Archer, "A Shropshire Poet," *Fortnightly Review* 70 o.s., 64 n.s. (August 1898): 271: "Mr. Housman is a
vernacular poet if ever there was one. He employs scarcely a word that is not
understanded of the people, and current on their lips."

Unlike Hardy, however, and unlike Hardy's great influence William Barnes, who wrote in an imaginatively reconstituted Dorset dialect, Sharp paid dialects sentimental rather than philological attention: a word like "drumly" was of interest to him because he saw it as a vaguely "Celtic" form fossilizing before his eyes, rather than what it was, a corrupt scrap of Burnsian literary Scots. Lionel Johnson's poem "Celtic Speech," though touched with something of this mood of linguistic regret, stresses (much as Hardy does) the elemental persistence of ancient speech. Sharp, however, cherishes its long failure, as this ecstatic inventory pronounced by his Celtic incarnation "Fiona Macleod" makes clear:

> Now we are a scattered band. The Breton's eyes are slowly turning from the sea, and slowly his ears are forgetting the whisper of the wind around Menhir and Dolmen. The Cornishman has lost his language, and there is now no bond between him and his ancient kin. The Manxman has ever been the mere yeoman of the Celtic chivalry; but even his rude dialect perishes year by year. In Wales a great tradition survives; in Ireland, a supreme tradition fades through sunset-hued horizons to the edge o'dark.[59]

Davidson, though no more scholarly or philologically informed than Sharp, was far more sensitive to literary imposture. He too recognized the exhaustion of the English high literary medium: "Our language is too worn, too much abused,/ Jaded and overspurred, wind-broken, lame—/ The hackneyed roadster every bagman mounts" (Davidson, *Smith*, p. 235), but he refused to abandon it for

[59] [William Sharp], "From Iona," in *The Sin Eater and Other Tales* (Edinburgh: Patrick Geddes, 1895), p. 13.

a language more worn-out still, the low Burnsian Scots of such nineteenth-century Burns imitators as Hector MacNeil and W. E. Aytoun:

> They drink, and write their senseless rhymes,
>   Tagged echoes of the lad of Kyle,
> In mongrel Scotch: didactic times
>   In Englishing our Scottish style
>   Have yet but scotched it: in a while
> Our bonny dialects may fade hence:
>   And who will dare to coin a smile
> At those who grieve for their decadence?[60]

Even its palpable decline could not move Davidson to take up the genuine Scots dialect for literary use; like Yeats, pressed by his ambitions to speak to the widest possible audience, he spoke in the standard dialect, the grapholect of English:

> These rhymsters end in scavenging,
>   Or in carrying coals, or breaking stones;
> But I am of a stronger wind,
>   And never racked my brains or bones.
> I rhymed in English, catching tones
> From Shelley and his great successors;
>   Then in reply to written groans,
> There came kind letters from professors.
>   (Davidson, "Ayrshire Jock," p. 48)

His own great successor, MacDiarmid, thought Davidson erred in choosing Shelley's dialect. All that Davidson wished to do could have been better done in Scots: "Social protest, espousal of the cause of the underdog, anti-reli-

---

[60] John Davidson, "Ayrshire Jock," *In a Music-Hall, and Other Poems* (London: Ward and Downey, 1891), p. 48.

gion, materialism, Rabelaisian wit, invective—all these find a place much more easily and prominently in the Scottish than in the English tradition."[61] But Davidson's choice of an "alien language," MacDiarmid conceded, did not thwart his genuine contributions: his widening of poetic subject matter to include scientific terminology in his later poems, the long blank-verse "Testaments," in which Davidson deludedly vested all his hopes of poetic immortality, and his attempt in his earlier poems to write a colloquial urban poetry.

It is largely for these urban ballads of the 1890s that Davidson is remembered, not least because T. S. Eliot remembered them: "Davidson had a great theme, and also found an idiom which elicited the greatness of the theme, which endowed this thirty-bob-a-week clerk with a dignity that would not have appeared if a more conventional poetic diction had been employed. The personage that Davidson created in this poem has haunted me all my life, and the poem is to me a great poem for ever."[62] Davidson's "Thirty Bob a Week," with its aggressive slang and stouthearted sentimentality, plainly declares its debt to Kipling's *Barrack-Room Ballads* (1892) and to the music-hall turns that lay behind Kipling's book:

> And it's often very cold and very wet,
>   And my missis stitches towels for a hunks
>   [i.e. a miser];
> And the Pillar'd Halls is half of it to let—
>   Three rooms about the size of travelling trunks.

---

[61] Hugh MacDiarmid, "John Davidson: Influences and Influence," in *John Davidson: A Selection of His Poems*, ed. Maurice Lindsay (London: Hutchinson, 1961), p. 51.

[62] T. S. Eliot, "Preface" to *John Davidson: Selection*, p. xii.

And we cough, my wife and I, to dislocate a sigh,
  When the noisy little kids are in their bunks.[63]

Those readers familiar with Davidson's "Testaments" will detect in this poem some of his obsessive themes: the new order revealed by science, the material nature of reality, the total power of the Nietzschean will:

I woke because I thought the time had come;
  Beyond my will there was no other cause;
And everywhere I found myself at home,
  Because I chose to be the thing I was;
And whatever shape of mollusc or of ape,
  I always went according to the laws.
      (Davidson, "Thirty Bob a Week," p. 96)

But Davidson handled tone and vernacular skillfully enough to make these themes function as dramatic characterization; in their place such themes serve as the auto-didactic "philosophy" of the lower-middle-class speaker as Davidson half-plaintively, half-aggressively ("I ain't blaspheming, Mr. Silver-tongue;/ I'm saying things a bit beyond your art") presents the rather bizarre combination of low slang and intellectual pretension that give this ballad its compelling effect of slight menace. Davidson explores the uneasy interpenetration of popular and intellectual culture again in the same volume, in his two songs set "To the Street Piano": the first describes in the rhythm of "Ta-ra-ra-boom-de-ay" the fortunes of a working-class woman before and after marriage, while the second teases the cosmic or apocalyptic meanings out of the popular waltz "After the Ball":

[63] John Davidson, "Thirty Bob a Week," *Ballads and Songs*, p. 93.

> After the spheral music
> > Ceases in Heaven's wide room,
> After the trump has sounded,
> > After the crack of doom,
> Never will any sweetheart
> > A loving message send,
> Never a blush light the darkness
> > After the end?[64]

Such tunes prelude the "Shakespeherian Rag" of Eliot's "Waste Land."

Somewhat less alloyed with intellectual matter are the six poetic "turns" performed by the six *artistes* of Davidson's *In a Music-Hall* (1891). If Davidson's command of colloquial language is less sure here, his effort to individualize his speakers through varying meters, from the vapid tetrameters of Stanley Trafford, "The Sentimental Star," to the professional roar ("I'm limber, I'm Antaean/ I chant the devil's paean") of Julian Aragon, "the famous California Comique," is largely successful. In the turn of Lily Dale, Davidson conveys both the raucous demotic voice ("Thin lips? Oh, you bet! and deep lines/ So I powder and paint as you see") and the sexual pungency of such boisterous music-hall stars as Bessie Bellwood and Marie Lloyd:

> So I give it them hot, with a glance
> > Like the crack of a whip—oh, it stings!
> And a still, fiery smile, and a dance
> > That indicates naughtiest things.[65]

And in the turn of Selene Eden, the veiled dancer, Davidson portrays the alluring synaesthetic whirl of vivid sexual

[64] John Davidson, "To the Street Piano," *Ballads and Songs*, p. 102.
[65] John Davidson, "Lily Dale," *In a Music-Hall*, p. 7.

promise ("My loosened scarf in odours drenched/ Showers keener hints of sensual bliss") and innocent aesthetic detachment that so fascinated Arthur Symons in the music-hall ballet:

> And soft, and sweet, and calm, my face
> Looks pure as unsunned chastity,
> Even in the whirling triple pace:
> That is my conquering mystery.[66]

As Yeats remarked at the time to his *Boston Pilot* readers, "No two attitudes towards the world and literature could be more different, and despite the community of subject no two styles could be more dissimilar than those of John Davidson and Arthur Symons."[67] Yeats seems to have meant by this that of the two poets, only Symons was treating the music-hall in the spirit of art; for Davidson's "Prologue" implied that the experience of the Glasgow music-hall, "rancid and hot," described in the volume, had been in fact his own. Symons's poems may have been no less autobiographical than Davidson's, but Yeats perceived them as arising from the pen of "a scholar in music halls" who studied such popular entertainments "for purposes of literature and remained himself, if I understand him rightly, quite apart from their glitter and din" (Yeats, "Rhymers' Club," p. 144). Yeats, who was not as intimate at this time with Symons as he would later become, here shows his bias against proletarian culture as well as a misunderstanding of Symons. We shall return to this bias, but it is worth noting at this point that despite his dislike of Davidson's music-hall poems ("I find my enjoyment

[66] John Davidson, "Selene Eden," *In a Music-Hall*, p. 11.
[67] W. B. Yeats, "The Rhymers' Club" [April 23, 1892], in *Letters to the New Island*, ed. Horace Reynolds (Cambridge, Mass.: Harvard University Press, 1934), p. 145.

checked continually by some crudity of phrase"), Yeats singled out for praise Davidson's poems about the dancer, "the haunting and wonderful Selene Eden" (Yeats, "Rhymers' Club," p. 145).

So, too, despite his prejudice, Yeats perceived that the fascination of Davidson and Symons with the music-hall, a fascination they shared with many other fin de siècle writers and artists (e.g. George Moore, Max Beerbohm, John Gray, Herbert Horne, Theodore Wratislaw, Selwyn Image, Stewart Headlam, Will Rothenstein, and Walter Sickert), marked an important moment in Victorian aesthetic culture, for it represented not simply a search for new subject matter, but

> the reaction from the super-refinement of much recent life and poetry. The cultivated man has begun a somewhat hectic search for the common pleasures of common men and for the rough accidents of life. The typical young poet of our day is an aesthete with a surfeit, searching sadly for his lost Philistinism, his heart full of an unsatisfied hunger for the commonplace. He is an Alastor tired of his woods and longing for beer and skittles. (Yeats, "Rhymers' Club," p. 146)

Yeats was not alone in his sarcasm, nor did the "Oxford-cum-Cockney" incongruities in the music-hall cult escape the notice of other contemporaries.[68] Dowson, for example, who fancied London lowlife, though never the music-hall, told a friend: "[I] met Image & Horne at midnight outside the 'back door' of the Alhambra! & was introduced to various trivial coryphées. There was something eminently grotesque in the juxtaposition. Horne very erect &

[68] See Cuthbert Wright, "Out of Harm's Way: Some Notes on the Esthetic Movement of the 'Nineties," *Bookman* [New York] 70 (1929-30): 234-43.

slim & aesthetic—& Image the most dignified man in London, a sort of cross in appearance between a secular abbé & Baudelaire, with a manner du 18me siècle—waiting in a back passage to be escort [*sic*] to ballet girls ~~whom they~~ ~~don't even~~--------!!! [*sic*]" (Dowson, *Letters*, p. 110). The moment, we would now say, marks an early and unmistakable sign of that disenchantment of culture with culture that, as Lionel Trilling said, characterizes modernism.

What bound Davidson to Symons in enthusiasm for the music-hall, then, was his sense that it assaulted Victorian notions of "respectability." "Rancid and hot," crammed with vociferous men and women shouting their approval or calling for more drink, the music-hall seemed to swarm with vibrant, forbidden, vulgar "life" to the artistic young men who sampled its offerings, even though by the 1890s, as Martha Vicinus has made clear, the ordinary working-man's music-hall had become quite respectable, and the larger halls like the Empire and the Alhambra in London were veritable palaces of art, catering to swells in formal dress.[69] George Moore welcomed the rich vulgarity of the " 'alls" in his *Confessions of a Young Man*:

> There is one thing in England that is free, that is spontaneous, that reminds me of the blitheness and nationalness [*sic*] of the Continent;—but there is nothing French about it, it is wholly and essentially English, and in its communal enjoyment and its spontaneity it is a survival of Elizabethan England—I mean the music-hall. . . . What delightful unison of enjoyment, what unanimity of soul, what communality of wit; all

[69] See Martha Vicinus, *The Industrial Muse: A Study of Nineteenth Century British Working-Class Literature* (New York: Barnes and Noble, 1974), pp. 235-85.

knew each other, all enjoyed each other's presence; in a word, there was life.[70]

The music-hall, Moore concluded, represented "a protest against the villa, the circulating library, the club" (Moore, *Confessions*, p. 147), all the institutions of Victorian bourgeois culture that so constricted and asphyxiated artistic life in the fin de siècle: "Something in the air of those ponderous institutions," declared Symons, "seems to forbid the exercise of so casual a freak as verse" (Symons, "Henley's Poetry," p. 188).

The claim that the music-halls were more vigorous than contemporary Victorian dramatic and literary art quickly led to the claim that the music-hall turn was itself an art; and here Symons and Davidson parted company, Symons joining those like Moore and Gray who urged the genuine aesthetic claims of popular culture upon critical attention. These partisans saw, for instance, that the music-hall had dispensed with the laborious theatrical realism of the legitimate Victorian stage productions: "no cascades of real water, nor London docks, nor offensively rich furniture, with hotel lifts down which some one will certainly be thrown, but one scene representing a street; a man comes on—not, mind you, in a real smock-frock, but in something that suggests one—and sings of how he came up to London, and was 'cleaned out' by thieves" (Moore, *Confessions*, p. 146). Music-hall initiates acclaimed the *artistes*' expressive gestures ("each look is full of suggestion; it is irritating, it is magnetic, it is symbolic, it is art" [Moore, *Confessions*, p. 147]), just as they applauded the bright quips and fresh cracks that banished the lumbering language of the high written tradition: Bessie Bellwood's

[70] George Moore, *Confessions of a Young Man*, ed. Susan Dick (Montreal and London: McGill-Queen's University Press, 1972), pp. 145-46.

brilliant vernacular improvisations were "no longer repellent vulgarity but art, choice and rare. . . . [C]urious, quaint, perverted, and are not these the *aions* and the attributes of art?" (Moore, *Confessions*, p. 146).

Here, of course, Moore is slyly assimilating aspects of music-hall performances to the emergent aesthetic of French Symbolism in order to mock himself and his readers. Yet clearly, popular culture *was* popular among fin de siècle aesthetes, not least because it could be shown to have its esoteric side accessible only to the hermeneutical powers of an elite:

> To the nineties the Music Hall was what the Russian Ballet was to the early neo-Georgian. . . . Like the Russian Ballet, the Music Hall gave men occasion to feel greatly superior to their fellows, and it was discovered that that pleasing song "You Cannot Tell Cigars by the Picture on the Box" had its symbolism and its true inwardness. It is true that the ignorant people of London went on enjoying their Music Hall merely as an agreeable evening diversion, even as the ignorant Russians enjoyed their ballets, but I have known young Englishmen, of great culture but rather weak wits, enter the Oxford with the trembling fervour of a neophyte entering a temple of the mysteries.[71]

To claim that music-hall performances represented serious art was to make one's position as a cultist and aesthete less marginal; for not only did the aesthete thus expand the sphere of art, and so the area of his special authority, but he more firmly secured the aesthetic permission, that is, the power of deciding what in fact constituted art, into his

---

[71] Edgar Jepson, *Memories of a Victorian* (London: Gollancz, 1933), p. 230.

own hands. If this tendency to find aesthetic complexity and "difficulty" in forms previously considered unartistic or aesthetically unproblematical seems peculiarly modernist, it is also the gesture of a self-aggrandizing elite. In vain did Max Beerbohm lampoon the "genteel gusto" of the music-hall cultists, and warn that they had foolishly driven vulgarity out of its most convenient haunt.[72]

At the same time, this self-parodic impulse among the music-hall aesthetes should not obscure from us the genuine contribution of the music-hall cult to the emergent modernist aesthetic. In this emergence, Symons's part was crucial, and he fulfilled it largely because he found in the art of the music-hall a new model for poetic language, one that freed it from the paralyzing choice between Pater's Euphuism and shapeless colloquial speech. Where Davidson briefly sought linguistic authenticity in the "real language" of the music-hall's lower-class audiences, Symons found a new expressive ideal in the music-hall's language of physical gesture, and specifically in the language of the dance.

Symons's role in assimilating French theories of the symbol to the image of the dancer has been extensively studied.[73] What deserves emphasis here is the anti-linguistic, or more properly, anti-verbal nature of his response to the dance. Symons gave the clearest expression of it in his essay "The World as Ballet" (1898), where he stressed that in the dance "[n]othing is stated, *there is no intrusion of words* used for the irrelevant purpose of describing; a

[72] See Max Beerbohm, "The Blight on the Music Halls" [first written in the 1890s], in *More* (New York: Dodd, Mead, 1922), pp. 129-36.

[73] See Frank Kermode, *Romantic Image* (New York: Vintage, 1957), pp. 49-91, 107-18; Ian Fletcher, "Explorations and Recoveries—II: Symons, Yeats and the Demonic Dance," *London Magazine* 7 (1960): 46-60; and Jan B. Gordon, "The Danse Macabre of Arthur Symons' *London Nights*," *Victorian Poetry* 9 (1971): 429-43.

world rises before one, the picture lasts only long enough to have been there: and the dancer, with her gesture, all pure symbol, evokes from her mere beautiful motion, idea, sensation, all that one need ever know of event."[74] Though Symons speaks of "the intellectual as well as sensuous appeal" of a living symbol like the dancer, the effect of his emphasis is to shift aesthetic authority from the intellectual *to* the sensuous, much as Keats (whose "Ode on a Grecian Urn" Symons is echoing here) did with the vatic and compelling dictum: " 'Beauty is truth, truth beauty,'— that is all/ Ye know on earth, and all ye need to know."

Similarly, Symons emphasizes the importance of visceral perception in understanding artistic performances, as when, for example, he says in *Spiritual Adventures* (1905) that the pianist Christian Trevalga's playing seemed to speak to his audiences "from somewhere inside their own hearts, in the little voices of their blood"; or when in another story from the same volume the painter Peter Waydelin says his delight in the music-hall comes from "the glitter, false, barbarous, intoxicating, the violent animality of the whole spectacle, with its imbecile words, faces, gestures, the very heat and odour, like some concentrated odour of the human crowd, the irritant music, the audience!"[75]

Symons's iterated insistence upon the visceral, animal knowledge of the blood, upon dance as "life, animal life, having its own way passionately" (Symons, "World as Ballet," p. 387), specifically challenges verbal language— "*no intrusion of words*"—rather than the possibility of ex-

---

[74] Arthur Symons, "The World as Ballet," in *Studies in Seven Arts* (London: Archibald Constable, 1906), p. 391. My emphasis.

[75] Arthur Symons, "Christian Trevalga," in *Spiritual Adventures* (London: Archibald Constable, 1905), p. 96; "The Death of Peter Waydelin," *Spiritual Adventures*, p. 160.

pressive language in general. Symons seems from the first to have been instinctively aware that music and dance and painting could be considered alternative human languages, equal or even superior to words; and he bestows this awareness upon his artist-protagonists in *Spiritual Adventures*. To the actress Esther Kahn, for instance, the "gestures of people always meant more . . . than their words; they seemed to have a secret meaning of their own, which the words never quite interpreted" (Symons, *Spiritual Adventures*, p. 54). And to the pianist Christian Trevalga, music, "comes nearer than any other of the human languages to the sound of these angelic voices. But painting is also a language, and sculpture, and poetry" (Symons, *Spiritual Adventures*, p. 111).

Symons thus grasps intuitively what contemporary linguists and philosophers were positing analytically, namely, that verbal language was simply one among a number of communicative sign systems, and one, moreover, endowed with a conventional rather than an inherent privilege over all the others. The young Oxford philosopher R. L. Nettleship, for example, argued that although speech "is the most widely spread form of symbolism . . . it does not follow that people who are deficient in the use of it are inarticulate."[76] Seeking a way round the word vs. thing impasse, Nettleship was willing to reduce words to "just a form of action like any other":

> I mean that one could define more or less the various powers of words (rhetorical, poetic, logical), and compare them with the powers of acting on men in other ways (by example, by look, by gesture, by music, pictures, &c.). It seems to me so enlightening to extend

[76] R. L. Nettleship, "Lectures on Logic," in *Philosophical Lectures and Remains*, ed. A. C. Bradley, 2 vols. (London: Macmillan, 1897), 1:129.

the physical notion of energy to everything (which is simply Aristotelianism), and to feel that *all* that we call things, properties, &c., are forms of action and re-action, and that this *is* "being."[77]

We encounter this same sense of liberation through a re-vision or redefinition of language when Symons and Yeats consider the dancer. Because they associated the Victorian tyranny of "abstraction" and "discursiveness" with the Spasmodic excesses and great-quarterly longueurs of ver-bal language, the gestural language of the dance seemed wonderfully fresh, immediate, and uncompromised by "impurities." Hence, of course, Symons's characteristic portrayal of the dancer as at once innocent and yet almost narcissistically or onanistically self-sufficient. Hence, too, his suppression of the *corps de ballet* in his dancer poems; in an early work like "Javanese Dancers" (1889), the dan-cer merges with her sister dancers ("Now swaying gently in a row,/ Now interthreading slow and rhythmically"), but in such later poems as "Nora on the Pavement" and "La Mélinite: Moulin Rouge," the dancer is seen set apart from the *corps*: "She dances for her own delight." To say that the narrators of Symons's poems find this self-suffi-ciency erotic is merely to insist upon the sensual, visceral basis of the gestural language.

Yet clearly to celebrate gesture in this way was to prefer a language even more "primitive" than the lower-class ver-naculars, for it was assumed that the more physically overt the linguistic sign, the cruder the mental capacity of the sign-maker. So, for instance, A. H. Sayce: "[T]here is abundant evidence to show that the lower we descend in the scale of humanity, the more important do gestures be-come in giving significancy to speech and determining the

[77] Nettleship, "Extracts from Letters," in *Philosophical Lectures*, 1:99.

sense and reference of each particular sentence."[78] Such "aesthetic Darwinists" as Grant Allen urged their readers in the 1890s to admit and embrace precisely this physical, sexual basis of human creativity:

> [E]verything high and ennobling in our nature springs directly out of the sexual instinct. . . . To it we owe the entire existence of our aesthetic sense, which is, in the last resort, a secondary sexual attribute. . . . The sense of beauty, the sense of duty; parental responsibility, paternal and maternal love, domestic affection; song, dance and decoration; the entire higher life in its primitive manifestations; pathos and fidelity; in one word, the soul, the soul itself in embryo—all rise direct from the despised 'lower' pleasures.[79]

Symons himself did not flinch from these pleasures in the 1890s. Dancers or "light loves," they all "seem to sum up in themselves the appeal of everything in the world that is passing, and coloured, and to be enjoyed; everything that bids us take no thought for the morrow, and dissolve the will into slumber, and give way luxuriously to the delightful present" (Symons, "World as Ballet," p. 389). In their sensual charm, their momentariness, their evanescence, the lower pleasures—the gestures of dance and of love–were for Symons the "truth" of Pater's "Conclusion," and in his brief poems of "primitive" syntax he sought to embody that truth in language with the spontaneity, as Yeats said, "of a gesture or of some casual emotional phrase."[80] It was this concerted effort at verbal gesture, at

---

[78] A. H. Sayce, "The Jelly-Fish Theory of Language," *Contemporary Review* 27 (April 1876): 718.

[79] Grant Allen, "The New Hedonism," *Fortnightly Review* 61 o.s., 55 n.s. (March 1894): 384, 387.

[80] Yeats, "Art and Ideas" [1913], in *Essays and Introductions*, p. 354.

reincarnating the disembodied voice, that long bound Yeats to Symons. But it was Symons's undissuadable devotion to fleeting sensuous impressions that at last sped Yeats on his own way. Thus did Symons's practice as a poet raise to visibility once again the exigent choices that lay before those who knew themselves to write in the post-philological moment, those who read Pater's *Marius* while yearning for the songs of the speaking voice.

V

Yeats and the Book of
the People

Ah, leave me still
A little space for the rose-breath to fill!
Lest I no more hear common things that crave;
. . . .
And learn to chaunt a tongue men do not know.
— YEATS, "To the Rose
Upon the Rood of Time"

W. B. Yeats appears as the culminating figure of fin de siècle Decadence not least because he so memorably portrayed himself in that light. Other great modern writers
were powerfully influenced by the Decadent ethos of the
fin de siècle—Pound, Eliot, and Stevens come first to
mind among the poets as Conrad, Joyce, Lawrence, and
Faulkner do among the novelists—but none dwelt there as
Yeats did. It is his own sumptuous commemoration of the
"Tragic Generation" in *The Trembling of the Veil* (1922)
that so insistently invites us to place him last in the processional line, to see him as a survivor of the wreck who now,
lingering on, stoppeth one in three, muttering in the hollow voice of Romantic survivors everywhere, "I only am
escaped to tell thee."

Yet sumptuous as it is, Yeats's account of the period is
not simply the result of glamorizing retrospection. As Ian
Fletcher points out, Yeats's account is, for a literary mem-

oir, remarkably accurate.[1] If in 1922 distance and disappointment helped to heighten the chiaroscuro in his portrait of the "Tragic Generation"—so that ballet girls became "harlots" and evenings of cheerful carousal became nights of "dissipation and despair"—Yeats's impulse to find pattern and symbol in fin de siècle events was something more than the self-justifying gesture of an aging man living on into an uncongenial time. The search for pattern in his *Autobiography* is, rather, cognate with the search for pattern and symbol Yeats conducted during the fin de siècle itself, part of his essentially religious predisposition to find the hidden tides and recurrent rhythms beneath all sublunary events.

This, especially, was the lure of the fin de siècle idea of cultural decadence. Even had Yeats not shared other interests with Symons, Dowson and Johnson, their sense—so often iterated in their poems—of an impending "end" would have attracted him, just as Mallarmé's sense of imminent revelation, the disturbed air about the veil of the temple, appealed to this thought. Though we may safely attribute some of the "fin de siècle, fin du globe" attitudinizing in the 1890s to journalistic sensationalism and what Northrop Frye has called a superstitious reverence for the decimal system of counting,[2] Yeats's interest in apocalyptic endings and revelations is far too thorough-going—

[1] See Ian Fletcher, "Explorations and Recoveries—II: Symons, Yeats and the Demonic Dance," *London Magazine* 6 (1960): 46-47.

[2] Cf. John Davidson, "Fin de Siècle," in *Sentences and Paragraphs* (London: Lawrence and Bullen, 1893), p. 122: "It is not so very long ago yet, although we have entered the last decade of the nineteenth century, since the phrase fin de siècle wakened up one morning and found itself famous. . . . It rides triumphant on the pen of every ready-writer; tyrannises over weak imaginations; and already, by sheer dint of its endeavour to be more than a phrase, has grown into something very like a fact."

persisting as it did long after the end of the nineteenth century—to be ascribed simply to passing artistic fashion. If, as J. L. Borges has said, "this imminence of a revelation which does not occur is, perhaps, the aesthetic phenomenon,"[3] Yeats's fascination with the crises of ending and renewal, the cruces that figure in such early collections as *Crossways* (1889), *The Rose* (1893), and *The Wind Among the Reeds* (1899), and made systematic in *A Vision* (1925), must instead be seen to arise from his desire to see the patterns and rhythms of aesthetic experience as the ground for all reality, including history.

Yeats, unlike many of his contemporaries in the 1890s, was nonetheless disinclined to see decadence, whether aesthetic or historical, as any sort of final "end," a disinclination that was to grow in strength once the end of the century passed without vouchsafing him any special vision. Despite all "those faint lights and faint colours and faint outlines and faint energies"[4] of nineteenth-century aesthetic Decadence, despite all the languor and savage appetites he was later to see in the first-century A.D. Roman world, decadence was usually not what it appeared to be: "When I think of the moment before revelation I think of Salome—she, too, delicately tinted or maybe mahogany dark—dancing before Herod and receiving the Prophet's head in her indifferent hands, and wonder if what seems to us decadence was not in reality the exaltation of the muscular flesh and of civilisation perfectly achieved."[5] What seemed to be cultural decadence was in reality the pause

---

[3] J. L. Borges, *Labyrinths*, quoted in Denis Donoghue, *William Butler Yeats* (New York: Viking, 1971), p. 17.

[4] W. B. Yeats, "The Autumn of the Body" [1898], in *Essays and Introductions* (New York: Collier, 1968), p. 191.

[5] W. B. Yeats, "Dove or Swan," in *A Vision*, rev. ed. [1937] (New York: Macmillan, 1956), p. 273.

before the peacock's cry, the moment when the descending foot turned to reascend the stair.

Yeats's relationship to the Victorian literary Decadence of his own youth, however, is considerably more complex. For if the idea of cultural decadence exerted a lifelong attraction over him, Victorian Decadence understood as a specifically literary phenomenon constantly wavered in its appeal, changing as Yeats's own artistic interests changed. Even in the 1890s, Yeats's estimate of literary Decadence had shifted in response to his own immediate artistic concerns, concerns so largely bound up with his ambitions for Ireland. When Yeats wished to contrast Ireland's literary situation to England's, he would thus emphasize the artificiality and exhaustion of the English literary medium, taking literary Decadence at its word. When, on the other hand, he wished to advance the claims of the new visionary art he believed was springing up in both England and Ireland as well as on the Continent, he became more scrupulous with the term, exchanging the aggressively polemical "Decadence" for the phrase "the autumn of the body" because, as he put it, "I believe the arts lie dreaming of things to come" (Yeats, "Autumn of the Body," p. 191).

Viewed thus externally, Victorian literary Decadence presented itself to Yeats as a useful weapon in the struggle to establish the Irish movement, providing him as it did with a dramatic principle of contrast between English and Irish writing, a contrast that worked for once in Ireland's favor. Viewed from within its philological preoccupations, however, Victorian literary Decadence emphasized precisely the linguistic basis of literary art upon which Yeats would rest so many of his later arguments for change. Although the Paterian and Decadent premise of linguistic artificiality as a literary ideal at first repelled him, other aspects of literary Decadence gradually appealed to his thought: its stress upon the richness, strangeness, and independent expressive power of language, for example, and Pater's notion of a learned elite, of scholars writing to the scholarly. So, too, the Decadent stylistic mode of "archaism and argot" would come to underlie Yeats's attempt in the later nineties to create an "aristocratic esoteric Irish literature"[6] that could speak to noble and beggar-man alike.

This is why, if much of Yeats's writing during the 1890s seems to be innocent of any Decadent consciousness of written language as a dangerously autonomous and artificial dialect, such stories as "The Devil's Book" (1892), "Rosa Alchemica" (1896), and "The Tables of the Law" (1897) nonetheless assume as their thematic center the Decadent *topos* of the fatal book. And it is why, even after the turn of the century, when "everybody got down off his stilts"[7] and Yeats, like his Rhymers' Club colleagues ten years before, turned away from the Paterian stylistic mode towards an ideal of the idiomatic speaking voice, even then literary Decadence would retain an honored place in his memory as an element of the "high talk" and high breeding required by his demanding ideal of poetic art.

Yeats's long career as a poet was thus continually to swerve between attraction toward and revulsion from the stylistic elaborations of literary Decadence. Aware of this shifting pattern, Yeats attempted to incorporate it into his own personal mythography: such swerves and changes belong to the *Hodos Chameliontos*, the delusive but necessarily shifting path of the artist. Seen from the perspective of Victorian literary history, however, such a pattern simply

---

[6] Yeats, a letter sent to John O'Leary, May 30, 1897. *The Letters of W. B. Yeats*, ed. Allan Wade (New York: Macmillan, 1955), p. 286.

[7] W. B. Yeats, "Introduction" to *The Oxford Book of Modern Verse: 1892-1935* (New York: Oxford University Press, 1936), p. xi.

recapitulates the fin de siècle hesitation between the two competing ideals of Pater's elaborate written language and the idiomatic speaking voice, with Yeats persisting in the fin de siècle ambition to accommodate both by finally rejecting neither.

In the beginning, then, Yeats, full of his youthful polemical purposes, stressed the difference between literary Decadence and literary Renaissance as he pointed to the contrast between "old" England and "young" Ireland: "England is an old nation, the dramatic fervor has perhaps ebbed out of her"; "England is old and her poets must scrape up the crumbs of an almost finished banquet, but Ireland has still full tables"; "In England I sometimes hear men complain that the old themes of verse and prose are used up. Here in Ireland the marble block is waiting for us almost untouched."[8] So too, the contrast between John Todhunter's *Helena in Troas* (1886), a poetic drama based on Greek myth, and Todhunter's collection of poems based on Irish folk tales is the contrast between "old age . . . and youth":

> *Helena* was as old as mankind. Old with words and thoughts and reveries handed down for ages; complex with that ever-increasing subdivision of thought and complexity of phrase that marks an old literature. . . . As a literature ages it divides nature from man and sings each for itself. Then each passion is taken from its fellows and sung alone, and cosmopolitanism begins, for a passion has no nation. . . . When a literature is old it grows so indirect and complex that it is only a possession for the few: to read it well is a difficult pur-

---

[8] W. B. Yeats, "Mr. William Wills" [August 3, 1889], in *New Island*, p. 69; "The Rhymers' Club," in *New Island*, p. 148; "The Irish National Literary Society" [November 19, 1892], in *New Island*, pp. 158-59.

suit, like playing on the fiddle; for it one needs especial training.[9]

Although (as Yeats became aware) there was a good deal of self-mockery involved in the Decadent postures of exhaustion and premature age, he was unpersuaded by it; that is, the satiric and self-parodic elements in Decadence only convinced him the more certainly of English complexity and cosmopolitanism. For this reason Yeats—"in all things pre-Raphaelite" during the 1890s,[10]—looked at Beardsley's satiric drawings "in despair at the new breath of comedy that had begun to wither the beauty that I loved, just when that beauty seemed to have united itself to mystery" (Yeats, *Autobiography*, pp. 222-23). In the same way, the music-hall poems of Symons and Davidson seemed to him plain evidence of the exhausted English tradition, a tradition indeed so exhausted that it could now renew itself only through a hectic search for alien and unlovely subjects.

As we have seen, Yeats at first took some comfort from the "scholarly" attitude of Symons's music-hall connoisseurship, but he must have soon realized that it was exactly the halls' "glitter and din" that Symons was savoring so judiciously. Symons's guileless but somewhat vacuous experimentation in music-halls—which Yeats was to deride gently in his autobiography ("O, Yeats, I was never in love with a serpent-charmer before" [Yeats, *Autobiography*, p. 224])—stimulated in Symons those fleeting "moods" and "sensations" he required to make real the distance from the Wesleyan chapels of his youth. To be sure, by the time Sy-

[9] Yeats, "The Children of Lir" [February 10, 1889], in *New Island*, pp. 191-92.
[10] W. B. Yeats, *The Autobiography of William Butler Yeats* (New York: Macmillan, 1965), p. 76.

mons came to recast his article "The Decadent Movement in Literature" as the book *The Symbolist Movement in Literature* (1899), he had learned from Yeats to say that "the visible world is no longer a reality, and the unseen world no longer a dream."[11] But in the early years of their acquaintance, Symons was pre-eminently a man "for whom the visible world exists," a man for whom the Gautier quote could not pall, and he seemed to Yeats, much as he seemed to Lionel Johnson, to be "a slave to impressionism, whether the impression be precious or no."[12] Thus where Symons saw in the waters off Rosses Point in Ireland an image of the fleeting succession of his own moods and caprices, Yeats was looking for something far more permanent—"the Immortal Moods," as he liked to call them—and was seeking "some symbolic language reaching far into the past and associated with familiar names and conspicuous hills that I might not be alone amid the obscure impressions of the senses."[13]

Yeats believed that programmatically "modern" poets like Symons exacerbated their difficulties by choosing to speak "in vulgar types and symbols,"[14] that is, by choosing for images the omnibuses and flaring gaslights of the impersonal modern world. But Yeats believed that even without making this choice, contemporary poets labored under heavy difficulties, simply because they lived "in a world of whirling change, where nothing becomes old and sacred." Beset by banality and ugliness outside themselves

[11] Arthur Symons, *The Symbolist Movement in Literature* (New York: E. P. Dutton, 1958), pp. 2-3.

[12] Lionel Johnson, quoted in Katharine Tynan, "A Catholic Poet," *Dublin Review* 141 (1907): 337.

[13] Yeats, "Art and Ideas," in *Essays and Introductions*, p. 349.

[14] W. B. Yeats, "Old Gaelic Love Songs" [October 1893], in *Uncollected Prose*, ed. John P. Frayne, 2 vols. (New York: Columbia University Press, 1907), 1:295.

and incoherence within, "we labour and labour, and spend days over a stanza or a paragraph, and at the end of it have made, likely as not, a mere bundle of phrases." Cut off from the undying human passions and beliefs, modern literature "dwindles to a mere chronicle of circumstance, or passionless fantasies, and passionless meditations."[15]

Given his Pre-Raphaelitism and his determined literary nationalism, Yeats naturally looked to the Irish past to guide him back to a genuine communion with those "creative powers behind the universe," the Immortal Moods: "One can only reach out to the universe with a gloved hand—that glove is one's nation, the only thing one knows even a little of."[16] And in the distant Irish or Celtic past, Yeats perceived that harmonious interdependence of poet and milieu he would later call "Unity of Being" and variously locate in the Irish eighteenth century and in Byzantium. In the Celtic past, the poet or man of passionate speech was divided neither from his surroundings nor from his own passion: "A peasant had then but to stand in his own door and think of his sweetheart and of his sorrow, and take from the scene about him and from the common events of his life types and symbols, and behold, if chance was a little kind, he had made a poem to humble generations of the proud" (Yeats, "Gaelic Love Songs," p. 295).

Yeats's early experiments with Irish folk ballads, and specifically Irish lyrics such as "The Lake Isle of Innisfree" (1890), belong, as Colin Meir has argued, to a consciously "popular" program of literary nationalism. With it, Yeats meant to avoid the obstreperous rhetorical patriotism of

---

[15] Yeats, "The Celtic Element in Literature" [1897], in *Essays and Introductions*, p. 185.

[16] Yeats, "Irish National Literature—III: Contemporary Irish Poets" [September, 1895], in *Uncollected Prose*, 1:380; "The Poet of Ballyshannon" [September 2, 1888], in *New Island*, p. 174.

such "Young Ireland" poets as Thomas Davis, but hoped at the same to reach Davis's broad audience. This ambition Yeats fully realized in "Innisfree" and "Down by the Salley Gardens" (1889), which, as Meir reminds us, "quickly became, and have since remained, the most widely known of all his work, the latter being sometimes accorded the final honour of 'author anonymous.' "[17]

As the decade of the 1890s progressed, however, Yeats was deflected from this genuinely popular poetic idiom. For one thing, his continuing battles with adherents of the Young Ireland view of national literature prompted him to distance himself from meretriciously popular poetic modes, from poems of jigging doggerel stuck with the inevitable bits of "green tinsel." So too, Yeats's devotion to an ideal of spiritual beauty, like the occult studies he pursued during the nineties in order to gain a vision of that beauty, led him away from a broadly accessible poetic idiom. Under the influence of the occult tradition, with its necessary emphasis upon the immensities and inexpressibilities of visionary experience, Yeats tended to perceive things Celtic through Rose-colored lenses. Moreover, because he lacked knowledge of Gaelic, Yeats responded only to generalized thematic elements in the translations of Gaelic literature he read at this time, rather than to their specific formal or linguistic qualities. So, for example, when he described J. J. Callanan's Gaelic translations, he dwelt upon "the immeasurable dreaming of the Gaelic literature."[18] In much the same way, when he urged the modern poet to "rid his verse of heterogeneous knowledge

[17] Colin Meir, *The Ballads and Songs of W. B. Yeats* (London and Basingstoke: Macmillan, 1974), p. 23. My account of Yeats's stylistic development follows Meir's illuminating linguistic analysis.

[18] Yeats, "Irish National Literature—I: From Callanan to Carleton" [July 1895], in *Uncollected Prose*, 1:362.

and irrelevant analysis," Yeats (invoking the formula of the Great Emerald Tablet) said the poet would thus make "the little ritual of his verse resemble the great ritual of Nature, and *become mysterious and inscrutable.*"[19]

This movement away from popular modes and towards a notion of the high and lonely path of the poet was accelerated, of course, when Yeats began reading Symbolist and Decadent writing. When he first urged his Irish readers to acquaint themselves with Celtic legends and tales, he tried to reassure them about "what is strange and *outré* in poems or plays or stories taken therefrom" by telling them to read simply "with the heart" rather than "with scholars' accuracy."[20] But as Yeats came under the influence of Symbolism and Decadence, he grew more receptive to what was strange and *outré*, and guided by the Paterian ideal of scholarship, began to value more highly the privileged achievements of learning and "sedentary toil."

Admittedly, Yeats had once been suspicious of what he called "scholasticism." To give one example, he identified his countryman Edward Dowden's careful, "scholastic" studies of Shakespeare and other major English literary figures with the pallid and passionless cosmopolitanism Yeats so hated. But as he became acquainted with such Rhymers' Club colleagues as Dowson, Horne, and Johnson, Yeats could see Pater's ideal of "a scholar writing to the scholarly" take living, persuasive form. In the rich language of later eulogy, Yeats said such men were "typical figures of transition, doing as an achievement of learning

[19] Yeats, "The Return of Ulysses" [1896], in *Essays and Introductions*, pp. 201-202. My emphasis.

[20] Yeats, "Ireland's Heroic Age" [May 17, 1890], in *New Island*, p. 107. That Yeats at this time still mistrusted Paterian "scholarship" is suggested by his allusion to Pater's formula "the appeal of a scholar to the scholarly" when he deprecated Todhunter's *Helena in Troas* as a "cosmopolitan" art product (Yeats, "The Children of Lir," p. 175).

and of exquisite taste what their predecessors did in care-
less abundance" (Yeats, *Autobiography*, p. 113). His acquaintance with Lionel Johnson, especially, made Yeats
feel the penalty of the "half civilised" Irish blood he shared
with Wilde. Yet Yeats recognized even during the fin de
siècle itself that Oxford men like Dowson and Johnson,
and those Englishmen without the university advantage
like Horne, created from within "mature traditions of all
kinds—traditions of feeling, traditions of thought, traditions of expression" (Yeats, "Irish National Literature—
I," p. 105). Whatever spasms of self-mistrust they might
individually experience as artists, such men, Yeats believed, could never suffer from his own deep sense of cultural crudity and dispossession:

> They write or paint or think or feel, and believe they
> do so to please no taste but their own, while in reality
> they obey rules and instincts which have been accu-
> mulating for centuries; their wine of life has mellowed
> in ancient cellars, and they see but the ruby light in
> the glass. In a new country like Ireland—and English-
> speaking Ireland is very new—we are continually re-
> minded of this long ripening by the immaturity of the
> traditions about us; if we are writers, for instance, we
> find it takes longer to learn to write than it takes an
> Englishman, and the more resolute we are to express
> the national character, or the more we understand the
> impossibility of putting our new wine into old bottles,
> the longer is our struggle with the trivial, the incoher-
> ent, the uncomely. (Yeats, "Irish National Litera-
> ture—I," p. 105)

The shift in Yeats's attitude towards scholarship will be
apparent. His earlier patriotic and essentially primitivistic
disdain for England's "almost finished banquet" has now

modulated into something close to envy. Yeats saw it was still true that the English writer who worked at the end of a depleted tradition required scholarship to write at all, for instead of the "language of Chaucer and Shakespeare, its warp fresh from field and market—if the woof were learned—his age offered him a speech exhausted from abstractions, that only returned to its full vitality when written learnedly and slowly" (Yeats, *Autobiography*, p. 95). But he now saw as well that writers from a "young" country like Ireland were no freer to create in the absence of tradition. Their very freedom from tradition was, indeed, disabling: "A young Englishman of little knowledge or power may write with considerable skill and perfect good taste before he leaves his university, while an Irishman of greater power and knowledge will go through half his life piling up in the one heap the trivial and the memorable, the incoherent and the beautiful, the commonplace and the simple" (Yeats, "Irish National Literature—I," p. 105). Except for the boisterous, pragmatically political idiom cobbled together by the Young Irelanders and their successors, there was no tradition of Irish literature in English. At best it resided as a fruitful implication in some of Douglas Hyde's translations from the Gaelic (1893). At worst it would have to be wholly fabricated, slowly and learnedly, under the curse of sedentary toil. The scholarly graces of Dowson and Johnson became for Yeats a synonym for this unrelenting labor of craftsmanship.

At the same time, Yeats was reluctant to set aside all hope of audience, particularly an audience among "the people." His anxiety concerning his audience surfaces most noticeably in *The Rose*, when he fears he may *"learn to chaunt a tongue men do not know,"*[21] and with an almost

---

[21] W. B. Yeats, "To the Rose upon the Rood of Time," *The Variorum Edi-*

querulous assertion when he adds his own name to those
of "Davis, Mangan, Ferguson," the poets of the popular
tradition:

> *Know, that I would accounted be*
> *True brother of a company*
> *That sang, to sweeten Ireland's wrong,*
> *Ballad and story, rann and song;*
> *Nor be I any less of them,*
> *Because the red-rose-bordered hem*
> *Of her, whose history began*
> *Before God made the angelic clan,*
> *Trails all about the written page.*
> (Yeats, "To Ireland in the Coming
> Times," pp. 137-38)

It is here not the least part of Yeats's difficulty that he must
justify his own "written page" against the less laborious
songs and ballads of the past; Yeats has denied himself the
Romantic's usual triumphant resort to the idea of his own
living and immortal breath—the resort he wonderfully
avails himself of later on in *The Wind Among the Reeds*
when he says with a proud flourish, "But weigh this song
with the great and their pride;/ I made it out of a mouthful
of air,/ Their children's children shall say they have lied"
(Yeats, "He thinks of those who have Spoken Evil of his
Beloved," p. 166).

Yeats sought to resolve this anxiety over audience by reconstituting his chosen audience, that is, by redefining
"the people" so as to exclude the commercial and philistine
middle classes who insisted upon green tinsel and a
thumping tune in their poetry. In the major essay in which

tion of the Poems of W. B. Yeats, ed. Peter Allt and Russell K. Alspach (New
York: Macmillan, 1957), p. 101. All subsequent citations of Yeats's poetry
are from this edition.

he undertakes to do this, "What is 'Popular Poetry'?" (1901), he appeals to an earlier time in Irish history when the audience for poetry comprised king and peasant, noble and beggar-man, as yet undivided from each other by (as Yeats would say a bit later) "the noisy set/ Of bankers, schoolmasters, and clergymen/ The martyrs call the world" (Yeats, "Adam's Curse," p. 205):

> Indeed, it is certain that before the counting-house had created a new class and a new art without breeding and without ancestry, and set this art and this class between the hut and the castle, and between the hut and the cloister, the art of the people was closely mingled with the art of the coteries as was the speech of the people that delighted in rhythmical animation, in idiom, in words full of far-off suggestion with the unchanging speech of the poets.[22]

Moreover, Yeats intuitively sensed that in the 1890s once again the art of the coteries and the art of the people were drawing together, because he could trace a deep likeness in the imaginative world of the Symbolists and Decadents on one hand and the unlettered Irish country-people on the other. Both groups shared a delight in the *outré*, in words full of far-off suggestion and verses that "keep half their secret to themselves" (Yeats, "Popular Poetry," p. 10). Hence, Yeats concluded, there was only one kind of good poetry, "for the poetry of the coteries, which supposes the written tradition, does not differ in kind from the true poetry of the people, which presupposes the unwritten tradition. Both are alike strange and obscure, and unreal to all who have not understanding" (Yeats, "Popular

[22] Yeats, "What is 'Popular Poetry'?" in *Essays and Introductions*, pp. 10-11.

Poetry," p. 8)—an echo of Pater's ideal of those " 'who have intelligence' in the matter," the ideal of the aesthetically competent few.

Indeed, in such poems as "The Man Who Dreamed of Fairyland" and, especially, "The Song of the Wandering Aengus," Yeats himself achieves this kind of new "popular" poetry, accessible to coterie and country-people alike. Esoteric images like "The silver apples of the moon,/ The golden apples of the sun," ("Wandering Aengus," p. 150) may shine with a special intelligence for the initiate, but their glimmering beauty is not occulted from the unelect—a feat of style that represents a version of Pater's Euphuism in its power to combine without dissonance or loss such divergent elements as archaism and argot. Even long after this time, when his dream of a single culture for the coteries and the country-people had failed, and he had acknowledged its failure, Yeats recurred to this first version of the "dream of the noble and the beggar-man" (Yeats, "The Municipal Gallery Revisited," p. 603), still seemingly convinced of the clear imaginative sympathy he had once seen to lie between aesthetic Decadence and unconscious peasant life:

> I can imagine an Aran Islander who had strayed into the Luxembourg Gallery, turning bewildered from Impressionist or Post-Impressionist, but lingering at Moreau's "Jason," to study in mute astonishment the elaborate background, where there are so many jewels, so much wrought stone and moulded bronze. Had not lover promised mistress in his own island song, "A ship with a gold and silver mast, gloves of the skin of a fish, and shoes of the skin of a bird, and a suit of the dearest silk in Ireland?" (Yeats, *Autobiography*, p. 215)

Grounded in the ancient Celtic legends (and hence in the Immortal Moods), this artistocratic esoteric literature reconciled at a deep level book and song. The Moods required, however, "a subtle, appropriate language or a minute, manifold knowledge for their revelation" (Yeats, "Irish National Literature—I," p. 106). Yeats apprehended this "mystic language" in his own passages of visionary experience.[23] He believed it was being enunciated as well in "Pater's jewelled paragraphs"[24] and in the faint lights and faint outlines of "the symbolical movement which has come to perfection in Germany in Wagner, in England in the Pre-Raphaelites, in France in Villiers de l'Isle-Adam, and Mallarmé, and in Belgium in Maeterlinck, and has stirred the imagination of Ibsen and D'Annunzio" (Yeats, "Celtic Element," p. 187), because in the Symbolist movement, and even in Pater, Yeats recognized a return to the "fountain of legends" much like his own return to Celtic beliefs.

Yeats was convinced that in the passionate tales of Deirdre and Cuchulain there opened "a more abundant fountain than any in Europe" (Yeats, "Celtic Element," p. 186)—unfamiliar enough to seem fresh and vivid, yet participating all the while in the great reservoir of imaginative experience that was the Anima Mundi. Thus centering his

[23] Yeats, "Notes to *The Wind Among the Reeds*" [1908], in *Variorum Poems*, p. 800: "I had sometimes when awake, but more often in sleep, moments of vision, a state very unlike dreaming, when these images took upon themselves what seemed an independent life and became part of a mystic language, which always seemed as if it would bring me some strange revelation." Deducting the gorse boughs, Yeats's visionary experience may be compared to Lucian Taylor's in *The Hill of Dreams*.

[24] Yeats, "A Ballad Singer" [September 12, 1892], in *New Island*, p. 138. It is worth pointing out that Yeats's description of his own reading of Pater's *Marius* here mirrors, in its dreamy mood and imagery of sunlight and shadows, the scene in *Marius*, Chapter 5, where the two young men read the "golden book" of Apuleius.

own poems in Celtic legends was not for Yeats simply a
way of shaping a usable past for Irish writers, but (as for
Pater's Flavian before him) a way of belonging to an imperial system rich in the world's experience, in short, a
way of overcoming the impoverishment of being an Irish
speaker of English:

> The mere sense that one belongs to a system—an im-
> perial system or organization—has in itself, the ex-
> panding power of a great experience; as some have felt
> who have been admitted from narrower sects into the
> communion of the catholic church; or as the old Ro-
> man citizen felt. It is, we might fancy, what the com-
> ing into possession of a very widely spoken language
> might be, with a great literature which is also the
> speech of the people we have to live among.[25]

What the English language could not be to Yeats, because
of his irritable Irish nationalist pride, the fountain of legends thus became—an imperial system. Far from being an
escape into a private subjective world, Celtic legends and
occult lore offered a release from that world, so that Yeats,
unlike his Rhymers' Club colleagues Symons and Dowson, might not be alone amid the obscure impressions of
the senses, so that he might not have to "make all out of the
privacy of [my] thought" (Yeats, *Autobiography*, p. 209).

This new mystic language of image and dream in *The
Wind Among the Reeds* seemed to baffle some of his reconstituted "popular" audience. But Yeats consoled himself
by reflecting that the "Catholic Church is not the less the
Church of the people because the Mass is spoken in Latin,
and art is not less the art of the people because it does not

---

[25] Walter Pater, *Marius the Epicurean: His Sensations and Ideas*, 2 vols.
(London: Macmillan, 1914), 2:26.

always speak in the language they are used to."[26] As is perhaps clearer now in a time of vernacular Masses than it was then, however, to deploy such an analogy came very near to conceding that one did in fact *"chaunt a tongue men do not know"*—an uncomfortable admission for a poet who once hoped that his poems might be sung by men at work in the fields. Yeats's sense of the difficulties inherent in an aristocratic esoteric literature continued to trouble him, even as he labored to produce such a literature.

Yeats's unease finds specific expression in the fatal book *topos* in the collection of stories entitled *The Secret Rose*, where elaborately wrought volumes of secret or forbidden knowledge tempt his timid narrator as he hesitates between pallid Christian orthodoxy and flame-colored mystical experience. In the first story, "Rosa Alchemica," for example, the fatal book is literally a text of initiation—the volume the narrator is given to study before he is inducted into the Order of the Alchemical Rose. Kept in "a curiously wrought bronze box," the book is adorned "with symbolical pictures and illuminations, after the manner of the *Splendor Solis*,"[27] designs that Yeats had reproduced on the actual cover of *The Secret Rose* volume. As William H. O'Donnell has observed, such volumes belong to the occult tradition of richly decorated books, specifically *grimoires* or magicians' manuals; stylistically, however, both the fatal book within the story and the story itself declare their descent from the elaborate artificial prose tradition of Pater and Wilde.[28]

[26] Yeats, "Ireland and the Arts" [1901], in *Essays and Introductions*, p. 207.

[27] W. B. Yeats, "Rosa Alchemica," in *The Secret Rose, Stories by W. B. Yeats: A Variorum Edition*, ed. Phillip L. Marcus, Warwick Gould, and Michael J. Sidnell (Ithaca and London: Cornell University Press, 1980), p. 141. All subsequent references to this story and to "The Tables of the Law" and "The Adoration of the Magi" are from this edition.

[28] William H. O'Donnell, *A Guide to the Prose Fiction of W. B. Yeats* (Ann

Yeats's treatment of the fatal book *topos* suggests that the independent shaping power of words that the fatal book usually represents—as for example in Wilde or Mallarmé—is not here specifically linguistic. Certainly, Yeats was attracted (thanks to Symons's translation) by Mallarmé's famous "enacted" description in "Crise de Vers" of words that "take light from mutual reflection, like an actual trail of fire over precious stones" (Yeats, "Autumn of the Body," p. 193). But Yeats viewed such elaborate language less as a power in its own right than as a beautiful form that would tempt one of the Immortal Moods to descend and fill it, much as a mood had once filled Edgar Allan Poe's wine cup and

> passed into France and took possession of Baudelaire, and from Baudelaire passed to England and the Pre-Raphaelites, and then again returned to France, and still wanders the world, enlarging its power as it goes, awaiting the time when it shall be, perhaps, alone, or, with other moods, master over a great new religion,

Arbor: UMI Research Press, 1983), p. 90. For Yeats's debt to the elaborate writing of Wilde's critical essays, cf. "Rosa Alchemica," p. 133: "[T]he more a man lives in imagination and in a refined understanding, the more gods does he meet with and talk with, and the more does he come under the power of Roland, who sounded in the Valley of Roncevalles the last trumpet of the body's will and pleasure; and of Hamlet, who saw them perishing away, and sighed; and of Faust, who looked for them up and down the world and could not find them"; and Oscar Wilde, "The Critic as Artist" [1890, 1891], in *The Artist as Critic: Critical Writings of Oscar Wilde*, ed. Richard Ellmann (New York: Random House, 1968), pp. 383-84: "We have whispered the secret of our love beneath the cowl of Abelard, and in the stained raiment of Villon have put our shame into song. We can see the dawn through Shelley's eyes, and when we wander with Endymion the Moon grows amorous of our youth. Ours is the anguish of Atys, and ours the weak rage and noble sorrows of the Dane." Michael Fixler makes the case for Huysmans's influence upon Yeats's prose in "The Affinities between J.-K. Huysmans and the 'Rosicrucian Stories' of W. B. Yeats," *PMLA* 74 (1959): 464-69; and F. C. McGrath urges the claims of Pater in " 'Rosa Alchemica': Pater Scrutinized and Alchemized," *Yeats-Eliot Review* 5 (1978): 13-20.

and an awakener of the fanatical wars that hovered in the gray surges, and forget the wine-cup where it was born. (Yeats, "Rosa Alchemica," pp. 143n.-44n.)

In tracing such a descent Yeats implicitly places his own writing last in the processional line, because his own prose style, with its hypnotic rhythms and invertebrate appositive structures, seeks to become one of those "beautiful shapes, which are but, as it were, shapes trembling out of existence" (Yeats, "Rosa Alchemica," p. 143) that will tempt the mood of Poe, Baudelaire, Rossetti, Swinburne, Pater, and Mallarmé to enter it and enlarge the surging gray apocalyptic wave. Literature, Yeats said, is "wrought about a mood, or a community of moods, as the body is wrought about an invisible soul,"[29] but in order to attract the beautiful moods, literature or literary style must be all but formless or "disembodied" like the beautiful moods themselves.

Because the style of the fatal book in "Rosa Alchemica" is manifestly the style of "Rosa Alchemica" itself, the story, too, is seemingly meant to function as a fatal book—"fatal" to the epoch of materialism and scepticism in which it appears. Yet finally, the apocalyptic "fatality" of both the initiation manual and "Rosa Alchemica" itself are put into question: for Yeats's book did not initiate a new historical phase, and the fatal book within Yeats's story does not even initiate the narrator. Presumably the initiation manual is destroyed by the outraged fishermen and women when they assault the Temple of the Alchemical Rose. The half-initiated narrator, who instinctively refused to yield his body to the immortal powers during his initiation, flees the peasants, only later to take up a somewhat less fanatical version of their Christian faith. By the end of

[29] Yeats, "The Moods" [1895], in *Essays and Introductions*, p. 195.

the story the narrator no longer hopes for visionary apocalypse but merely for "peace." The only outward evidence of his experience with the Immortal Moods is in his literary style: his writings "have grown less popular and less intelligible" (Yeats, "Rosa Alchemica," p. 126).

Yeats traces the same sort of retreat from mystical commitment in the next story, "The Tables of the Law." In that story, Owen Aherne shows the narrator a great treasure—the single surviving copy of Joachim of Flora's "secret book," *Liber inducens in Evangelium aeternum*. Encased in a bronze casket wrought by Benvenuto Cellini, with a cover enriched by silver filigree and pages gilded and illuminated by a minor Renaissance master, "this terrible book . . . this amazing book" is another inverted Bible. Specifically, it is a gospel of antinomianism, with one part devoted to a rewritten Decalogue and another to a geographically and morally relativistic survey of human laws. The narrator, unable with his lamely "commonplace" arguments to dissuade Aherne from going forth with his fatal book to gain secret adherents, does not meet with his friend for ten years. When he does, he finds a broken man, afflicted with "a leprosy that even eternity cannot cure" (Yeats, "Tables of the Law," p. 163). Aherne can neither return to ordinary Christian faith nor approach any nearer the mystical ecstasy. At the end of the story, the narrator sees Aherne ringed by immortal torch-bearing figures sorrowing over him—figures that Aherne himself cannot see—thus confirming that the narrator, too, exists between two worlds. But when the figures turn toward the narrator as if "to fling their torches upon me, so that all that I held dear, all that bound me to spiritual and social order, would be burnt up" (Yeats, "Tables of the Law," p. 164), the narrator flees.

The accelerating withdrawal from the mystical world

depicted in the first two stories continues in the third, "The Adoration of the Magi." Here Yeats's narrator neither tells of his own experience nor depicts the experience of someone he knows and has observed. Instead he reports, at a distance of "some years," the tale told him by strangers—three old Irish countrymen who claim to have witnessed the birth of the new avatar. So too, the immortal powers themselves have been distanced: in "Rosa Alchemica" the narrator danced with an immortal august woman; in "The Tables of the Law" the narrator "saw, or imagined that I saw" a ring of purple-robed immortals. In "The Adoration of the Magi," however, the narrator sees nothing of the mystical world himself, but merely transcribes second-hand the experience of the three old men—and even their experience is largely auditory rather than visionary.

This withdrawal of sustained visionary experience is expressed stylistically in *The Secret Rose*: by the decreasing length of each successive story and by the decreasing stylistic elaboration within each story. Thus the lavishly rhythmical, highly colored writing of "Rosa Alchemica" (e.g. "I had gathered about me all gods because I believed in none, and experienced every pleasure because I gave myself to none, but held myself apart, individual, indissoluble, a mirror of polished steel" [Yeats, "Rosa Alchemica," pp. 127-28] gives way to the less metaphorical periods of "The Tables of the Law": "He had the nature, which is half monk, half soldier of fortune, and must needs turn action into dreaming, and dreaming into action; and for such there is no order, no finality, no contentment in this world" (Yeats, "Tables of the Law," p. 151). And these in turn yield to the still plainer, more nearly colloquial prose of "The Adoration of the Magi": "They took off their great-coats, and leaned over the fire warming their hands, and I saw that their clothes had much of the country of our own time, but a little also, as it seemed to me, of the town life of a more courtly time" (Yeats, "Adoration," p. 165).

In this way, the three stories—which are more profitably read as a unit rather than in the usual way as Yeats's increasingly unsuccessful experiment in prose-writing—enact the ebbing of the mystical powers they describe. By the third story, there is not only no fatal book to serve as an embodying form or vehicle for the Immortal Moods, but the narrator now looks upon written language as an effective screen or defense *against* the Immortal Moods, those dreadful illusions, as he now calls them, "which come of that inquietude of the veil of the temple" (Yeats, "Adoration," p. 165): "I have grown to believe that there is no dangerous idea which does not become less dangerous when written out in sincere and careful English." Such a thought expressed in such a style is the literary equivalent of the narrator's experiential decision no longer to "live an elaborate and haughty life, but seek to lose myself among the prayers and the sorrows of the multitude" (Yeats, "Adoration," pp. 171-72), praying "in poor chapels, where frieze coats brush against me as I kneel" (Yeats, "Adoration," p. 172), with a prayer made long ago to help a peasant "who had suffered with a suffering like mine," that is to say, with a poem translated out of the Gaelic.

The thematic and stylistic movement within Yeats's *Secret Rose* story sequence thus foreshadows the famous stylistic change in his poetry that became remarkable after the fin de siècle with the publication of *In the Seven Woods* (1903). During the time around the actual turn of the century, Yeats, like his prose narrator in *The Secret Rose*, turned away from elaborate style—"that artificial, elaborate English so many of us played with in the 'nineties," as Yeats himself later called it, "that extravagant style/ He had learnt from Pater."[30] He returned to the speaking voice of the Irish peasant, to "that simple English [Augusta Gregory] had learned from her Galway countrymen" (Yeats, "1925 Notes," p. 173). Because Yeats's stylistic self-transformation has been so assiduously studied by his critics, I shall stress only two points here: first, that Yeats's return to the voice represents a belated version of the reaction against Paterian Euphuism initiated by Pater's followers in the 1890s; and secondly, that Yeats's return to the voice, chiefly because it was part of a Romantic nationalist movement of liberation against an invasive, oppressive foreign culture, was more specifically linguistic than the anti-Paterian reaction of Wilde and the Rhymers' Club poets.

The first point needs little elaboration. Just as Yeats in the 1890s detested his contemporaries' nostalgia for the eighteenth century, only to succumb to it himself years later,[31] so his reaction against Pater's stylistic idealization of written language followed—years after his contemporaries turned against Pater's dead language—the lines and language of their rejection. Hence, for example, Yeats implicitly criticizes J. M. Synge's earliest work for its Paterian faults, for its "morbidity," the result of "too much brooding over methods of expression, and ways of looking upon life, which come, not out of life, but out of literature, images reflected from mirror to mirror."[32] And so too, he criticizes George Russell (Æ) for writing the "dead language" of the nineties. With a fine, unforgiving detach-

[30] Yeats, "Notes to *The Secret Rose*" [1925], in *Variorum Stories*, p. 173; "The Phases of the Moon," *Variorum Poems*, p. 373.

[31] See Linda Dowling, "The Aesthetes and the Eighteenth Century," *Victorian Studies* 20 (1977): 357-58, 375-76.

[32] Yeats, "Preface to the First Edition of *The Well of the Saints*" [1905], in *Essays and Introductions*, p. 298.

ment from his earlier stylistic self, Yeats declared that Russell "writes 'dream' where other men write 'dreams,' a trick he and I once shared, picked up from William Sharp perhaps when the romantic movement was in its last contortions. Renaissance Platonism had ebbed out in poetic diction, isolating certain words and phrases as if they were Platonic Ideas."[33] As the reference to Platonism makes clear, behind Æ and William Sharp lurks the stylistic shade of Pater, whose "golden sentences" and "jewelled paragraphs" in *Marius the Epicurean* enunciated "the Platonic theory of spiritual beings having their abode in all things without and within us" (Yeats, "A Ballad Singer," pp. 137, 138), and as they did so sought to make of literary style itself a haunting, imperishable presence.

The turn of the century changed all that, or at least Yeats was prepared to write and remember as if it had. We may wish to trace the motives for his stylistic change to his friendship with Lady Gregory, his experience of writing plays for performance, his reading of Nietzsche, his passing conviction that the new "objective" age had begun, or to Maud Gonne's marriage, but whatever its biographical or artistic origins, the change is best viewed, as Colin Meir has argued, as a return rather than a new departure:

> Seeking qualities of beauty, strangeness and mystery, what one might call the subtle evidence of the soul, Yeats was led for a time to exaggerate one element of the Gaelic tradition and ignore its matter-of-factness, its realism. It is not until after 1900 that he begins to recognise the distinctive features of Hyde's use of Anglo-Irish syntax and idiom, and to praise it for its concreteness, its lack of abstraction, its characteristics of "living speech." In doing so, he comes to a much

[33] Yeats, "My Friend's Book" [1932], in *Essays and Introductions*, p. 415.

clearer view of the nature of his native heritage, and develops an aesthetic which again takes its starting point from what is simple and direct. (Meir, *Ballads and Songs*, p. 36)

Like the narrator of the "Rosa Alchemica" sequence, Yeats, having for a period during the later nineties fled common men, returns to live in their midst. His earlier fin de siècle acquiescence in the literary artist's desire to be "mysterious and inscrutable," "less popular and less intelligible" is now portrayed as at best a misleading turn in the *Hodos Chameliontos*, the shifting path of the artist: "There are two ways before literature—upward into ever-growing subtlety, with Verhaeren, with Mallarmé, with Maeterlinck . . . or downward, taking the soul with us until all is simplified and solidified again."[34]

At worst, however, the mystic language of the fin de siècle search "for an almost disembodied ecstasy" (Yeats, "Autumn of the Body," p. 194) has simply become "that conventional language of modern poetry which has begun to make us all weary" (Yeats, *"Well of the Saints,"* p. 298), a language of abstraction (e.g. "dream," "rose") almost as impersonal, finally, as the language it was first invented to combat, namely, "the impersonal language . . . of necessities of commerce, of Parliament, of Board Schools, of hurried journeys by rail" (Yeats, *"Well of the Saints,"* p. 301). The attempt to create a mystic language for noble and beggar-man alike by writing slowly and learnedly had resulted, it now seemed with the new century, in an esoteric aristocratic lingo that could be understood only with difficulty and spoken not at all: "[W]e have begun to forget that literature is but recorded speech and even when we

---

[34] Yeats, "Discoveries: Personality and the Intellectual Essences" [1906], in *Essays and Introductions*, pp. 266-67.

write with care we have begun to write with elaboration that which could never be spoken."[35]

When Yeats began with the new century to choose the second path of simplicity and solidity, he insisted upon a spoken idiom "of those who have rejected, or of those who have never learned the base idioms of the newspapers." If his new path no longer led him to the Aran Islander's *outré* imaginative world, neither did it lead him to the proletarian idiom of the cities. Instead it led him "downward" to the common speech of the Irish peasant and to the Irish soil itself:

> John Synge, I and Augusta Gregory, thought
> All that we did, all that we said or sang
> Must come from contact with the soil, from that
> Contact everything Antaeus-like grew strong.
> We three alone in modern times had brought
> Everything down to that sole test again. . . .
> (Yeats, "The Municipal Gallery Revisited," p. 603)

The phonetic play on soil/sole, of course, underlines the new importance Yeats and the others discovered in the spoken word. Dissatisfied with his own earlier experiments in phonetically reproducing the Irish dialect (e.g. "I saw the sorrowful dhrames o' the world dhriftin' above it, like a say as it slept in the night, and I skimmed the foam o' them with a noggin, and made mesel' a body, and it was love for your love o' me that made me do it, Owen"[36]) and perhaps remembering the sarcasms directed at the "provincial" dialect of William Sharp ("[O]ne cannot help asking whether this is to be the common tongue of the future Renaissance of Romance. Are we all to talk Scotch, and to

---

[35] W. B. Yeats, "The Irish Dramatic Movement: Samhain 1902," in *Explorations* (New York: Macmillan, 1962), p. 95.

[36] Yeats, "The Devil's Book" [1892], in *Variorum Stories*, p. 193.

speak of the moon as the 'mune,' and the soul as the 'saul'?"[37]), Yeats looked instead for a literary model of spoken language to "turns of speech out of Gaelic" (Yeats, "Samhain: 1902," p. 94), that is, to the non-phonetic renderings of the Anglo-Irish dialect produced by Douglas Hyde and Lady Gregory.

Yeats's debt to the Anglo-Irish dialect is syntactical rather than dictional: "I must seek, not as Wordsworth thought, words in common use, but a powerful and passionate syntax."[38] Colin Meir has argued that Yeats did not at first understand *how* Anglo-Irish syntax made for a more concrete style and a more "embodied" poetic presence or personality[39]; but plainly Yeats knew *that* it did so, for his insistence upon "passionate syntax" never abated. If Yeats's linguistic understanding of the Anglo-Irish dialect was essentially intuitive, his defense of that dialect was aggressively polemical—carried on partly in the same spirit of linguistic nationalism that had once moved the founders of scientific language study in the beginning of the nineteenth century as they struggled to advance the claims of the German language against the cosmopolitan hegemony

[37] Arthur Galton, "An Examination; of Certain Schools and Tendencies, in Contemporary Literature: Suggested by the Title to a Volume of Modern Poems [i. e. Sharp's *Romantic Ballads and Poems of Phantasy*]; and by the Theories Propounded in the Introduction to Them," *Century Guild Hobby Horse* 4 (1889): 101: "Mr. Sharp's language is not antique, it is provincial; it is mixed with a large quantity of Lowland Scotch"; Wilde, "A Note on Some Modern Poets," in Ellmann, p. 99.

[38] Yeats, "A General Introduction for my Work" [1937], in *Essays and Introductions*, pp. 521-22.

[39] It does so largely by laying greater emphasis on the noun than is the case in standard English. See Meir, *Ballads and Songs*, pp. 65-90. Cf. Yeats, "General Introduction," p. 515: "Gaelic is incapable of abstraction." For Yeats's reason for not writing in Gaelic himself, see "General Introduction," p. 520: "I begged the Indian writers present to remember that no man can think or write with music and vigour except in his mother tongue. . . . I could not more have written in Gaelic than can those Indians write in English; Gaelic is my national language, but it is not my mother tongue."

of French, and partly in the same spirit of linguistic anti-prescriptiveness that moved the modern descriptive linguists.[40] Yeats's study and appropriation of elements from the Anglo-Irish dialect thus made his one of the voices from the circumference—from Merioneth and the Liffey and the Dee[41]—that the linguistic guardians at "the very centre" of literary London had long warned against. Yeats's eccentric syntax heralded the implosion of "provincial" and colonial dialects upon the English grapholect that has since characterized twentieth-century literary and linguistic history.[42]

Hence Yeats's return to his earlier nationalist tactic of

[40] Cf. Yeats, "Samhain: 1902," p. 94: "Even Irish writers of considerable powers of thought seem to have no better standard of English than a schoolmaster's ideal of correctness."

[41] Cf. Grant Allen, "Letters in Philistia," *Fortnightly Review* 55 o.s., 49 n.s. (June 1891): 957: "London and England no longer compose our whole British world. Connemara and Donegal, Caithness and the Lewis, Glamorgan and Merioneth, have taken heart of grace to assert their right to a hearing in the counsels of our complex nation."

[42] For Yeats's non-standard syntax, see John Holloway, "Style and World in 'The Tower,'" in *An Honoured Guest: New Essays on W. B. Yeats*, ed. Denis Donoghue and J. R. Mulryne (New York: St. Martin's, 1966), pp. 88-105. For the enrichment and invigoration of literary English in the twentieth century by circumferential dialects, see George Steiner, "Linguistics and Poetics," in *Extra-territorial: Papers on Literature and the Language Revolution* (London: Faber and Faber, 1972), pp. 149-50: "There is the profoundly disturbing question of linguistic entropy. . . . Is there in languages—Hebrew and Chinese being the only decided exceptions—a life cycle of prodigal growth, confident maturity and gradual decline? Are the critical elements behind the fact that twentieth-century English literature, with the exception of D. H. Lawrence, is so largely the product of American and Irish poets, novelists, playwrights, essayists, economic, political, social, or linguistic? . . . To an observer, it is very nearly an unavoidable conclusion that English as it is spoken and written in England today is an enervated, tired version of the language as compared with the almost Elizabethan rapacities and zest of American English and of the breathless literature it is sending into the world. Which is cause, which is effect? . . . [T]he question itself is of the utmost importance: it may well be that cultures and societies die when their uses of language atrophy."

making invidious linguistic and literary comparisons with the English. The revival of Gaelic in Ireland, he declared, is no mere patriotic antiquarianism, but the noble effort "to restore what is called a more picturesque way of life, that is to say, a way of life in which the common man has some share in imaginative art"—in short, a way to "be the less English."[43] Again we hear about the "full tables," the "untouched marble block" of Ireland: "Ireland, her imagination at its noon before the birth of Chaucer, has created the most beautiful literature of a whole people that has been anywhere since Greece and Rome, while English literature, the greatest of all literatures but that of Greece, is yet the literature of a few" (Yeats, "Living Voice," p. 474). With the failure of the English folk imagination in the sixteenth century ("but a handful of ballads about Robin Hood") came the artificial cosmopolitan dialect of Euphuism, "compounded of the natural history and mythology of the classics."[44] And some form of Euphuism—aristocratic, heterogeneous—has been the English literary dialect ever since. Yet "how [Euphuism] injured the simplicity and the unity of the speech!" Even Shakespeare, with his verbal web "woven of threads that have been spun in many lands" (Yeats, "Stratford-on-Avon," p. 109), lived in a time of spreading imaginative penury "when solitary great men were gathering to themselves the fire that had once flowed hither and thither among all men" (Yeats, "Stratford-on-Avon," p. 110). And because Shakespeare's glory as a poet was preserved only by "a narrow class," the poor

[43] W. B. Yeats, "Literature and the Living Voice," *Contemporary Review* 90 (1906): 474.

[44] Yeats, "At Stratford-on-Avon" [1901], in *Essays and Introductions*, p. 110. Despite Yeats's deprecation of Euphuism, Pater's influence upon the diction ("web," "fire") and the ideas of this essay is marked. See Leonard P. Nathan, "W. B. Yeats's Experiments with an Influence," *Victorian Studies* 6 (1962-63): 66-74.

Gaelic rhymer "leaves a nobler memory among his neigh-
bours" than Shakespeare left among the burgers of Strat-
ford.

If Yeats's reading of English literary history seems eccentric, his explanation of Shakespeare's "narrow" fame
remains interesting:

> [T]he good English writers, with a few exceptions
> that seem accidental, have written for a small culti-
> vated class; and is not this the reason? Irish poetry and
> Irish stories were made to be spoken or sung, while
> English literature, alone of great literatures because
> the newest of them all, has all but completely shaped
> itself in the printing press. (Yeats, "Living Voice,"
> p. 474)

There may be a recollection in this of Wilde's remarks on
"the introduction of printing, and the fatal development of
the habit of reading amongst the middle and lower
classes." But as an explanation it is wonderfully useful, for
Yeats is able to gather within it some of his favorite
themes: the deadly English dependence on mechanism,
the joyless English devotion to the knowledge that can be
got from books, the pushing, parvenu character of the English literary imagination ("the newest of them all") and, on
the other side, the importance to poetry of the spoken
word, of "personality, the breath of men's mouths" (Yeats,
"Samhain: 1902," p. 95), the importance of distinctly felt
nationality in literature, and the saving imaginative vitality of the Irish *Volk* ("[T]o belong to any aristocracy, is to
be a little pool that will soon dry up. A people alone are a
great river").[45]

[45] Yeats, "The Galway Plains" [1903], in *Essays and Introductions*,
p. 214.

Chapter V

For the first few years of the new century Yeats set about trying to put his beliefs into practice—on the stage of the Abbey Theater and on the psaltery, the curious stringed instrument his friend Florence Farr plucked as she spoke his verse. Ronald Schuchard has made the persuasive case that "Yeats's attendant dream of a revived oral culture, partially inspired by the continuing existence in western Ireland of what he called the 'culture of the cottage,' was consciously conceived in direct opposition to what he called Arnold's 'culture of scholarship,' an impossible culture for Ireland."[46] There was, of course, an earlier Arnoldian Yeats: we discover him in the young man who in 1892 wrote his American readers from a table in the "big, florid new" Irish National Library protesting that "on all sides men are studying the things that are to get them bodily food, but no man among them is searching for the imaginative and spiritual food to be got out of great literature" (Yeats, "Irish Literary Society," pp. 154-55). But this Arnoldian Yeats had disappeared by fifteen years later. Still more years later, Yeats's ideal cultural embodiments— "Hard-riding country gentlemen" (Yeats, "Under Ben Bulben," p. 639)—could easily be mistaken for Arnold's anaesthetic "Barbarians."

Arnold's way to culture, to "the best that has been thought and said," was through the book: "culture is *reading*," he insisted.[47] But the book, as Yeats now perceived it, was inimical to the ideal culture he wished Ireland to have. He desired an oral, communal culture, while the

[46] Ronald Schuchard, "The Minstrel in the Theatre: Arnold, Chaucer and Yeats's New Spiritual Democracy," in *Yeats Annual, No. 2*, ed. Richard J. Finneran (London: Macmillan, 1983), p. 4.

[47] Matthew Arnold, "Preface to the First Edition of *Literature and Dogma*," in *Complete Prose Works*, ed. R. H. Super, 11 vols. (Ann Arbor: University of Michigan Press, 1960-77), 7:162.

book besought the eye in silence, dividing the reader from
his fellows and from his very thought:

> When one takes a book into the corner, one surrenders
> so much life for one's knowledge, so much, I mean, of
> that normal activity that gives one life and strength,
> one lays away one's own handiwork and turns from
> one's friend, and if the book is a good one is at some
> pains to press all the little wanderings and tumults of
> the mind into silence and quiet.[48]

Besides, as Yeats knew from the first, "Ireland . . . is not a
reading nation" (Yeats, "Irish Literary Society," p. 155),
her people are "too restless and sociable to be readers"
(Yeats, "Living Voice," p. 476). Hence the antagonism
between "the old world that sang and listened" and the
new world "that reads and writes" (Yeats, "Living Voice,"
p. 474) also comprises the antagonism between Ireland
and England. There is something un-Irish, alien and unnatural in "our exaggerated love of print and paper,"
something perverse, like "the craving of a woman in child-
bed for green apples" (Yeats, "Living Voice," p. 475). It
is as if Yeats is fashioning a new fatal book out of English
Board School texts and proletarian penny thrillers. For he
sees that the book *is* decadent, an outworn toy about to be

[48] Yeats, "Living Voice," p. 475. The theme of imaginative fragmentation
or paralysis through overmuch reading of books continues in the later
poems: "I seek an image, not a book./ Those men that in their writings are
most wise/ Own nothing but their blind, stupefied hearts" (Yeats, "Ego
Dominus Tuus," p. 370); "Climb to your chamber full of books and wait,/
No books upon the knee . . . (Yeats, "To Dorothy Wellesley," p. 579). Cf.
Donoghue, *Yeats*, p. 18: "In Ireland, where the governing art is rhetoric,
proof of power is voice. Irish history is elucidated not in books but in
speeches. . . . Hence, too, the value ascribed to gesture. . . . Even when a
book is allowed, it must be 'a written speech/ Wrought of high laughter,
loveliness and ease' [Yeats, 'Upon a House Shaken by the Land Agitation,'
p. 264]."

dropped from listless fingers as the eyes stray elsewhere: "I myself cannot be convinced that the printing press will be always victor, for change is inconceivably swift. . . . [How the change is to come,] I do not know, but that the time will come I am certain" (Yeats, "Living Voice," pp. 474-75).

In fact Yeats was already hearing the change in 1906, when he heard passé music-hall tunes penetrating Galway and other western Irish towns with "a rhythm as pronounced and as impersonal as the noise of a machine" (Yeats, "Living Voice," p. 473). For in the wake of the music-hall tunes followed the vaudeville, the cinema, the radio, the television, more flecks in "this filthy modern tide" (Yeats, "The Statues," p. 611). Already he heard in the musician's meaningless lengthening of vowels, the singer's "lo-o-o-o-o-ve," one of the "causes that are bringing about in modern countries a degradation of language" (Yeats, "Living Voice," p. 481)—the Shakespeherian Rag, full of words that are "so broken and softened and mixed with spittle that they are not words any longer."[49]

Yet in a sense Yeats remained supremely indifferent, gay: "Of the many things, desires or powers or instruments, that are to change the world, the artist is fitted to understand but two or three, and the less he troubles himself about the complexity that is outside his craft, the more will he find it all within his craft, and the more dextrous will his hand and his thought become" (Yeats, "Living Voice," p. 475). In later years the complicatedly clanking gyres of *A Vision* would orchestrate all the comings and goings of such change. But it is a measure of Yeats's imaginative loftiness—or at least his imperviousness to the in-

[49] Yeats, "Discoveries: The Musician and the Orator" [1906], in *Essays and Introductions*, p. 268.

conveniences of disconfirming evidence—that even in 1906 he could transform the grand icon of English book-worship and bibliophilia, William Morris's Kelmscott Chaucer, into a presiding symbol for the new unmediated *oral* culture he hoped to make for Ireland:

> In every art, when it seems to one that it has need of a renewing of life, one goes backwards till one lights upon a time when it was nearer to human life and instinct, before it had gathered about it so many mechanical specialisations and traditions. . . . William Morris, for instance, studied the earliest printing, the founts of type that were made when men saw their craft with eyes that were still new, and with leisure, and without the restraints of commerce and custom. And then he made a type that was really new, that had the quality of his own mind about it, though it reminds one of its ancestry, of its high breeding as it were. (Yeats, "Living Voice," p. 477)

Morris had renewed the book by going backwards, by recalling the time before the book, before men read, when "the ear and the tongue were subtle, and delighted one another with the little tunes that were in words." So too, Yeats, in the intensity of his special quest for a communal oral culture, could ignore the fact that the founding "volume paramount" of English literature—the King James Bible—was a *book*, and portray it as simply another example of his own presiding ideal of "living speech":

> [W]e must found good literature on a living speech. English men of letters found themselves upon the English Bible, where religious thought gets its living speech. Blake, if I remember rightly, copied it out twice, and I remember once finding a few illuminated

pages of new decorated copy that he began in his old age. Byron read it for the sake of style, though I think it did him little good; and Ruskin founded himself in great part upon it. Indeed, we find everywhere signs of a book which is the chief influence in the lives of English children. The translation used in Ireland has not the same literary beauty, and if we are to find anything to take its place we must find it in that idiom of the poor, which mingles so much of the same vocabulary with turns of phrase out of Gaelic. (Yeats, "Samhain: 1902," p. 94)

The only book for Ireland was to be no book at all: "The book of the people" (Yeats, "Coole Park and Ballylee, 1931," p. 492).

With the failure to make a new oral and communal culture out of bawneen jackets, psalteries, and "this theatre of speech"—a failure that finds its obvious symbol in the riots in 1907 at the Abbey over Synge's "Playboy of the Western World"—Yeats followed the veering *Hodos Chameliontos* and turned back once more towards aristocratic ideals. For despite all its sinewy, passionate syntax, and despite all his insistence that a poem is nothing more than "an elaboration of the rhythms of common speech" (Yeats, "Modern Poetry," p. 508), Yeats's later poetry hardly courts the common reader:

> No! Greater than Pythagoras, for the men
> That with a mallet or a chisel modelled these
> Calculations that look but casual flesh, put down
> All Asiatic vague immensities,
> And not the banks of oars that swam upon
> The many-headed foam at Salamis.[50]

[50] Yeats, "The Statues," p. 610. Yeats's idea of the actual power of imaginative culture to repel its enemies here recalls Coleridge's conviction that

These lines from "The Statues" are not "mysterious and inscrutable" in the old way of the nineties; they are "difficult" in the knotty modernist sense of the word. Reading them, the astonished Irish peasant would likely derive little hermeneutical help from recalling his old song about the fish-skin gloves. Yet in Yeats's return to a more exclusive idea of poetic audience towards the end of his life, he does not, of course, return to the artificial, elaborate English he had played with in the nineties. It might still be true that "without fine words there is no literature" (Yeats, "Living Voice," p. 477), but he had since learned that to give the impression "of an active man speaking . . . certain words must be dull and numb" (Yeats, *Autobiography*, p. 291). The extravagant style he had learned from Pater persists only as trace elements in the later work, in the moments of sumptuous assonance in the poems ("casual flesh," "All Asiatic vague immensities") and, certainly, in the gorgeous periods of the *Autobiography*.

Pater's disciples, especially the "Tragic Generation" poets Johnson and Dowson, mattered to the later Yeats, as Harold Bloom has said, "in the style of their lives, and their stance as poets, rather than in their actual work."[51] And indeed, Yeats summons these two slim, besotted spectres whenever he meditates upon the poet's high calling and high sacrifice:

> *You had to face your ends when young—*
> *'Twas wine or women, or some curse—*
> *But never made a poorer song*

"civilization" more than "fleets, armies, and revenue, forms the ground of [a nation's] defensive and offensive power." S. T. Coleridge, *On the Constitution of Church and State*, ed. John Colmer, in *The Collected Works of Samuel Taylor Coleridge*, ed. Kathleen Coburn, 16 vols. (Princeton: Princeton University Press, 1976), 10:43.

[51] Harold Bloom, *Yeats* (London and Oxford: Oxford University Press, 1970), p. 28.

That you might have a heavier purse,
Nor gave loud service to a cause
That you might have a troop of friends.
You kept the Muses' sterner laws,
And unrepenting faced your ends,
And therefore earned the right—and yet
Dowson and Johnson most I praise—
To troop with those the world's forgot,
And copy their proud steady gaze.
  (Yeats, "The Grey Rock," p. 273)

Yet even when he does not call by name upon the "Companions of the Cheshire Cheese" or rail against the slovenliness of an age in which "No Oscar ruled the table" (Yeats, "The Statesman's Holiday," p. 626), Yeats may be seen to invoke the Decadent ideal of elaborate, artificial language. For the "stilts" that everybody climbed down from in 1900, the year that everybody also gave up the other fin de siècle affectations of absinthe, madness, and suicide, are cognate with the stilts and ladders and long legs—the unnatural structures of elevation and vision—Yeats repeatedly seeks to mount in his last poems: Michelangelo on the high scaffolding beneath the Sistine ceiling, *"Like a long-legged fly upon the stream/ His mind moves upon silence"*; and Malachi Stilt-Jack, a "Daddy-long-legs upon his timber toes," still stalking on, though with a shortened stride ("What if my great-granddad had a pair that were twenty foot high,/ And mine were but fifteen foot, no modern stalks upon higher"); and the speaker of "The Circus Animals' Desertion," ladderless, disillusioned, with nothing left but the memory of "[t]hose stilted boys" he once was.[52]

[52] Yeats, "Long-legged Fly," p. 618; "High Talk," pp. 622-23; "The Circus Animals' Desertion," p. 629.

The elaborate language of fin de siècle literary Decadence *was* stilted, and when the century changed, Yeats, like old Malachi, had to take to chisel and plane in order to amend his gait. But as the real decadence of "this foul world in its decline and fall" spread out around him in the 1930s, Yeats remembered the high mode of literary Decadence, and he kept turning back to the "beautiful lofty things" that he had once heard fulfill that high mode in speech: "Standish O'Grady supporting himself between the tables/ Speaking to a drunken audience high nonsensical words," the crazed girl who voiced "No common intelligible sound/ But sang, 'O sea-starved, hungry sea' "[53]—grand arabesques of anger and insanity in which the speaking voice tries to match its high ambition against the printed page. Dreading to live where all the ladders start, unable to imagine a poetry without some kind of high talk, Yeats at the end clung to his Decadent stilts. No modern stalks upon higher.

[53] Yeats, "A Bronze Head," p. 619; "Beautiful Lofty Things," p. 577; "A Crazed Girl," p. 578.

INDEX

Symonds, John Addington, 120,
152–53, 153n, 182, 182n, 220
Symons, Arthur, x, 120n–21n,
150, 150n, 151n, 175, 204n,
210, 214–22, 216n, 217n, 224,
233–36, 238–43, 245, 250, 261,
263; "Decadent Movement in
Literature," 134, 143, 150–51,
214, 239–40
synecdoche, 205
Synge, John Millington, 268, 271,
280

T., M., 63n
"talkee-talkee." *See* language: spo-
ken dialects in
Tauber, Abraham, 101n
Temple, Ruth Z., 147n
Tennyson, Alfred, 33–34, 52, 54,
61, 72, 94, 124, 127, 141–42,
196, 205, 224
Thesing, William B., 221n, 227n
Thompson, Francis, 202
Thornton, R.K.R., 142n, 151n,
179, 180n, 209, 216–17
Thorpe, Benjamin, 51–52
Timko, Michael, 33n
Todhunter, John, 249, 254n
Tooke, John Horne, xiii, xv, 8, 14,
48–49, 50, 53–54, 58–60, 60n,
169
Townsend, Benjamin, 224n
Trench, Richard Chenevix, 41–42,
47–50, 52, 60–61, 62, 63, 86n–
87n, 96, 98–99, 124
Trilling, Lionel, 235
Turnbull, Andrew, 223n
Tylor, E. B., 56, 72, 78n

unutterability *topos*, 161–62
urban pastoral, 221–23, 224

Valéry, Paul, 206
Varro, 88

Verhaeren, Emile, 270
Verlaine, Paul, 206–208, 208n,
212n, 220
Vicinus, Martha, 235
Victoria, Queen, 72–73
Villiers de l'Isle-Adam, Philippe-
Auguste, 260
Villon, François, 212, 212n, 263n
Virgil, 142
Volksstimme, 15, 23–24, 31, 33,
35, 37, 63, 67, 82, 83–84, 103,
109, 275
Voltaire, 8n

Wagner, Richard, 144, 260
Ward, Anthony, 127
Warton, Thomas, 53
Watts, Thomas, 43n
Weintraub, Stanley, 146, 147
Wellek, René, 7n
Whistler, J.A.M., 220
White, Gleeson, 208n
White, Joseph Blanco, 29n
White, R. G., 91
Whitman, Walt, 214, 220
Whitney, William Dwight, 73–77,
74n, 78, 82, 92, 95
Wilde, Oscar, ix–x, 3–4, 23, 40,
61, 72, 72n, 104, 143, 156–57,
160, 163–64, 170n, 176n, 178,
180–81, 182–88, 183n, 185n,
186n, 190, 212, 212n, 219, 224,
255, 262–63, 268, 271–72, 275,
282; "Critic as Artist," 173n,
184, 187, 263n; *Dorian Gray*,
143, 156, 160n, 170–72, 173,
186; "Salome," 173, 187–88
Wilkinson, Elizabeth M., 76n
Willoughby, L. A., 24, 76n
Wolf, F. A., 55
Wordsworth, Dorothy, 23
Wordsworth, William, 15–17, 21,
23, 25, 27–28, 30–32, 38, 49,
83, 91, 119, 137, 150, 161, 181,

LIBRARY OF CONGRESS CATALOGING-IN-
PUBLICATION DATA

Dowling, Linda C., 1944–
Language and decadence in the Victorian fin de siècle.

Includes index.
1. English literature—19th century—History and criticism.   2.
Decadence (Literary movement).   3. Linguistics—History—
19th century.   4. Philology—History—19th century.   5. Neogrammarians.   6. Language and culture.   I. Title.
PR468.D43D69   1986   820'.9'008   86–15135
ISBN 0–691–06690–6 (alk. paper)